D0149599

Praise for

fault lines

"This book by Voddie Baucham is a gift to the bride of Jesus. The hallways of history point to moments when the Church was called to stand firm. The call of the Christian is to 'contend for the faith once delivered to the saints' (Jude 3). The difficulty with social justice is that it appears to be virtuous and it sounds 'Christian' when it's being employed by Christian leaders. However, social justice is one of the most devious and destructive movements the Church has faced in the last hundred years. Voddie Baucham, like a capable doctor, diagnoses the problem and in a skillful manner directs his readers to the biblical solution."

—JOSH BUICE, Ph.D., pastor of Pray's Mill Baptist Church in Douglasville, Georgia, and founder and president of G3 Ministries

"Voddie Baucham has a gift for very clear writing about the complex history and terms and bottom-line relevance of Critical Race Theory. The weaving of the stories and the reporting with the solid and clear teaching is perfect. I always learn something when I read Voddie on this topic, even though I am a smart fellow and have been studying this stuff a while. His long interest in it and concern about it shows. *Fault Lines* is great. I shall be requiring it of my students."

—MARK DeVINE, Ph.D., associate professor of divinity at Samford University's Beeson Divinity School

"Just as under the guise of Liberation Theology Marxism was smuggled into the Catholic Church, so under the guise of Social Justice/Critical Race Theory, Marxism is being smuggled into evangelical churches across the country. Through a mixture of autobiography, incisive analysis, and a careful sifting of the statements made and positions taken by Critical Race theorists, Voddie Baucham exposes the anti-biblical, anti-God presuppositions upon which CRT is founded. This book is a must-read for all Christians, but especially for evangelicals who, in the name of justice and compassion, have been lured into supporting a movement that denies, in the most radical way, that we are all creatures made in the image of God but fallen into sin."

—LOUIS MARKOS, Ph.D., professor of English and scholar in residence at Houston Baptist University and author of *Atheism on Trial: Refuting the Modern Arguments Against God*

"Voddie Baucham has a long-established reputation for faithfulness and boldness, but this gracious, convictional, sometimes humorous, and always biblical book is an inestimable contribution to the Church's consideration of race, ethnicity, and related ideologies. The theological work is precise; the personal narrative is arresting and moving; the cultural analysis is razor-sharp, and driven not by buzzwords but by data. Even as Baucham renders critique, he does so in love, with a spirit of upbuilding. This is a fantastically courageous book, and it will single-handedly shift the conversation, anchoring Christ's blood-bought church in sound scriptural doctrine, not sinking sociological sand."

—OWEN STRACHAN, Ph.D., associate professor of Christian theology at Midwestern Baptist Theological Seminary and author of the forthcoming book *Christianity & Wokeness*

fault lines

fault lines

The Social Justice Movement and Evangelicalism's Looming Catastrophe

Voddie T. Baucham Jr.

SALEM
BOOKS
an imprint of Regnery Publishing
Washington, D.C.

Salem Books™ is a trademark of Salem Communications Holding Corporation
Regnery® is a registered trademark of Salem Communications Holding Corporation

ISBN: 978-1-68451-180-8
eISBN: 978-1-68451-201-0

Library of Congress Control Number: 2020948290

Published in the United States by
Salem Books
An Imprint of Regnery Publishing
A Division of Salem Media Group
Washington, D.C.
www.SalemBooks.com

Manufactured in the United States of America

10 9 8 7 6 5

Books are available in quantity for promotional or premium use.
For information on discounts and terms, please visit our website:
www.SalemBooks.com.

It is the truth which is assailed in any age which tests our fidelity. It is to confess we are called, not merely to profess. If I profess, with the loudest voice and the clearest exposition, every portion of the truth of God except precisely that little point which the world and the devil are at that moment attacking, I am not confessing Christ, however boldly I may be professing Christianity. Where the battle rages the loyalty of the soldier is proved; and to be steady on all the battle-field besides is mere flight and disgrace to him if he flinches at that one point.

—Elizabeth Rundle Charles

CONTENTS

Thought Line

1989 was a banner year. Not because the World Wide Web was invented, the Berlin Wall came down, Nintendo came out with the Gameboy, and I met and married the woman of my dreams. Those were all big, but four other things happened in 1989 that were at least as big—things that shaped the current war being waged in our midst.

Harvard Law professor Derrick Bell and some colleagues held a conference in Wisconsin, where Critical Race Theory was officially born. Bell's protege, Kimberlé Crenshaw, introduced the idea of Intersectionality in her paper "Demarginalizing the Intersection of Race and Sex: A Black Feminist Critique of Antidiscrimination Doctrine, Feminist Theory and Antiracist Politics."[1] Peggy McIntosh published "White Privilege: Unpacking the Invisible Knapsack."[2] And two other Harvard professors, Marshall

---

[1] Kimberlé Crenshaw, "Demarginalizing the Intersection of Race and Sex: A Black Feminist Critique of Antidiscrimination Doctrine, Feminist Theory, and Antiracist Politics," *University of Chicago Legal Forum*, Vol. 1989, Issue 1, Article 8, https://chicagounbound.uchicago.edu/cgi/viewcontent.cgi?article=1052&context=uclf.

[2] Peggy McIntosh, "White Privilege: Unpacking the Invisible Knapsack," working paper, https://www.racialequitytools.org/resourcefiles/mcintosh.pdf.

Kirk and Hunter Madsen, published their little-known but monumentally influential book *After the Ball: How America Will Conquer Its Fear & Hatred of Gays in the 90s*.[3]

All of these publications have one thing in common. They are all the product of the same worldview: Critical Social Justice (CSJ), which is the subject of this book.

In order to understand CSJ, we must first understand where it came from. Rather than a glossary or a timeline, I want to give you what I call a thought line. Here is a very brief sketch of the development of the ideas this book will address.

The Roots of CSJ

Karl Marx's Conflict Theory

German philosopher Karl Marx was the leading architect of the most dominant school of thought within sociology, known as Conflict Theory. Marx viewed society as a group of different social classes all competing for a limited pool of resources such as food, housing, employment, education, and leisure time.[4]

Antonio Gramsci and Hegemony

Simply put, hegemony is what takes place when a dominant group imposes its ideology on the rest of society: "thus social control is achieved through conditioning rather than physical force or intimidation."[5]

---

[3] Marshall Kirk and Hunter Madsen, *After the Ball: How America Will Conquer Its Fear & Hatred of Gays in the 90s* (New York, New York: Doubleday, 1990).

[4] Heather Griffiths, *Introduction to Sociology 2e* (OpenStax, 2015).

[5] Robin DiAngelo and Özlem Sensoy, *Is Everyone Really Equal?: An Introduction to Key Concepts in Social Justice Education* (Multicultural Education Series) (New York, New York: Teachers College Press, Kindle Edition), 73.

Italian Marxist Antonio Gramsci developed this concept to explain how domination and control are maintained not only through coercion, but also through the voluntary consent of both the oppressed and their oppressors to maintain the status quo. Gramsci redefined hegemony as "a complex interlocking of political, social, and cultural forces"[6]

Frankfurt School and Critical Theory

After the Marxist revolution failed to topple capitalism in the early twentieth century, many Marxists went back to the drawing board, modifying and adapting Marx's ideas. Perhaps the most famous was a group associated with the Institute for Social Research in Frankfurt, Germany, which applied Marxism to a radical interdisciplinary social theory. The group included Max Horkheimer, T.W. Adorno, Erich Fromm, Herbert Marcuse, Georg Lukács, and Walter Benjamin and came to be known as the Frankfurt School.

These men developed Critical Theory as an expansion of Conflict Theory and applied it more broadly, including other social sciences and philosophy. Their main goal was *to address structural issues causing inequity.* They worked from the assumption that current social reality was broken, and they needed to identify the people and institutions that could make changes and provide practical goals for social transformation.

Putting It All Together

In order to understand Critical Theory, it is important to understand how the words "critical" and "theory" are used.

In the social sciences, "critical" is "geared toward identifying and exposing problems in order to facilitate revolutionary political change."[7] In other words, it implies revolution. It is not interested in reform. Hence, we do not "reform" the police; we "defund" the police or abolish them. "It is more

---

[6] Dino Franco Felluga, *Critical Theory: The Key Concepts* (Oxfordshire, United Kingdom: Taylor and Francis, Kindle Edition, 2015), 127–28.

[7] Helen Pluckrose and James Lindsay, *Cynical Theories* (Durham, North Carolina: Pitchstone Publishing, Kindle Edition, 2020).

interested in problematizing—that is, finding ways in which the system is imperfect and making noise about them, reasonably or not—than it is in any other identifiable activity, especially building something constructive."[8]

This is complicated by the fact that Critical Theory denies objective truth. "An approach based on critical theory calls into question the idea that objectivity is desirable or even possible," write Özlem Sensoy and Robin DiAngelo in *Is Everyone Really Equal?* "The term used to describe this way of thinking about knowledge is that knowledge is … reflective of the values and interests of those who produce it."[9] But this is only half the puzzle.

The word "theory" can be used in two ways in the social sciences: as an abstract noun (as in "I have a theory about that") or as a proper noun, as in Critical Theory. According to the New Discourses Encyclopedia:

> Theory—treated as a proper noun and thus capitalized—is an appropriate catch-all term for the thinking behind Critical Social Justice, especially at the academic level. It is the set of ideas, modes of thought, ethics, and methods that define Critical Social Justice in both thought and activism (that is, theory and praxis). In a meaningful way, Theory is the central object—the canon and source of further revelation of canon—of Critical Social Justice. That is, *Theory is the heart of the worldview that defines Critical Social Justice.*[10]

In other words, Critical Theory is not just an analytical tool, as some have suggested; it is a philosophy, a worldview.

Critical Race Theory

Perhaps the most important concept to grasp for the purposes of this book is Critical Race Theory (CRT). "Critical Race Theory is an outgrowth

---

[8] Pluckrose and Lindsay, *Cynical Theories.*

[9] DiAngelo and Sensoy, *Is Everyone Really Equal?*, 29.

[10] "Theory: Social Justice Usage," New Discourses, https://newdiscourses.com/tftw-theory.

of Critical Legal Studies (CLS), which was a leftist movement that challenged traditional legal scholarship."[11]

There has been much debate over CRT within evangelical circles recently. Some have accused those of us who are leery of CRT of creating a straw man and labeling everything we disagree with or that makes us uncomfortable as CRT. Therefore, it is important that I allow CRT to define itself in order to demonstrate that when I refer to this ideology, I am not making things up, taking them out of context, or building a straw man. I am merely taking its founders and practitioners at their word.

According to the UCLA Luskin School of Public Affairs:

> CRT recognizes that racism is engrained in the fabric and system of the American society. The individual racist need not exist to note that institutional racism is pervasive in the dominant culture. This is the analytical lens that CRT uses in examining existing power structures. CRT identifies that these power structures are based on white privilege and white supremacy, which perpetuates the marginalization of people of color. CRT also rejects the traditions of liberalism and meritocracy. Legal discourse says that the law is neutral and colorblind, however, CRT challenges this legal "truth" by examining liberalism and meritocracy as a vehicle for self-interest, power, and privilege.[12]

Many discussions of CRT have referenced this definition, and with good reason. First, it is as clear and succinct a definition as you will find. Second, it captures the essence and major tenets of CRT. Third, it comes from a source that has led the charge for CRT in recent years, which means, fourth, that it is a case of proponents of CRT defining themselves. Note also that this definition, without using the word "worldview,"

---

[11] "What Is Critical Race Theory?," UCLA School of Public Affairs, Critical Race Studies, https://spacrs.wordpress.com/what-is-critical-race-theory.

[12] Ibid.

describes precisely that. One way to define a worldview is "an analytical lens one uses to examine the world."

According to Richard Delgado, the worldview of CRT is based on four key presuppositions:

Racism is Normal: ... the usual way society does business, the common, everyday experience of most people of color in this country.[13]

Convergence Theory: "Racism advances the interests of both white elites (materially) and working-class whites (psychically), large segments of society have little incentive to eradicate it."[14] This means *whites are incapable of righteous actions on race and only undo racism when it benefits them*; when their interests "converge" with the interests of people of color.

Anti-Liberalism: [CRT] questions the very foundations of the liberal order, including equality theory, legal reasoning, Enlightenment rationalism, and neutral principles of constitutional law.[15]

Knowledge is Socially Constructed: Storytelling/Narrative Reading is the way black people forward knowledge vs. *the Science/reason method of white people*. Minority status, in other words, brings with it a presumed competence to speak about race and racism. The "legal storytelling" movement urges black and brown writers to recount their experiences with racism and the legal system and to apply their own unique perspectives to assess law's master narratives.[16]

---

[13] Richard Delgado, *Critical Race Theory* (Third Edition) (New York, New York: New York University Press, Kindle Edition), 8.

[14] Ibid., 9.

[15] Ibid., 3.

[16] Ibid., 11.

While this is a well-established summary, Tara Yosso, one of the most-cited academics on Critical Race Theory, expands Delgado's fourth tenet with a very important dimension:

The centrality of experiential knowledge. CRT recognizes that the experiential knowledge of People of Color is legitimate, appropriate, and critical to understanding, analyzing and teaching about racial subordination....[17]

Intersectionality

If Derrick Bell is the father of CRT, then he is the grandfather of Intersectionality. The idea was popularized by Bell's Harvard Law School protege, Kimberlé Crenshaw, and is best summed up in her two seminal papers: "Demarginalizing the Intersection of Race and Sex: A Black Feminist Critique of Antidiscrimination Doctrine, Feminist Theory and Antiracist Politics," published in 1989, and "Mapping the Margins: Intersectionality, Identity Politics, and Violence Against Women of Color," published in 1991. I offer the full titles as they give a glimpse into Crenshaw's worldview. Put simply, Intersectionality is about the multiple layers of oppression minorities suffer. For instance, if a black person has one layer of oppression, a black woman has two, a black lesbian woman has three, etc. The *Encyclopedia of Diversity and Social Justice* offers a helpful summary:

Our experiences of the social world are shaped by our ethnicity, race, social class, gender identity, sexual orientation, and numerous other facets of social stratification. Some social locations afford privilege (e.g., being white) while others are oppressive (e.g., being poor). These various aspects of social inequality do not operate independently of each other; they

---

[17] Tara J. Yosso, "Whose Culture Has Capital? A Critical Race Theory Discussion of Community Cultural Wealth," *Race Ethnicity and Education* 8, no. 1 (August 23, 2006), https://www.tandfonline.com/doi/pdf/10.1080/1361332052000341006.

interact to create interrelated systems of oppression and domination. The concept of intersectionality refers to how these various aspects of social location "intersect" to mutually constitute individuals' lived experiences.[18]

There are volumes written on these concepts, and I commend them to you. I have benefitted greatly from the work of people like Neil Shenvi, Helen Pluckrose, James Lindsay, and a host of others. Their work is thorough, insightful, and much-needed in these times. I also recommend diving into the sources I have cited here and throughout this book for an inside look at what CRT and Intersectionality say about themselves.

---

[18] Sherwood Thompson, *Encyclopedia of Diversity and Social Justice* (Lanham, Maryland: Rowman & Littlefield Publishers, Kindle Edition, 2015), 435.

Introduction

At 5:12 a.m. on April 18, 1906, a temblor deep inside the earth's surface shook the San Francisco Bay Area. It was followed 25 seconds later by a 7.9-magnitude earthquake which lasted between 45 and 60 seconds. It came to be known as the Great San Francisco Earthquake, one of the most significant of all time. According to the U.S. Geological Society, "The earthquake was felt from southern Oregon to south of Los Angeles and inland as far as central Nevada" and ruptured 296 miles of California. Yet the significance of the San Andreas Fault and its cumulative effects would not be fully recognized until the advent of plate tectonics more than half a century later.

Over the next century, San Francisco would experience even more seismic, culture-changing events—but it would not be the ground that would shake.

Another Kind of Earthquake in San Francisco

In late 1966, white police officers in San Francisco caught three teens joyriding in a stolen car through a mostly black neighborhood called

1

Hunters Point. The teens ditched the car and fled on foot as the police chased them. One of boys, sixteen-year-old Matthew Johnson, ignored a cop's warning to stop running—and the cop shot him four times, killing him instantly. San Franciscans rioted for three days in protest, wreaking such havoc that the mayor eventually called in assistance from two thousand National Guard troops with tanks to help local and state police quell the violence.

On May 25, 2020, George Floyd, a forty-six-year-old black man, was arrested for allegedly using a counterfeit bill at a Minneapolis store. He died as a white police officer knelt on his neck for nearly nine minutes to subdue him. As a result, nearly eight thousand protests—many of them violent—rocked 2,500 cities from coast to coast for four months.[1] Those events, combined with subsequent calls to "defund the police"—some of which passed—showed many Christians for the first time the shakiness within our culture and underscored it for the rest.

But this fault line is not new. It has been quietly forming underneath our feet for a long time around the area of social justice, and the Church must be awake and aware of what it means and where it comes from. Otherwise, we will fall victim to it—as many leading Christian voices already have.

The Nature of the Coming Catastrophe

Why are people and groups like Thabiti Anyabwile, Tim Keller, Russell Moore, the Southern Baptist Convention, the Ethics and Religious Liberty Commission, 9Marks, the Gospel Coalition, and Together for the Gospel (T4G) being identified with Critical Social Justice on one side of the fault, and people like John MacArthur, Tom Ascol, Owen Strachan, Douglas Wilson, and the late R.C. Sproul being identified on the other? There are groups and ministries that have embraced CRT, and those are

---

[1] "Demonstrations & Political Violence in America: New Data for Summer 2020," ACLED, September 3, 2020, https://acleddata.com/2020/09/03/demonstrations-political-violence-in-america-new-data-for-summer-2020.

problematic. But there is a larger group that is sympathetic to it because of their desire to fight what they see as a problem of racial injustice. Most of the groups I will mention in this book fall into the latter category.

It is not a stretch to say we are seeing seismic shifts in the evangelical landscape. But is it an exaggeration to call this a coming catastrophe?

I don't think so. John MacArthur calls it "the greatest threat" to the Gospel in his lifetime—and he had a front-row seat to the debates over both inerrancy and lordship salvation.[2] What do I, MacArthur, and myriad other pastors and leaders see on the horizon that leads to such drastic statements?

Before I answer that question, let me first tell you what I do *not* see as the root of the problem.

Our Problem Is Not Growing Ethnic Tensions

O. J. Simpson. Rodney King. Michael Brown. Tamir Rice. Trayvon Martin. Breonna Taylor. George Floyd. Just say these names and you can divide a room. On one side will be people who see the incidents those names represent as evidence of America's "systemic racism." The others will argue that they were isolated incidents, at least some of which represented justifiable actions taken by the police. Chances are the discussion will not end in agreement, or even one side moving slightly toward the other. Instead, they will simply continue slipping past each other along the fault line.

Growing ethnic tension is *a* problem—but it is not *the main* problem. While troubling, it is no match for the truth of the Gospel and the unity it creates among those who embrace it. In fact, such tensions represent an opportunity for Christ's followers to demonstrate the truth of Paul's words:

> For he himself is our peace, who has made us both one and
> has broken down in his flesh the dividing wall of hostility by

---

[2] John MacArthur, "Social Injustice and the Gospel," Grace to You blog, August 13, 2018, https://www.gty.org/library/blog/B180813.

abolishing the law of commandments expressed in ordinances, that he might create in himself one new man in place of the two, so making peace, and might reconcile us both to God in one body through the cross, thereby killing the hostility. (Ephesians 2:13–16)

Ethnic tensions are only a problem for Christians who forget this truth or subordinate it to a competing ideology (whether that be on the left or the right). When that happens, a fault line appears: those on one side "press the text" of the Bible, while those on the other see that approach as short-sighted and insensitive. The problem is not ethnic tension, but the fundamental assumptions that drive our assessment of and subsequent approaches to it.

Our Problem Is Not Political Divisions

Friends in the U.S. have half-jokingly asked if I moved my family to Zambia in 2015 to escape "Trump's America." I may not have been present for the 2016 election, but I was definitely connected and aware.

I started writing and speaking on political issues in 2008, during Barack Obama's first run for the White House. At that time I warned repeatedly of his culturally Marxist worldview. I also warned that an Obama presidency would not heal, but rather deepen ethnic tensions in America. I also warned much the same regarding both Hillary Clinton and Donald Trump in 2016.

But neither was "the problem." On the one side of the election debate were Christians who saw immorality as reason enough to swallow hard and vote for Trump in the hopes of stemming the tide of illegal immigration and abortion. On the other side were those who saw inequalities in health care, income, and immigration as reason enough to swallow hard and vote for Clinton in the hopes of stemming a different tide.

Our Problem Is Social Justice versus Biblical Justice

Those belonging to the social-justice crowd present themselves as the only ones pursuing justice, to the exclusion of all who disagree with their assessments—who, by that definition, are pursuing injustice.

Perhaps the most troubling aspect of the current struggle is that it mischaracterizes Christians that way too. On one side are "compassionate" Christians who are "concerned about justice." On the other are "insensitive" Christians who are "not concerned about justice." This is wrong.

I have pursued justice my entire Christian life. Yet I am about as "anti–social justice" as they come—not because I have abandoned my obligation to "strive for peace with everyone, and for the holiness without which no one will see the Lord" (Hebrews 12:14), but because I believe the current concept of social justice is incompatible with biblical Christianity.

This is the main fault line at the root of the current debate—the epicenter of the Big One that, when it finally shifts with all its force, threatens to split evangelicalism right down the middle. Our problem is a lack of clarity and charity in our debate over the place, priority, practice, and definition of justice.

The current cultural moment is precarious. The United States is on the verge of a race war, if not a complete cultural meltdown. And the rest of the Western world seems to be following suit. Tensions are rising in every place the African slave trade has left its indelible mark.

However, as much as I love and want the best for America, I am far more concerned about the precarious moment facing evangelicals. I am not a pessimist. I believe the Lord's Church will survive until He comes, and this moment is no exception. God's people have faced other—and I would argue more significant—obstacles in the past. I don't think anyone would say that what we are dealing with here rises to the level of the Spanish Inquisition or the Protestant Reformation in terms of threatening our unity. There is nothing like the drowning of the Anabaptist martyr Felix Manz on our current radar screen. Nevertheless, there is trouble afoot.

Navigating through the Issue

The goal of this book is not to avoid the looming trouble. In fact, I believe that to be neither possible nor desirable. The trouble has arrived. It will not go away any time soon, and the division it is causing is necessary. I chose the fault line metaphor because I believe it not only describes the catastrophe, but also the aftermath.

There are two competing worldviews in this current cultural moment. One is the Critical Social Justice view—which assumes that the world is divided between the oppressors and the oppressed (white, heterosexual males are generally viewed as "the oppressor").[3] The other is what I will refer to in these pages as the biblical justice view in order to avoid what I accuse the social-justice crowd of doing, which is immediately casting its opponents as being opposed to justice. (In evangelical circles, that paints us as opposed to God Himself, since every effort has been made to demonstrate that "social justice is a Gospel issue.") There are plenty of sincere, though perhaps naive Christians who, if they knew the ideology behind it, would run away from the term "social justice" like rats from a burning ship. (As legendary economist Friedrich Hayek once said, "I have come to feel strongly that the greatest service I can still render to my fellow men would be that I could make the speakers and writers among them thoroughly ashamed ever again to employ the term 'social justice'.")

The current moment is akin to two people standing on either side of a major fault line just before it shifts. When the shift comes, the ground will open up, a divide that was once invisible will become visible, and the two will find themselves on opposite sides of it. That is what is happening in our day. In some cases, the divide is happening already. Churches are splitting over this issue. Major ministries are losing donors, staff, and leadership. Denominations are in turmoil. Seminary faculties

---

[3] James Lindsay identifies Critical Social Justice as "the intentional combination of Critical Theory, Postmodern Theory, and Social Justice." Triggernometry, "Why Social Justice Is Dangerous - James Lindsay," YouTube, August 12, 2020, https://www.youtube.com/watch?v=SUdGLrW3_uI (19:30).

are divided with some professors being fired or "asked to leave." Families are at odds. Marriages are on the rocks. And I don't believe the fracture in this fault line is yet even a fraction of what it will be.

No, I am not writing this book to stop the divide. I am writing to clearly identify the two sides of the fault line and to urge the reader to choose wisely.

Nonetheless, addressing this topic usually leaves me open to attacks from people who will accuse me of "being a sellout," "trying to curry favor with white people," not being informed about the struggles black Americans currently face, or just not understanding "the black perspective." Anyone who knows me will find those things laughable—so let me begin by telling you my story.

CHAPTER ONE

A Black Man

I was born on the San Andreas Fault. More specifically, I was born in Los Angeles, California, on March 11, 1969. This was the end of the Great Migration between 1915 and 1970 that saw somewhere between five and ten million blacks leave the South in search of a better life. This migration took place along very specific routes to the North and West and landed large swaths of the black population in cities like New York, Boston, Detroit, Oakland, Los Angeles, and other major urban areas.

"It was during the First World War that a silent pilgrimage took its first steps within the borders of this country," writes Isabel Wilkerson in her compelling and eye-opening book *The Warmth of Other Suns*. I can see the expressions on the faces of my grandparents as she describes the organic, almost unnoticed nature of the movement: "The fever rose without warning or notice or much in the way of understanding by those outside its reach. It would not end until the 1970s and would set into motion changes in the North and South that no one, not even the people doing the leaving, could have imagined at the start of it or dreamed would take nearly a lifetime to play out."[1]

My family was among those who trod those well-worn paths. My third-great paternal grandfather, Nazarin, was born a slave in North Carolina in 1835. On my mother's side, I have been able to trace my third- and fourth-great-grandparents back to slavery in Alabama, Virginia, and Texas between the 1830s and 1860s. Both my maternal grandmother and paternal grandfather came from Texas, while my maternal grandmother made her way up I-10 from Louisiana. They all eventually found their way to the City of Angels, where they, along with scores of other immigrants, made a life for themselves and their loved ones that offered more promise than they ever could have hoped for in the land they left.

My father was born in Los Angeles. My mother didn't arrive there until 1961 at the age of ten; she grew up in Midland, Texas—one of seven children from four different men. She spent most of 1960 living with her father in Odessa while my grandmother—who was unmarried at the time—went to Los Angeles to get established before sending for my mother, her older brother, and her younger sister. Three older siblings had already left home and started families of their own, and a seventh, the youngest of the bunch, was living with her father in Tyler. (My grandmother would marry the man I called my grandfather the year I was born. He was twenty years her senior—and white.)

Mom and her siblings spent two days on a bus from Midland to Los Angeles. Like many who undertook similar journeys, they had only a loaf of bread and some fried chicken. "We had enough chicken for two days, but we ate it all the first day," my mother recounted as she told me her story again not long ago. "We didn't have any money, so the second day we just went hungry." They arrived in Los Angeles and went from a temporary apartment to a permanent home in the Imperial Courts projects in Watts. "We didn't go outside to play," my mother told me.

---

[1] Isabel Wilkerson, *The Warmth of Other Suns* (New York, New York: Knopf Doubleday Publishing Group, Kindle Edition, 2010), 19–20.

"There was so much asphalt. We were used to playing in fields and trees." She was also shocked by the regular fights in the projects where she lived.

My mother met my father a few years later when they both attended Jefferson High School in South Central Los Angeles. My dad was a handsome multi-sport athlete. He stood six and a half feet tall with broad shoulders, a booming voice, and a personality that was more imposing than his stature. My mom stood five foot four and more than held her own. She had a keen mind, a sharp wit, and an infectious smile. She was a stellar student destined for great things. Their high school romance turned into a teenage pregnancy, a shotgun wedding, and a brief marriage that could not withstand their personal differences or my father's departure for university and eventual pursuit of a career in professional football.

I have seen pictures of the three of us together when I was a toddler, but my parents were not a couple long enough for me to have any memories of our time as an intact family. I would be haunted by this reality for decades to come.

A Child of Desegregation

I remember the day when I was in third grade that my school sent me home with a special letter to give to my mother—one that would have a much greater impact than I could have imagined. It informed her that I would be bussed across town to an elementary school in Pacific Palisades.[2]

I don't particularly remember my mother's reaction to it other than her relief that at least this time it didn't have anything to do with my misbehavior. (Yes, I was that much of a troublemaker. In fact, I was such a troublemaker that the principal made a deal with me: if I stayed out of his office for the last three weeks of the term, he would take me out to eat anywhere I wanted to go.) What I do remember is the discussion we had the night before I got on that bus for the first time. My mother reminded me that, though we did not have much, we did have

---

[2] Robert Lindsey, "Los Angeles Busing Ends after Three Years," *New York Times*, April 21, 1981, https://www.nytimes.com/1981/04/21/us/los-angeles-busing-ends-after-3-years.html.

our good name, and whether I liked it or not, I was going to have to uphold that name.

She also reminded me that I was a black boy about to walk into an all-white school, and this meant that our family name was not my only concern. As she spoke, I did not have the sense that I was a child being instructed, but a soldier being commissioned. I remember feeling like I was about to step onto a stage and assume a role in a drama that, up until then, I had only witnessed from a distance and would rather not participate in.

But my participation was not optional. I had to get on that bus.

They Don't Want Us Here

My time in the Palisades is a blur. My few memories of the semester I spent there are not pleasant. I don't think I had a particularly bad time, but the incidents that stand out to me shaped the way I thought about the world. Two of them demonstrate how my racial identity developed.

The first was the fact that my fellow bussees and I weren't wanted there. At least that's the way I saw it. Looking back on it, I realize there were several issues, both political and historical, that I could not possibly have understood. To the adults, bussing was an issue involving the National Association for the Advancement of Colored People (NAACP), the Los Angeles Unified School District, the State of California, the federal courts, and the history of segregation in the United States. But for us kids, it just felt like we were being forced to go someplace where people didn't want us around.

That semester had a tremendous impact on my understanding of what it meant to be black in America. I may have been too young to understand the complex, multi-layered drama going on around me, but I could definitely understand what it meant to feel unwelcome. I could also understand, perhaps for the first time, what it meant to be poor and disadvantaged. By the time we got off the bus in Pacific Palisades, we were keenly aware that 1) we weren't in South Central anymore, and 2) these people had a lot more money than we did.

The Day I Didn't Get Expelled

The second thing that always stands out in my mind when I think about my time in the Palisades is the day I didn't get expelled. The talk my mother had with me was very effective. I was on the straight and narrow when I got off that bus. We all were—partly because we were in a strange environment, but also because we all felt like we were under a microscope. Nevertheless, it didn't take long for trouble to find me.

I have heard it said that you "never forget the first time a white person calls you a nigger." That was certainly the case for me, but not because I'd never heard it before. I'd actually heard it all my life. People had used it to refer to me, and I had used it to refer to others. When black people used the word, it was a rather benign moniker, even a term of endearment. But from a white person's mouth, it was a weapon being used to demean and dehumanize me.

The little boy who said it probably had no idea what he was doing. He used the word like it was a new toy with which he was learning to play. However, when he saw my reaction to it, he used it with greater fervor. He had struck a nerve, and like any kid on the playground who feels like he has figured out how to get the upper hand, he continued to strike at that nerve.

The boy would say the word, then run and stand by our teacher. At first I stopped short, not wanting to get the teacher involved. But after a few rounds of this, I had had enough. That time, as the boy stood next to the teacher, looking smug and satisfied, I calmly walked up to him and punched him in the chest as hard as I could. He dropped like a sack of potatoes. The teacher began yelling, "What is wrong with you?!" I looked at her and said, "He kept calling me *nigger*."

The teacher took us both to the principal's office, where both of our parents were called. What happened next is a bit of a blur. My mother came to the school. She did not tell me that what I did was right, or even justified. She didn't say that someone calling me a name, even *that* name, gave me the right to resort to violence. However, she did say that we were little boys playing a grown-up game and that there was teaching to be done. That boy needed to learn something, and so did I. That boy needed to be disciplined, and so did I. And we both were. (We also ended up sitting together at lunch most days after that.)

Lessons My Mother Taught Me

My mother shaped my thinking about who I was and what I was capable of. She never said or did anything to cause me to believe that my blackness was a curse or a limitation. She gave me a sense of agency and accountability that remains with me to this day. She did this by advocating for me, protecting me, disciplining me, and sacrificing for me. There are myriad examples of this, but four stories in particular have always stood out in my mind.

My Mother Protected Me

The life of a single mother raising a son in Los Angeles in the late 1970s and early 1980s was tough. There were drugs, gangs, crime, poverty, and a host of other traps to which a young man could fall prey. People often ask how I came out of all that unscathed. My answer is always the same: Frances Baucham. My mother was a tough, smart, hard-working, no-nonsense woman who did not suffer fools. Growing up, there were two things I never doubted: 1) my mother loved me, and 2) if I got out of line, she'd kill me!

One day, as a friend and I were walking home from the store, we took a routine shortcut through the back of a nearby housing project. As we walked and talked, we didn't notice two young men following us. Suddenly, out of nowhere, they rushed us. One of them shoved a gun in my face while the other searched me and my friend for money and/or drugs. We had neither, so they took the bag of groceries we had just bought and ran off.

Not long after that incident, my mother decided it was time for a change of scenery. So we packed our things, got on a Greyhound bus, and for the next three days we crossed the United States to end up in Buford, South Carolina, where we would spend the next year and a half living with my mother's oldest brother, Luther Sanders, and his wife before moving to Texas, the place I still call home. Not only would I go to high school, college, and seminary in Texas, but it is also where I met and married my wife, welcomed all nine of my children, and started my ministry. I often say, "I am a Californian by birth, but a Texan by the grace of God!"

Luther (or Uncle Kid, as we called him) was and is a hero. He is a laid-back, soft-spoken, slow-talkin' Southerner. If you were to meet him, you might mistake him for a simple country boy. You would be wrong. Uncle Kid served for twenty-two years in the United States Marine Corps and survived two tours in Vietnam. He spent part of his time in the Marines as a drill instructor, some in K9 training and handling, and later became a certified scuba diver. Uncle Kid was so committed to the Corps that after 9/11, he walked onto the closest base and tried to reenlist. He was in his fifties at the time.

I could write an entire book about Uncle Kid. Perhaps someday I will. But for now, you just need to know that when my mother saw I needed something she felt she couldn't provide for me by herself in Los Angeles, she knew where to go. It was the best thing that could have happened to me, and words are inadequate to express my gratitude.

My Mother Sacrificed for Me

My mother graduated from the University of the Incarnate Word in San Antonio, Texas, in 2000. She was forty-nine years old. I remember sitting in the audience and crying like a baby. My wife was rubbing my back and hugging my neck, and our children were asking, "What's wrong with Daddy?" I couldn't explain it at the time, but I would go on to use that moment to impress upon my children the value of sacrifice.

My mother graduated from college at forty-nine because she got pregnant at seventeen. Yes, she made a moral choice that cost her. However, not everyone faced with the consequences of that same moral dilemma decided to do what my mother did. Some chose abortion. (It wasn't legal in the 1960s, but it was available.) Others chose to leave the child with a relative, while still others put their child in the system.

I do not presume to understand the circumstances that led other women to make different choices. This is not about them. My point is simply this: When they called my mother's name and she walked across that stage to receive her diploma, her classmates and teachers applauded her because of the tenacity and determination she showed in working and going back to school in her forties. I, on the other hand, applauded her for the sacrifices she made earlier in life by working and raising a son by herself in her twenties and thirties. By the time my mother graduated from college, I had two bachelor's degrees, a Master of Divinity, and was finishing a doctorate.

Some people see their parents' diplomas on the wall as motivation for them to follow in Mom's or Dad's footsteps and get a degree. I had already done that. What I hadn't done yet was raise my children and launch them into adulthood. My mother's diploma said, "This is what sacrifice, determination, and redemption looks like." My mother was neither a perfect woman nor a perfect parent. But in her imperfection, she showed me what it looks like to sacrifice for your kids.

My Mother Advocated for Me

My wife, Bridget, is often amazed by the stories my mother has told her about my days in elementary school. She finds it hard to fathom how much of a troublemaker I was. One of the stories my mother often tells is of the day she came to visit my class (probably for a parent/teacher conference about my behavior). My mother always had a job or two, so she would drop by the school whenever she could. That day she dropped by during reading time.

As she met with the teacher, she noticed that the books on my group's table were different than those the other groups were reading. She asked about it and was told that my group was at a lower reading level. At that point, my mother called me to the teacher's desk, gave me a look that shook me to my core, then turned to the teacher and said, "Give me a book."

The teacher reached for one of the readers on her desk. "No," my mother corrected her, "give me *your* book." The teacher protested, assuring my mother that her book was far beyond my reading level, at which point my mother simply pointed to the book and held out her hand; the teacher handed her the book. My mother opened it to a random page, handed it to me, then folded her arms and said, "Read this, son."

I knew I was in trouble. There was no way out. If I fumbled through the book, my mother would know I was playing dumb at school. However, if I read it, my teacher would know I had been, well, playing dumb at school. Either way, I knew I would be toast when I got home. So I did the only thing I could; I began to read the book. The teacher, a rather pale white woman, began to grow increasingly red. Her jaw dropped and her eyes doubled in circumference. She tried to speak, but the words wouldn't come out. I finished the passage, handed the book to my mother, then turned and walked back to my group.

But it wasn't over. Before I could get back to the table, my mother said, "Oh, no ... that's not your group anymore." She then told the teacher, "I see that all his little buddies are at that table. Voddie doesn't care about reading as much as he cares about being with his homeboys." And she was right. I was a little black boy growing up in South Central Los Angeles during the heyday of the Crips and Bloods. It wasn't "cool" to hit the books, so I underperformed so as not to stand out.

But not that day. That day, Frances Baucham had come to class. That day, she reminded me (and my teacher) that she, not the streets, had the last word.

My Mother Disciplined Me

Several years after that incident, my mother would remind me once again that when it came to academics, Frances Baucham *did not play!*

It all started with a progress report. These were report cards sent home midway through the semester to give parents an idea how their children were doing; mine contained a C in one subject. When my mother saw that, she went ballistic! Space doesn't allow for the long story, but the short version is she told me I couldn't play football. Not that I couldn't play in the next game; she told me I couldn't even go to *practice.*

The next day I told our head coach, Diz Reeves, what had happened. (Coach Reeves was a living legend in Texas football, and in Texas, that's saying a lot.) He immediately brought me into his office, sat down behind his desk, and called my mother to "straighten things out." What happened next was epic!

Coach started out trying to reason with my mother. The conversation went something like this:

> Coach Reeves: Ms. Baucham, remember, this was only a progress report.
> Mom: I am aware of that, Coach.
> Coach Reeves: I assure you, Voddie will bring the grade up by the end of the semester.
> Mom: Oh, trust me, I know he will. At least, he'd better.
> Coach Reeves: Your son is one of the smartest players I have ever coached.
> Mom: This is not about how dumb your other players are, this is about what I expect from my son.

I can't recall exactly what my mother said after that. What I can tell you is that Coach Reeves's side of the conversation suddenly turned into a series of "Yes ma'ams," "No ma'ams," and then, "I understand." Finally, he hung up the phone, looked at me, and said,

"Son, you better get that grade up, and I hope your momma lets you come back next week."

My mother and Coach Reeves would go on to become the best of friends. Years later, he would say, "I wish every one of my players had a mother like Frances Baucham." And he would tell the story often of the time he lost his best player for a week, not because he was flunking a class, but because his mother would not tolerate a C on a progress report. I was performing below my ability and below my mother's expectations. And in my house, that was simply unacceptable.

I would go on to excel academically for the rest of my life. In high school, I was not only a captain on the football and track teams; I was also a leader of our student government, a peer counselor, an officer in the Spanish Club and the Math Club, a member of the Honor Society, listed in *Who's Who Among American High School Students*, a member of Mu Alpha Theta (a national high school and junior college honor society for mathematics), a Merit Scholar, and graduated near the top of my graduating class of over four hundred students. I would eventually attend college on a football scholarship, but I saw that as a means to an end—and that end was not football. My first three recruiting visits were to Rice University (the Harvard of the South), West Point, and the United States Air Force Academy.

So What?

You may be asking, "This book is about Critical Race Theory and the Church. What does all of this have to do with that, social justice, and the current conversation about race in America?"

The answer is: EVERYTHING!

I grew up poor, without a father, and surrounded by drugs, gangs, violence, and disfunction in one of the toughest urban environments imaginable. Yet through all of that, I didn't just survive; I thrived! Not because of government programs or white people "doing the work of anti-racism"; I thrived in large part because, by God's grace, my mother protected me, sacrificed for me, advocated for me, and disciplined me.

Black people often take offense when they hear me speak about the importance of family and personal responsibility. The attitude Jesse Jackson expressed when he was caught on a hot mic saying he wanted to "cut [President Barack Obama's] nuts off" when he heard him "talking down to black people" is both real and common. There are those to whom any response to the plight of black people in America that emphasizes something other than systemic racism, white supremacy, or white privilege is seen as "blaming the victim."

Advocates of this victim mentality think the only thing that can cause a man like me to focus on the centrality of family and personal responsibility is internalized racism, a lack of sensitivity, catering to white folk, being out of touch with blackness and/or the black experience, or all of the above. Well, those people don't know me. They don't know my story. And, in fact, until you hear everything else I have to say, you don't know my story either. It took more than a strong mother and a bus ride to South Carolina to save me.

CHAPTER TWO

A Black Christian

T here is a major debate among black evangelicals as to whether, in discussing and applying our faith in the midst of the current cultural crisis, the priority should be on our blackness or our Christianity. In other words, are we Christians or black people first? This may seem strange to non-black Christians. However, I assure you, it is a real issue and is relevant to the topic of this book.[1] I have wrestled with this question since coming to faith, and I have fallen on both sides of it at different times—all of which I will detail in this chapter.

The question of the proper order of faith and ethnicity is critical to understanding the various positions people take in the broader social-justice debate—one with which all people must wrestle, regardless of their ethnicity. However, for black Christians, this concept has often been difficult to embrace for several reasons.

Black Nationalists have often argued that Christianity is the white man's religion and that whites used it to encourage slaves to be docile. My

---

[1] Kimberlé Crenshaw, *Mapping the Margins: Intersectionality, Identity Politics and Violence against Women of Color*, https://www.racialequitytools.org/resourcefiles/mapping-margins.pdf.

childhood hero, Malcolm X, for example, "denounced Christianity as a religion designed for slaves." He also saw "the Negro clergy as the curse of the black man, exploiting him for their own purposes instead of seeking to liberate him, and acting as handmaidens of the white community in its determination to keep the Negroes in a subservient position."[2] This is very similar to Marx's insistence that "religion is the opiate of the masses." So when Black Nationalism is combined with Marxism (as it often is), an especially virulent strain of anti-Christian sentiment forms. Therefore, for many black people, coming to faith in Christ requires addressing this objection not only in and for one's own self, but also for one's peers.

Providentially, the Bible does not leave us to answer this question in the dark. This is exactly what Jesus meant when He said:

> Do not think that I have come to bring peace to the earth. I have not come to bring peace, but a sword. For I have come to set a man against his father, and a daughter against her mother, and a daughter-in-law against her mother-in-law. And a person's enemies will be those of his own household. (Matthew 10:34–36)

The Gospel is not something that merely sits on top of our identity. When we come to Christ, our identity is transformed completely. As Paul tells us, "From now on, therefore, we regard no one according to the flesh. Even though we once regarded Christ according to the flesh, we regard him thus no longer. Therefore, if anyone is in Christ, he is a new creation. The old has passed away; behold, the new has come" (2 Corinthians 5:16–17).

A New Creation

I am not a Christian because I was raised to be one. (I wasn't.) Nor am I a Christian because I was smart enough to figure it out, good

---

[2] Malcolm X, *The Autobiography of Malcolm X* (New York, New York: Random House Publishing Group, Kindle Edition, 2015).

enough to find my way, or lucky enough to meet the right people. I am a Christian because the grace of God found me when I wasn't even looking. I am a Christian because of God's miraculous intervention in my life.

That intervention came in October 1987 on the campus of New Mexico State University—a place where I wasn't even "supposed to be." My uncle had talked me out of going to the Air Force Academy, and all the big schools had already allocated their allotment of scholarships. That left NMSU. I had only visited because the strength coach, Gil Reyes, was a legend. It turned out he would leave for the University of Nevada-Las Vegas before I even got there. My plan was to play a season at NMSU before heading on to greener pastures, which is exactly what I did ... eventually.

I was the starting tight end at NMSU by my second practice. In my first game against the University of Texas at El Paso (UTEP), I caught 10 passes for 106 yards. The campus was abuzz with people who wanted to know why this new "Blue Chip" recruit was slumming at NMSU.

However, one guy had different motives for wanting to know me. His name was Steve Morgan. He was a Campus Crusade staffer, and he heard that I was involved with the Fellowship of Christian Athletes, so he met with me to talk about leading a Bible study to reach the football players with the Gospel. It took him about five minutes to learn that 1) he had been misinformed, and 2) I didn't know Jesus from the Man in the Moon. He tried to take me through the Four Spiritual Laws, but that wasn't registering with me. Eventually, he backed up, held up his Bible, and—being a Wisconsin boy—gave me his best Vince Lombardi impression: "Voddie, *this* is a Bible."

We spent the next two or three weeks meeting together as he answered my questions and helped me delve deeper into biblical truth. Eventually, he taught me how to find my own answers, and I began to search the Scriptures daily.

Every conversion is a miraculous event. Scripture makes it clear that every man is dead in sin, prone to pursue the passions of his flesh, and under satanic influence (Ephesians 2:1–3). As a result, men, in and of themselves, do not turn to God and obey Him. In fact, man is incapable of doing so (Romans 8:8); the Bible tells us, "No one understands; no one seeks for God. All have turned aside; together they have become worthless; no one does good, not even one" (Romans 3:11–12). This goes beyond mere ignorance. In fact, the Bible makes it clear that men are in fact "hostile to God" (Romans 8:7). As the prophet Isaiah says, "All we like sheep have gone astray; we have turned—every one—to his own way" (Isaiah 53:6).

I remember the day I realized this. Steve had asked me how sure I was that I would go to Heaven when I died. Being the arrogant and ignorant young man I was, I figured my odds were "better than most" and said, "About 90 percent." Steve looked at me and—instead of being impressed, as I thought he would be—asked me a question that changed my life.

"What if I can give you the other 10 percent?"

That question stayed with me for the next several days until finally, on Friday, November 13, 1987, as I sat in the NMSU locker room after practice waiting for Steve, I could hold back no longer. I understood what it meant to be a sinner and that I could not save myself.

I lay down on the floor and said, "God, that thing You did for Steve that he's been telling me You want to do for me? Now's good." I believed the Gospel. I repented of my sin. And God saved me.

For me, the miracle of salvation took place my first year in college. However, it started long before that. Technically, it started before the foundation of the world (Ephesians 1:4), but looking back, I see God's providential work intensifying my last two years of high school.

During my junior year, my cousin Jarmal was murdered in California. Going back to Los Angeles for his funeral affected me tremendously. I thought about the way our paths diverged and could not fathom why things ended so differently for us. I also began to think about my life in significantly more profound ways. The next year I decided to go to the Air Force Academy, then got talked out of it only to be "forced" to spend a season in Las Cruces, New Mexico (which is Spanish for "the crosses"). Talk about divine appointments. Look at God!

Afrocentric Christian

I met my wife, Bridget, during my sophomore year in college in January 1989. I married her on June 30 that year. Our daughter, Jasmine, was born ten months after that. I was playing football and studying pre-law and international business at Rice University in Houston, having transferred there after a year at NMSU. Bridget was in her senior year as an education major across town at Texas Southern University. I spent two and a half years at Rice before transferring to Houston Baptist University (HBU) in 1991.

A dear friend from that era recently sent me a photo that elicited a multi-layered response. I smiled as I reminisced about the good old days. I shook my head in dismay at being reminded of the folly of youth and sighed as I pondered what others must have thought of me at that time. This photo of me, my friend, and his fiancée captured the enigmatic nature of my early Christian life in a single frame, and it instantly reminded me of at least two undeniable realities.

One was how young I was. It was taken when I was married, a father, and fully immersed in Christian ministry at the ripe old age of twenty-two.

It also reminded me how Afrocentric I was at that time. There I stood, an HBU ministry student who would go on to win the prestigious Riverside Scholarship (a full scholarship to the Southern Baptist seminary of my choice) for being an outstanding theology student, and I was wearing a T-shirt featuring Martin Luther King Jr., Malcolm X, and Elijah Muhammad! I assure you, it doesn't get much more Afrocentric than that.

Nor did my Afrocentrism stop at wearing T-shirts. Not only was I a member of Omega Psi Phi—a black fraternity known for having its members brand a Greek letter on their arms—but I also helped get it back onto the NMSU campus after it had been suspended. I had married a woman from an historically black college and was one of the founders of the Black Student Fellowship at HBU. At that point in my life, I was most certainly more black than Christian.

HBU didn't have a football team, so when I transferred there from Rice, I lost my scholarship. I was twenty-two years old with a wife and a new daughter, and I had no idea how I was going to pay for my last year of college; I only knew I had to get it done. I had secured a full-time job, and Bridget had graduated and was teaching school by then. But we were still struggling. Providentially, as a Southern Baptist institution, HBU offered a substantial tuition break for ministry students who belonged to a Southern Baptist church. So we became Southern Baptists!

I remember the discussion with the registrar like it was yesterday. I asked her two questions: 1) What is a Southern Baptist church? and 2) Where do I find a black one? As I think about those questions, I am struck by how uncontroversial they were. It made as much sense to the registrar that I would be looking for a black church as it did that I would be looking for a Southern Baptist one. She was no more taken aback by the fact that I didn't want to go to church with white people than she was by the fact that I didn't want to pay full tuition.

A Season in the Desert

Bridget and I ended up joining Holman Street Baptist Church, where Reverend Manson Johnson was the pastor. (Johnson was quite the character. He preached every Sunday in a tuxedo with tails. I kid you not!)

The next year was tough. I had gone from being a big-time college football player contemplating a career in the NFL and a sought-after speaker within the Fellowship of Christian Athletes to a struggling ministry student who, all of a sudden, had zero opportunities coming his way.

But God knew exactly what He was doing. That season in the desert, having my pride crushed, was just what I needed to prepare me for my next season of life and ministry. I had to go from building a reputation on *my story* to building a ministry on *His story*. That season also helped me learn to build a ministry by investing in others rather than riding my reputation.

HBU required all students to double major. I was there to get a Bachelor of Arts in Christianity. Since I was a senior when I transferred, there was no time for dreaming. I was closest to completing a sociology degree, so *voila!* I became a sociology major. This would figure prominently in my life and ministry.

Always an Advocate

There is a passage of Scripture tucked away in the book of Job that has always served as a motivational guide for me in terms of serving others:

> When I went out to the gate of the city, when I prepared my seat in the square, the young men saw me and withdrew, and the aged rose and stood; the princes refrained from talking and laid their hand on their mouth; the voice of the nobles was hushed, and their tongue stuck to the roof of their mouth. When the ear heard, it called me blessed, and when the eye saw, it approved, because I delivered the poor who cried for help, and the fatherless who had none to help him. The blessing of him who was about to perish came upon me, and I caused the widow's heart to sing for joy. I put on righteousness, and it clothed me; my justice was like a robe and a turban. I was eyes to the blind and feet to the lame. I was a father to the needy, and I searched out the cause of him whom I did not know. I broke the fangs of the unrighteous and made him drop his prey from his teeth. (Job 29:7–17)

I think it is very important to read passages like this carefully. Our tendency is to rip it, kicking and screaming, from its context and fit it neatly into our system of moralism or legalism. However, that would be a mistake. In fact, that is precisely the mistake made by many an eager Social Justice Warrior (SJW). They take texts like this and immediately conclude, "We must advocate for justice for the oppressed!"

Ibram X. Kendi captured this sentiment in a recent tweet contrasting his "Liberation Theology" with what he called "Savior Theology." According to Kendi, we are not here to see people delivered from the penalty and power of sin. On the contrary, "the job of the Christian is to liberate oppressed people from their oppressors."[3] (We will revisit Kendi's theology, philosophy, and influence throughout this book.)

While I am no fan of Kendi or Liberation Theology, I have always taken the call to advocacy seriously. In many ways, it has characterized my adult life.

When I left football and found myself in need of a job to pay tuition, the first ones I landed were in the field of social work. I worked at Houston Achievement Place, which offered everything from counseling and skills training for families to foster-care placement for children. After graduating from HBU, I went to Southwestern Baptist Theological Seminary in Fort Worth, Texas, and supported my family through a job at a similar facility until I landed a position as minister of missions at Cornerstone Baptist Church in Arlington. There I served under Pastor Dwight McKissic … until I got fired for a youthful zeal for justice that turned into an act of defiant insubordination. (Speaking of youthful zeal, it was Pastor McKissic who confronted me about my Afrocentric T-shirts. But that's another story for another day.)

During those years, I worked in two different group homes with kids whose stories were similar to my own: poor kids from rough neighborhoods whose fathers were not in the picture. They were being educated

---

[3] Ibram X. Kendi (@DrIbram), "And the White savior idea informs what I call 'savior theology.' That the job of the Christian is to save all those backward, savage, lowly humans. Thank God I learned liberation theology. That the job of the Christian is to liberate oppressed peoples from their oppression," Twitter, September 27, 2020, 3:54 p.m., https://twitter.com/dribram/status/1310306763359555587?s=12.

in inferior schools and living in environments where drugs, gangs, and violence were the norm. However, unlike me, these kids had not been able to escape. For them, things had gotten so bad that they had to be taken out of their homes.

Working in those environments was a natural extension and expression of both my upbringing and my education. Both my parents spent most of their careers in social work–related fields. My mother eventually retired as a victims' advocate in the Bexar County court system in San Antonio, Texas, and my father had several social work–related jobs in boys' homes, community centers, and at least one juvenile detention center. When I think about my successes in life, I don't think, "I pulled myself up by my own bootstraps." Rather, I think, "He raises up the poor from the dust; he lifts the needy from the ash heap to make them sit with princes and inherit a seat of honor. For the pillars of the earth are the LORD's, and on them he has set the world" (1 Samuel 2:8).

I don't take this truth as an invitation to simply sit and wait for God to "do something" for the widow, the orphan, or the poor. In fact, I have pursued advocacy work because I recognize that God uses His people to deliver the oppressed.

I point this out because at the heart of the current debate over racism lies a false dichotomy that says, "Either you are on the side of the oppressed" (read: an SJW), or you are 1) shutting down the conversation about racial injustice, 2) ignoring minority voices, and 3) upholding (or internalizing) white supremacy. One pastor friend put it this way in a private email:

"I cannot help but feel that much of the dispute … comes down not to a disagreement on principles, but to a disagreement on historical judgments. [One] crowd *doesn't see race in America as a significant problem worth addressing*, while the [other] does."

There is, however, an alternative explanation—one I will present more fully hereafter.

But first, back to my story.

Welcomed and Wanted

From the time I arrived at HBU, I was welcomed into Southern Baptist life. My professors went out of their way to disciple and mentor me. Men like Randy Hatchett and David Capes did more than just teach me; they invested in me. Like most of the men I met thereafter, they were genuine brothers who were well aware of the Southern Baptist Convention's (SBC) racist history and determined to see it continue to make strides in ethnic relations.

This welcoming attitude continued when I got to seminary. Shortly after turning in my first paper in a New Testament survey class, my professor called me in for a meeting. I thought I had done something wrong. However, he said he saw promise in my work and wanted to encourage me to keep after it. He had seen many promising black students in his day, but few continued their academic pursuits. Many failed to complete their M.Divs. The ones who did usually went on to greener pastures in churches that would pay them far more than the academy. Rare was the black student who would go on to doctoral-level work.

During my doctoral studies, I went from being welcomed to being courted. Paige Patterson was, at that time, a famous (or infamous, depending on your perspective), larger-than-life figure in the SBC, a key player who helped free it from the grips of liberalism to become the first Protestant denomination ever to recover its conservative moorings in the 1990s. This involved deliberately positioning candidates for key positions in the Convention.

Patterson was president of Southeastern Baptist Theological Seminary while I was studying for my doctorate there. I never had a class with him, but he took notice of me and other black doctoral students. In fact, he took specific steps to invest in me. He made it clear that he wanted to see me become not just a professor at an SBC seminary, but president of one of them—or even the first black president of the Convention.

As my star began to rise, I preached at every one of the six SBC seminaries, a number of state conventions, and twice at the pastors' conference of the annual meeting. I was also appointed as a committee chairman at the annual SBC meeting in New Orleans. Nor was this merely Patterson's doing. There was no shortage of leaders willing to help me gain more prominence there.

That is, until I committed what amounted to two tactical errors which would end any hopes I had of serving in high SBC offices.

In 2004, two things happened: 1) the SBC voted to boycott Disney because of its aggressively pro-homosexual agenda, and 2) my good friend Bruce Shortt, along with the *Baptist Banner* publisher T.C. Pinckney, proposed a resolution asking Southern Baptists to leave government schools (which I openly opposed). The following year, Bruce and I combined those ideas.[4] If Disney's actions warranted a boycott, then government schools, whose pro-homosexual agenda was already in full swing, certainly deserved the same treatment.

To be clear, Bruce and I were both homeschooling dads and staunch advocates of Christian education. We both saw government schools as places to which no Christian should send their child unless there was absolutely no alternative, and we chided churches for not offering those alternatives. To say that this was and is a minority view in the SBC is a gross understatement; over 85 percent of Southern Baptists send their children to government schools. Moreover, the SBC lags far behind other Christian groups in advocating for or providing Christian education alternatives. In fact, among Christian government-school teachers, the SBC has the highest representation of any denomination. Needless to say, I was not winning friends and influencing people by putting my name on this resolution. However, I saw the threat of the LGBTQIA+ movement and the entire social-justice juggernaut, of which it is but the tip of the spear, as a clear and present danger.

Ironically, after being mocked, ridiculed, and dismissed, I was invited to do a radio interview with Albert Mohler, the president of Southern

---

[4] Religious Herald, "Proposed SBC Resolution Encourages Churches to Investigate Homosexuality in Public Schools," Baptist News Global, June 13, 2005, https://baptistnews.com/article/proposedsbcresolutionencourageschurchestoin-vestigatehomosexualityinpubl/#.X2ClJi10fOQ.

Baptist Theological Seminary and arguably the most respected Southern Baptist thinker and theologian of the modern era. Much to my surprise, he flat-out endorsed our resolution![5] In fact, although we only called for an investigation of public schools with a view toward further action, Mohler went further, saying, "I believe that now is the time for responsible Southern Baptists to develop an exit strategy from the public schools." His support was so unequivocal that the SBC later adopted our resolution. Nonetheless, I would forever be labeled as "a radical" in the eyes of many.

My second error came in the form of a blog post a few years later when I dared to identify myself openly as a Calvinist. It has been said that the only thing the leaders of the conservative resurgence hate more than the liberalism they successfully rooted out of the Convention are its lingering vestiges of Calvinism. This anti-Calvinist faction included my friend and benefactor, Paige Patterson. Though we remain friends, it was no secret that my position put me outside the camp.

The Blessing of the Blacklist

If you think I am complaining about the aforementioned reversal of fortune, you are sorely mistaken. I am grateful to have been a part of the SBC and for all the help and encouragement I received along the way. I appreciate every brother and sister who reached out to me during my formative years. More than merely welcoming, I found my SBC brethren to be downright eager to bridge ethnic divides. (That is why, unlike many revisionist historians, I see not the slightest hint of hypocrisy or duplicity in its 1995 statement on slavery and racism.)[6]

---

[5] Bob Allen, "Proposed SBC Resolution Seeks 'Exit Strategy' from Public Schools," Good Faith Media, April 26, 2006, https://goodfaithmedia.org/proposed-sbc-resolution-seeks-exit-strategy-from-public-schools-cms-7273.

[6] Southern Baptist Convention, "Resolution on Racial Reconciliation on the 150th Anniversary of the Southern Baptist Convention," June 1, 1995, https://www.sbc.net/resource-library/resolutions/resolution-on-racial-reconciliation-on-the-150th-anniversary-of-the-southern-baptist-convention.

As one of, if not the first, black itinerant preachers in the Conference of Southern Baptist Evangelists, I was constantly bombarded with invitations to preach at local churches and associations and to lecture at Southern Baptist colleges and seminaries. My first book was not the result of my reaching out to publishers, but of the SBC publisher B&H Publishing's reaching out to me to see if I had any material I wanted to turn into a book. So when things changed for me in the SBC, I knew better than to assume it had anything to do with my melanin. On the contrary, the way I saw it, my reversal of fortunes represented the height of acceptance: Patterson and others changing their posture toward me proved they saw me as anything but a token. They treated me exactly the way they treated white Southern Baptists who held positions they considered contrary to the Convention's best interests. I saw things the way one of the first black head coaches in the NFL did: it's not when they hire one of us, he said, but when they fire one of us that you know we're being treated as equals.

He Has Made the Two into One

In 1990, University of Colorado head football coach Bill McCartney founded Promise Keepers. The movement spread like wildfire, eventually filling stadiums nationwide with tens of thousands of men, training them to become God-fearing husbands and fathers. However, McCartney, who was used to working with young men from diverse backgrounds, was disappointed with the "whiteness" of the crowds. Consequently, diversity became a central focus and theme of the movement.

I remember taking part in several Promise Keepers events in the mid-1990s. Up to that point, I had never seen such a drive for diversity among believers. Then in 1995, the Southern Baptist Convention passed a resolution repenting of its racist history. Suddenly, I found myself surrounded by people calling for racial reconciliation.

But instead of being encouraged, I was convicted. I had spent my short Christian life pursuing segregation. At HBU, I made sure I was able to find a black SBC church to help me meet the requirement for a half scholarship. I was very active in my black fraternity, and I had also helped found the Black Student Fellowship. When I got to Southwestern Seminary, I immediately looked for another black SBC church, then combed the job-placement boards until I found a position at another black SBC church. And I had only recently stopped wearing Black Power paraphernalia. Now here I was speaking at PK events that highlighted racial reconciliation!

Eventually, this conviction led to action. *I was not aware of, nor had I ever met, a black pastor who was working for or even passionate about racial reconciliation.* Not one had ever lamented the fact that their church was 99 percent black, or that the remaining 1 percent included exactly zero white members. I am not saying that was the entirety of the black church experience, or that those leaders were evil or ungodly—only that for the first time, I was coming face-to-face with brothers who, through tear-stained eyes, were begging God to diversify His church, and all of them were white.

I did not condemn my pastor at the time. (Nor do I now.) I just knew I had to do something. So I decided then and there that I would not continue to live and serve in environments where everybody looked like me. I didn't announce it. I didn't challenge or even invite others to join me. I just did it.

Fenton Moorhead was one of those brothers whose passion for racial reconciliation, imperfect though it may have been, was real and tangible. We met when he invited me to preach at an Urban Boys Camp put on by Sugar Creek Baptist Church in Sugar Land, Texas, every year. They brought hundreds of young men from inner-city Houston to a campsite for a week of worship, teaching, mentoring, recreation, and fellowship. I spent a week preaching at that camp and getting to know Pastor Moorhead. In 1996, I took a position on the staff of his predominantly white church. I believed then, as I do now, that the Lord called me not only to that position, but to the broader pursuit it represented. However, if I said it was always a happy journey, that would be a lie. That position, like the next two decades of my ministry, was fraught with difficulty and hardship.

It was a challenge for me personally. I struggled over the years to strike a balance between working to promote unity and working to make it a non-issue. I didn't want to be "the black guy" on staff. I just wanted to serve the body. I was constantly aware of this tension. But whether I liked it or not, I *was* the black guy on staff—usually, the first black guy ever to be on staff. I was also constantly aware of the fact that in many ways, I was a stranger in a strange land. These people had different worship styles, leadership styles, came from different backgrounds, watched different shows, and in many ways lived very different lives than the other people I knew. On the other hand, I came to realize that, underneath all of that, they were the same as me. They battled the same demons, struggled with the same ups and downs, wanted the same things, and feared the same things I did. In the end, these were my brothers and sisters in Christ. So, regardless of the challenges and difficulties, I stayed the course.

That season of life was not only a challenge for me; it was also a challenge for my wife and children. Our two oldest were born in 1990 and 1993, respectively. Their only memories of their spiritual upbringing are in the context of being extreme ethnic minorities who also had the "privilege" of living in the fishbowl that plagued all pastors' kids. They grew weary of statements that were sometimes insensitive, and sometimes downright racist. They also grew weary of having to live in the shadow of a father who, besides having dragged them into environments where they were ethnic "others," also had a propensity for being the occasional theological lighting rod.

In addition to challenging me and my family, that season was also a challenge for the churches I served. It took me a while to realize that my family and I were not the only ones who struggled under the weight of my decisions. Churches that decided to reach outside their ethnic comfort zones to bring me on staff took great risks and faced great challenges as well. They were accused of tokenism, had to figure out whether and when it was OK to challenge or disagree with me—and on rare occasions, had to deal with objections from members who didn't want me on staff. These churches also had to learn to navigate a new ethnic landscape in a changing culture.

Finally, according to some, that season in my life was a challenge for black churches that I didn't serve. One of the most stinging charges I faced after leaving the world of predominantly black churches was that I was guilty of "robbing the black church" of her best and brightest. To some, the idea of well-educated, gifted, experienced ministers of the Gospel who could have been serving the black church (but weren't) was treason of the highest order. And some were not shy about telling me so. One black pastor, after complimenting me on the sermon I had just delivered to his congregation, said, "It's a shame that brothers like you take your gifts and go serve white folks."

Back to Africa

In the summer of 2006, I had the chance to go to Africa for the first time. It was a life-changing experience. Like many young black American men, I had always wanted to go there. Part of my attraction to the idea was rooted in the Black Power stream of identity to which I had migrated. I had imbibed the myth of having "come from kings and queens," had claimed every Egyptian achievement as my heritage in spite of my obvious West-African roots, and was awash in kente cloth and a love for Swahili, even though it was only spoken by a small minority of Africans and probably was not the language of my ancestors. Yes, I was itching to go to the Motherland.

That first visit was magical! I landed in Zambia the last week of August with my oldest son, Trey (Voddie III). We were there for the Annual Zambia Reformed Family Conference put on by the Reformed Baptist Church Association of Zambia (ReBCAZ). We stayed in the home of Pastor Conrad Mbewe. Everything about the two weeks we spent there was amazing: The fellowship was sweet, the ministry was fruitful and refreshing, and the cultural experience was far more than we could have anticipated. When I got home, Bridget asked me how it went. I just looked at her and said, "I think I want to be buried there!"

Eight years later and six trips later, the Lord made it as clear to Bridget as He had to me that we were being called to Zambia. ReBCAZ was starting the African Christian University (ACU), a semi-classical liberal arts university committed to a biblical worldview, academic excellence, and theological fidelity. Bridget looked at me during a family trip that took us to Kenya, Zambia, and South Africa, and said, "You need to be here!" That was in August 2014.

One year later, we sold our home, packed everything we owned in a couple of Maersk intermodal containers, and with our seven youngest children in tow, put our hand to the plow on African soil. As of this writing, we have been in Lusaka, Zambia, for five years.

A New Perspective

Living in Africa has given me a new perspective on many things. First, it has given me a renewed appreciation for God's providence. I see His hand in American history in ways I hadn't appreciated before—not only in establishing what I believe is the greatest Republic in the history of the world, but also in allowing me to be born, educated, and trained for the ministry there. Most Africans would give all they had to get to America. Ironically, I didn't have to do that because my ancestors were forced to give all they had as African slaves.

I have also broadened my perspective on slavery. A visit to the Slave Tree in Ndola, Zambia, poignantly reminded me that, contrary to popular belief, white slavers did not come to Africa and track through the bush to find and capture slaves; they bought them from other Africans who had already enslaved them. It was sobering to realize that my ancestors—far from being kings and queens—were actually debtors, criminals, or conquered people who were sold to Westerners by their own kinsmen. And thank God they sold them to the Westerners and not the Arabs! The Arab slave trade lasted more than thirteen centuries and was far more brutal; few Africans sold to the Arabs even survived the journey.[7]

Finally, living in Africa for the past five years has broadened my perspective on social justice in two major ways:

1) I have come to understand that the Critical Social Justice (CSJ) movement is global. Just like people in the U.S. are arguing that racial disparities are *de facto* evidence of racism and white supremacy, the global version of CSJ is arguing that the same is true in regard to global inequities. Thus, power and resources must be redistributed not only within nations, but between them. And since America is the wealthiest nation on earth, guess who needs to "check their privilege" and divest themselves of power the most?

2) I have come to realize that culture does matter, that not all cultures are equal, that Christian culture has produced the highest levels of freedom and prosperity and the lowest levels of corruption and oppression in the world, and that transforming culture is a laudable and worthwhile goal.

An Unexpected Assignment

As ACU got off the ground, we found ourselves with a ragtag bunch of volunteers and a few full-time staffers. We started with ten students while we were in the midst of moving from registration as an institution to the more formal accreditation process—and with me teaching Introduction to Sociology.

Though I chaired the Theology Department and served as dean of the School of Divinity, neither excited me since administration is not my

---

[7] David Gakunzi, "The Arab-Muslim Slave Trade: Lifting the Taboo," Jerusalem Center for Public Affairs, September 3, 2018, https://jcpa.org/article/the-arab-muslim-slave-trade-lifting-the-taboo. The Arab slave trade was notorious for brutality, rape, castration, and high mortality rates. This is one reason there are so few surviving black populations in the Arab world as compared to the West.

thing. But teaching Introduction to Sociology for two years was an absolute blast! Getting reacquainted with the literature was like diving into a pool of current affairs—only this pool was the fountainhead from which the ideas that drove current affairs sprang. We used the most popular Intro to Sociology textbook in the world since 1) there is a shortage of sociology textbooks written from a biblical worldview, 2) I wanted to show the students what was "out there" beyond our worldview, and 3) it gave us a great opportunity to analyze contemporary culture using its own source material. It also helped re-immerse me in the foundational ideas I had been dealing with since the beginning of my ministry.

Many people who hear me speak about issues like postmodernism, cultural Marxism, neo-Marxism, Critical Theory, the Frankfurt School, and Intersectionality assume that I am either parroting a particular evangelical trope or trying to put on airs. However, few realize that I have been talking about these things for nearly two decades, or that my educational background is in the behavioral sciences. My first book, *The Ever-Loving Truth: Can Faith Thrive in a Post-Christian Culture?*, is rife with references to cultural, sociological, and philosophical ideas from the perspective of cultural apologetics. I was warning about the Frankfurt School at homeschool conferences in the mid-2000s, and many people at that time thought I was out to lunch. It was only later, as the social-justice debate heated up, that Americans started to notice the ground underneath them was vibrating.

But by then, I was far away in Zambia.

In fact, the response of Zambians to recent racial incidents in the United States served as a catalyst for me to write this book. The police in Zambia do not "protect and serve" the citizenry; they "protect and serve" themselves, usually to your property. They generally do not respond to crime, so you don't "call the cops" here. Most often, you see them stopping cars, looking for violations. When they find one, they pull motorists over to the side of the road where fines are paid ... in cash! They also beat thieves and other criminals upon arrest—and recording such an incident with a cell phone will earn you similar treatment.

So when Zambians began to ask me questions about the murderous and corrupt American police hunting down black men, I could not remain silent. I began to tell the stories and raise the issues that I will share with you in the next chapter.

CHAPTER THREE

Seeking True Justice

G od clearly condemns injustice. He is also clear in His condemnation of falsehood and lies. The most succinct statement of this is found in the Decalogue. The Ninth Commandment simply states, "You shall not bear false witness against your neighbor" (Exodus 20:16). However, this commandment carries more weight than one can imagine. Falsehood and lies are reprehensible because they not only harm those to and/or about whom they are told, but they also blaspheme the very character and nature of the God Who is truth (John 14:6), whose very Word is truth (Psalm 119:43, 160; John 17:17), and whose very essence is that of "the Father of lights, with whom there is no variation or shadow due to change" (James 1:17). Moreover, God is clear about His attitude toward falsehood and its implications:

> There are six things that the LORD hates, seven that are an abomination to him: haughty eyes, a lying tongue, and hands that shed innocent blood, a heart that devises wicked plans, feet that make haste to run to evil, a false witness who

breathes out lies, and one who sows discord among brothers.
(Proverbs 6:16–19)

There are falsehoods in the current cultural moment that tick every one of these boxes. As such, these falsehoods must be confronted.

Colin Kaepernick

On September 1, 2016, San Francisco 49ers quarterback Colin Kaepernick decided to kneel during the National Anthem before his team's last preseason game to protest police violence against black people.

Numerous articles lionized Kaepernick as a modern civil-rights hero, claiming that he was a "figurehead for a movement of NFL players" protesting *"police killings of unarmed black Americans."*[1] There had been several such stories in the news at the time. I always thought Kaepernick was protesting the killings of Trayvon Martin, 17, of Miami Gardens, Florida, in 2012; Michael Brown, 18, of Ferguson, Missouri, in 2014; and Tamir Rice, 12, of Cleveland, Ohio, also in 2014. Mind you, even if that were the case, I did not see his protest as valid for reasons I will detail in this book.

However, I was shocked and more than a little disappointed when I learned that the real flashpoint for Kaepernick was a case that had even less merit than these: In an interview with NBC News, Kaepernick explained he was protesting a deadly December 2015 confrontation between San Francisco police officers and a twenty-six-year-old man named Mario Woods.[2] The fact that Kaepernick and others saw the Woods case as a legitimate cause for protest is quite telling.

---

[1] Mark Bain, "Nike's Kaepernick Ad Is What Happens When Capitalism and Activism Collide," *Quartz*, September 29, 2018, https://qz.com/1400583/modern-corporate-social-activism-looks-like-nikes-kaepernick-ad.

[2] David K. Li, "Colin Kaepernick Reveals the Specific Police Shooting That Led Him to Kneel," NBC News, August 20, 2019, https://www.nbcnews.com/news/us-news/colin-kaepernick-reveals-specific-police-shooting-led-him-kneel-n1044306.

Three aspects of the Mario Woods case belie the claims of Kaepernick's crusade and reveal the true fault lines that lie beneath.

We hear over and over that taking a knee during the National Anthem is an act of protest against police brutality as evidenced by the rampant hunting and killing of "innocent, unarmed, black men." However—like several of the other black men shot or killed by police in 2020, whom we will discuss later—Woods was neither innocent nor unarmed. In fact, when confronted by the San Francisco police, Woods reached into his pocket and produced a knife nearly eight inches long.[3]

Second, Woods was a threat to both the police and the public. The police were responding to a reported stabbing. The victim had been taken to a nearby hospital, where he gave a description of his assailant; police were dispatched to the scene, where they found and confronted Woods. At that point, Woods drew his knife and refused all five responding officers' attempts to stop him from using it. According to a report released after a year-long internal investigation, "These included verbal commands, O.C. spray, Less Lethal Force options including: 40mm ERIW and the 12 gauge ERIW bean bag rounds." None of these options achieved the desired effect; Woods continued to brandish his knife and did not surrender.

One bystander who captured the events on his phone can be heard saying, "Drop that knife," and again, "Drop that knife, homeboy!" Someone asks, "Did they shoot him?" Another bystander responds, "They're using rubber bullets." Woods was hit multiple times by these "less-than-lethal" rounds, once taking him to the ground. However, he got up and continued to threaten police and civilians. In the end, "Woods continued directly towards" the five officers facing him until he was "less than ten feet" away. Only then did they open fire.

This incident was tragic, to be sure. However, to cite it as an example of police brutality that warrants national protest stretches credulity. Especially when that protest is characterized as a movement to raise awareness

---

[3] San Francisco Police Department memorandum, June 12, 2018, https://www.sfchronicle.com/file/462/2/4622-151045735-_responsive_1%20(1).pdf.

of the killing of "unarmed black men." More importantly, cries for "Justice for Mario Woods" and the ensuing Kaepernick protest reveal a kind of cognitive dissonance that underlies much of the Critical Social Justice movement. Understanding the ideology that lies at the root of this cognitive dissonance is key to recognizing the fault line it represents.

Real Justice Requires Truth

Beyond confronting falsehoods in general, our pursuit of justice must also be characterized by a pursuit of truth. Much has been said recently about seeking justice, and I could not agree more. However, we must be certain that we pursue justice on God's terms. For instance, we must bear in mind that "A single witness shall not suffice against a person for any crime or for any wrong in connection with any offense that he has committed. Only on the evidence of two witnesses or of three witnesses shall a charge be established" (Deuteronomy 19:15, cf. Matthew 18:16; 2 Corinthians 13:1; 1 Timothy 5:19; Hebrews 10:28). This is critical in our quest to adhere to the Lord's admonition that "You shall do no injustice in court. You shall not be partial to the poor or defer to the great, but in righteousness shall you judge your neighbor" (Leviticus 19:15). How much of our current debate about justice is rooted in these principles?

My goal when I hear about "injustices" is to bear in mind that I am biased. I am a single witness with limited information, and I carry a ton of baggage. So when I am evaluating people's testimonies and pleas, and when people are shouting, "Justice for George, Ahmaud, Breonna, Trayvon!" or anyone else, I always want to bear in mind the words of John 7:51: "Does our law judge a man without first giving him a hearing and learning what he does?" I also want to remember that "the one who states his case first seems right, until the other comes and examines him" (Proverbs 18:17), which is why "if one gives an answer before he hears, it is his folly and shame" (Proverbs 18:13).

Today, people are rioting and demanding justice before knowing the facts, and in most cases, without ever considering the aforementioned principles. And here is the key: *People are ignoring these principles because the standard of justice upon which their pleas are built does not come from the God of the Scriptures.* While that may be fine for others, those of us who claim to know Christ are held to a different standard.

Exposing the False Narrative

In a now-famous tweet, NBA star LeBron James wrote, "We're literally hunted EVERYDAY/EVERYTIME we step foot outside the comfort of our homes!" (emphasis his).[4]

A *New York Times* headline proclaimed last June: "'Pandemic within a Pandemic': Coronavirus and Police Brutality Roil Black Community." The story quoted a protest organizer who said, "I'm just as likely to die from a cop as I am from COVID."[5] Not to be outdone, the *Washington Post* headlined a story: "Police Killing Black People Is a Pandemic, Too," with a subhead stating, "State violence is a public health crisis."[6] Vox echoed that claim, citing National Academy of Sciences research that suggests "one in every 1,000 black men and boys can expect to be killed by police in this country."[7] Al Jazeera even

---

[4] LeBron James (@KingJames), "We're literally hunted EVERYDAY/EVERYTIME we step foot outside the comfort of our homes! Can't even go for a damn jog man! Like WTF man are you kidding me?!?!?!?!?!? No man fr ARE YOU KIDDING ME!!!!! I'm sorry Ahmaud(Rest In Paradise) and my prayers and blessings sent to the.....," Twitter, May 6, 2020, 6:06 p.m., https://twitter.com/KingJames/status/1258156220969398272.

[5] Sheryl Gay Stolberg, "'Pandemic within a Pandemic': Coronavirus and Police Brutality Roil Black Communities," *New York Times*, June 7, 2020, https://www.nytimes.com/2020/06/07/us/politics/blacks-coronavirus-police-brutality.html.

[6] Osagei K. Obasogie, "Police Killing Black People Is a Pandemic, Too," *Washington Post*, June 5, 2020, https://www.washingtonpost.com/outlook/police-violence-pandemic/2020/06/05/e1a2a1b0-a669-11ea-b619-3f9133bbb482_story.html.

[7] Frank Edwards, Hedwig Lee, and Michael Esposito, "Risk of Being Killed by Police Use of Force in the United States by Age, Race—Ethnicity, and Sex,"

joined the chorus with an entire website called Know Their Names, which features black men and women killed by the police (apparently regardless of the circumstances).[8] No wonder the chairman of Black Lives Matter of Greater New York told Fox News, "If this country doesn't give us what we want, then we will burn down this system and replace it!"[9]

All of this stems from and perpetuates the perception that police are killing unarmed black men. And if you think I am being misogynistic by excluding women from the phrase, just do a quick web search. It's not just me.

"A search of the archive reveals that NPR has used the phrase [unarmed black man] 82 times in the past year. Five of those were head-lines," writes Kelly McBride in an insightful piece for the Poynter Institute.[10] She notes that of those eighty-two uses, twenty-six came "in newscasts read at the top of the hour." Sixty-five of them occurred in the 187 days after Ahmaud Arbery, a twenty-five-year-old Georgia man, was killed in February 2020, and McBride's article was published on August 31, 2020. But over that same time period, the phrase "'unarmed white man' does not appear anywhere in NPR's coverage."[11]

In case you are wondering about the absence of the phrase "unarmed white man," it was not due to lack of opportunity. Eleven of those were killed by police over that 187-day span.

Proceedings of the National Academy of Sciences of the United States of America, August 20, 2019, https://www.pnas.org/content/116/34/16793.

[8] Alia Chughtai, "Know Their Names: Black People Killed by the Police in the US," Al Jazeera, https://interactive.aljazeera.com/aje/2020/know-their-names/index.html.

[9] Meghan Roos, "BLM Leader: We'll 'Burn' the System Down If U.S. Won't Give Us What We Want," *Newsweek*, June 25, 2020, https://www.newsweek.com/blm-leader-well-burn-system-down-if-us-wont-give-us-what-we-want-1513422.

[10] Kelly McBride, "'Unarmed Black Man' Doesn't Mean What You Think It Means," Poynter Institute, August 31, 2020, https://www.poynter.org/ethics-trust/2020/unarmed-black-man-doesnt-mean-what-you-think-it-means.

[11] Ibid.

Stephen O'Brien was killed by police in Floresville, Texas, the day after Arbery on February 24; Christopher Palmer was killed in Manila, Arkansas, on March 4; Kenneth Mullins was killed in Edison, California, on March 6; Brian Marksberry and Aaron Tolen were killed in Humble, Texas, and Wasilla, Alaska, on March 8; John Hendrick was killed in Linwood, North Carolina, on March 26; Zachary Gifford was killed in Brandon, Colorado, on April 9; Giuseppe Particianone was killed in Philadelphia, Pennsylvania, on April 10; Nicholas Bils was killed in San Diego, California, on May 1; Tyler Hays was killed in Sale Creek, Tennessee, on May 19; and Jeffrey Stott Haarsma was killed in St. Petersburg, Florida, on August 7.

But you didn't hear any of their names, did you?

By the way, please don't miss the fact that while police killed these unarmed white men, they did not kill Arbery. Arbery's murder would fall under another category that people would rather forget: intraracial violence. I'll say more about that later.

The High Cost of False Narratives

On the morning of October 5, 2016, a female officer in Chicago was nearly beaten to death because she was afraid to use her weapon. "She thought she was going to die," her superintendent told reporters the next day. "She knew that she should shoot this guy, but she chose not to, because she didn't want her family or the department to have to go through the scrutiny the next day on national news."[12]

This is just one example of how false narratives cost our society. There is one statistic underlying most of those narratives.

"The police are two and a half times more likely to shoot and kill a black man than a white man." If you are like me, you have heard this number cited in sermons, read it in articles and blogs, and seen it in

---

[12] "Chicago Police Officer Says She Feared Using Gun While Being Beaten," ABC 7 News, October 6, 2016, https://abc7chicago.com/chicago-police-officer-afraid-to-use-gun-beaten-eddie-johnson/1543015.

headlines everywhere you looked. And at first blush, it seems to make sense. More white people are killed by police (armed or unarmed), but black people make up only 13 percent of the population, so the ratio matters. Right?

Maybe.

I am not a mathematician. However, I did take and pass statistics in college. (It almost killed me, but I got through.) And one thing I took away from that experience is the maxim "correlation is not causation." I have been reminded of this almost daily in recent years as I have been bombarded with statistics, but particularly with the oft-repeated 2.5-to-1. The implication is that this stat "proves" systemic racism. Whenever you hear this mantra, I hope you remember Proverbs 18:17: "The one who states his case first seems right, until the other comes and examines him." And this "one who states his case" must be examined in light of 1) the nature of the claim itself, 2) the individual cases that are frequently cited as evidence of the claim's veracity, and 3) the inconvenient truth about interracial violence in America. When we examine the 2.5-to-1 stat in these ways, we discover it does not hold up.

Extensive Research

The best research on the topic of fatal officer-involved shootings (FOIS) has been clear, as were the findings of Harvard economist Roland G. Fryer Jr. in a forthcoming study. "On the most extreme use of force, FOIS," he writes, "we find no racial difference in either the raw data or when contextual factors are taken into account."[13] Fryer was actually surprised by his findings.

Meanwhile, a National Academy of Sciences study ignited controversy when its authors proclaimed, "We find no evidence of anti-Black or anti-Hispanic disparities across shootings, and White officers are not

---

[13] Roland G. Fryer Jr., "An Empirical Analysis of Racial Differences in Police Use of Force," *Journal of Political Economy*. Forthcoming.

more likely to shoot minority civilians than non-White officers."[14] More fundamentally, the researchers noted that "using population as a benchmark makes the strong assumption that White and Black civilians have equal exposure to situations that result in FOIS," which is the only way the 2.5-to-1 ratio could be viewed as *prima facie* evidence of police bias. Instead, they noted that contrary to the accepted narrative, "If there are racial differences in exposure to these situations, calculations of racial disparity based on population benchmarks will be misleading."[15] In other words, the 2.5-to-1 ratio, taken at face value, is actually misleading.

So what is the answer? If we shouldn't rely on a univariate analysis of FOIS, what should we do? The National Academy of Sciences points out that criminologists have known the answer to this question for some time: "Researchers have attempted to avoid this issue by using race-specific violent crime as a benchmark, as the majority of FOIS involve armed civilians." Perhaps most astonishing is the discovery that "[w]hen violent crime is used as a benchmark, anti-Black disparities in FOIS disappear or even reverse."[16] In other words, it is white people who are actually shot at disproportionately high rates when the number of interactions with police is tallied up.

The idea of racial motivation being a factor in these shootings is further contradicted by Fryer's finding that

> [f]or white officers, the probability that a white suspect who is involved in officer-involved shooting has a weapon is 84.2 percent. The equivalent probability for blacks is 80.9 percent.

---

[14] David J. Johnson, Trevor Tress, Nicole Burkel, Carley Taylor, and Joseph Cesario, "Officer Characteristics and Racial Disparities in Fatal Officer-Involved Shootings," *Proceedings of the National Academy of Science* 116, no. 32 (August 6, 2019): 15877–15882; first published on July 22, 2019. Their study was attacked immediately as racist. One researcher was demoted from his position at Michigan State University for citing it. Eventually, the authors retracted the study, though it was peer reviewed and they still stand behind their findings. Moreover, the findings mirror those of a similar study in 2015.

[15] Ibid.

[16] Ibid.

A difference of 4 percent, which is not statistically significant. For black officers, the probability that a white suspect who is involved in an officer-involved shooting has a weapon is surprisingly lower, 57.1 percent. The equivalent probability for black suspects is 73.0 percent. The only statistically significant differences by race demonstrate that black officers are more likely to shoot unarmed whites, relative to white officers.[17]

It must be noted that these findings and others have been attacked as biased, inaccurate, and downright racist. However, they remain the best work on the topic.

But there is a more fundamental problem with the 2.5-to-1 ratio. If we apply the same logic across the board, we find systemic injustice in police shootings based on sex, age, geographic region, population, and a host of other factors. Consider two obvious and clear examples: sex and age.

Example One: Men versus Women

According to a database maintained by the *Washington Post*, 96 percent of the 5,542 people killed by police since 2015 were men. If we use the same logic employed by those who claim the black/white shooting stats prove racial bias, wouldn't we have to conclude that the overwhelming disparity in the male/female stats proves misandry? Of course no one is making this claim. Why? Because in this case we readily admit that a univariate analysis is inadequate to explain the disparity. We also know that the majority of violent crimes are perpetrated by males,[18] which is the top predictor of violent interactions with police.

---

[17] Fryer, "An Empirical Analysis of Racial Differences in Police Use of Force."

[18] Örjan Falk, Märta Wallinius, Sebastian Lundström, Thomas Frisell, Henrik Anckarsäter, and Nóra Kerekes, "The 1% of the Population Accountable for 63% of All Violent Crime Convictions," *Social Psychiatry, Psychiatry and*

Example Two: Children and Old Men versus Young Men

Another example that proves this point is the disparity in the age of people killed by police. The age breakdown of the U.S. population is as follows:

Under 18 = 74.2 million, or 24 percent

18–44 = 112.8 million, or 36.5 percent

Over 44 = 121 million, or 39.4 percent

However, the statistics on Americans killed by police don't match up. Of the 5,542 people killed by police since 2015, 101 (2 percent) were under the age of 18; 2,736 (49 percent) were between the ages of 18 and 44; and 1,454 (26 percent) were over age 44. Note that both the young and the old are underrepresented relative to their population stats, and those in the middle are overrepresented. Is this *prima facie* evidence of age discrimination? Or is it a function of something else? "The relationship between aging and criminal activity has been noted since the beginnings of criminology," note Jeffery T. Ulmer and Darrell Steffensmeier in their paper "The Age and Crime Relationship."[19] "Age is a consistent predictor of crime, both in the aggregate and for individuals." And guess which of the three age groups is overrepresented in committing violent crime? Eighteen- to forty-four-year-olds.

The relationship of these variables is even more pronounced when looking at those killed while unarmed. Of the 355 unarmed people killed by police since 2015, the age breakdown was:

Under 18 = 14 (4 percent)

18–44 = 292 (82 percent)

Over 44 = 44 (12 percent)

Epidemiology 49, no. 4 (2014): 559–71. Published online October 31, 2013, doi: 10.1007/s00127-013-0783-y.

[19] Jeffrey Todd Ulmer and Darrell J. Steffensmeier, "The Age and Crime Relationship: Social Variation, Social Explanations," in *The Nurture Versus Biosocial Debate in Criminology: On the Origins of Criminal Behavior and Criminality* (Thousand Oaks, California: SAGE Publications Inc., 2014), 377–96, https://pennstate.pure.elsevier.com/en/publications/the-age-and-crime-relationship-social-variation-social-explanatio.

In other words, in terms of representation by age, 36.5 percent of the population accounts for 82 percent of those killed by police while unarmed.

Bonus: The Killing of Police

Another fact that should give pause to those who rely on the 2.5-to-1 trope is related to the killing of police by civilians. A 2015 *Washington Post* analysis found that "511 officers [were] killed in felonious incidents and 540 offenders from 2004 to 2013. Among the total offenders, 52 percent were white, and 43 percent were black."[20] Ambush killings of officers are nearly evenly split racially: "There were 304 officers killed in ambush attacks from 1980 to 2013, with 371 offenders involved in those deaths. The percentage of black and white offenders in ambushes were about the same: 44 percent were white, and 43 percent were black."[21]

Remember, blacks represent approximately 13 percent of the population and 23.6 percent of the FOIS cases in the *Washington Post* database, compared to whites at 60 percent of the population and 45.3 percent of FOIS. The argument is that the overrepresentation of blacks in the FOIS data is *prima facie* evidence of racist police brutality. But anyone who takes that position will find it difficult to escape the implication of these numbers related to the killing of police.

Simply put, we must be careful when we hear and/or draw conclusions. We must reject simplistic, univariate analyses as a basis for sweeping accusations of bias. The 2.5-to-1 stat is an example of the aforementioned "single witness" being allowed to establish a charge. It is as inappropriate to use that stat to "prove" police bias as it is to use the stats on the killings of police to "prove" inherent bias in black people.

---

[20] Michelle Ye Hee Lee, "Are Black or White Offenders More Likely to Kill Police?," *Washington Post*, FactChecker Analysis, January 9, 2015.

[21] Ibid.

But what about the cases themselves? Do they prove the case for racial injustice?

The Unique Nature of Individual Cases

Many argue that the ways in which black people have been killed by police sets them apart and, along with the other witness of statistical disparity, more than establishes the case. Here again, "The one who states his case first seems right, until the other comes and examines him," so we must examine this witness since "If one gives an answer before he hears, it is his folly and shame" (Proverbs 18:13).

Space limitations require me to be selective and brief, which will undeniably open me up to charges of bias (as though my opponents in this debate need an excuse for that). Nevertheless, my goal here is not to adjudicate these cases, but merely to demonstrate the fact that the way they have been covered by the media is insufficient, slanted, and unjust in terms of the accusations they are used to levy. That being said, I have chosen cases that are recent, well-known, and have generated and maintained a great deal of public outcry.

George Floyd

Many view the now-ubiquitous George Floyd case as the part that represents the totality of police killings of unarmed black men. Minneapolis mayor Jacob Frye, in response to Floyd's death, said, "Being black in America should not be a death sentence."

Others in the Christian camp made it clear that the Floyd case was the smoking gun in the question of racial injustice. "If you are a Christian leader and you remain silent on racial injustice, idk why you are even in ministry!" tweeted Eric Mason, pastor of Epiphany Fellowship in Philadelphia and author of *Woke Church,* on May 27. Then, assuming the posture of a social media watchdog, he continued, "I've peeked at some of your timelines. There are posts but not about these matters...."

"I haven't been able to focus on much at all since I saw the horrific video of George Floyd's murder," wrote pastor and Christian hip-hop artist Shai Linne in an article for the Gospel Coalition's website. Then, making the clear connection between Floyd and every other case, regardless of merit or circumstances, he continued, "But it's not just the video of this one incident. For many black people, it's never about just one incident."[22]

Space does not permit me to go on. Suffice to say, the idea of the Floyd case as the part that represents the whole is almost universal. But is that accurate? Was George Floyd's killing unique? Was it evidence of a particular callousness toward black men on the part of police?

Have you heard of Tony Timpa? Like Floyd, "Timpa wailed and pleaded for help more than 30 times as officers pinned his shoulders, knees and neck to the ground,"[23] reported the *Dallas Morning News* in August 2016. Timpa, a thirty-two-year-old schizophrenic, called the police himself, saying he was off his meds and needed help. When police arrived, Timpa had already been handcuffed by a security guard. Three Dallas Police Department officers restrained Timpa for nearly fourteen minutes as he pleaded, "You're gonna kill me! You're gonna kill me! You're gonna kill me!" Eventually, Timpa went limp, at which time the officers mocked him and made jokes. In the end, when the paramedics finally came and put Timpa's flaccid body on a stretcher, one officer said, "I hope we didn't kill him." But they had.

The *Dallas Morning News* "first reported Timpa's death in a 2017 investigation that showed police refused to say how a man who had called

---

[22] Shai Linne, "George Floyd and Me," Gospel Coalition, June 8, 2020, https://www.thegospelcoalition.org/article/george-floyd-and-me.

[23] Cary Aspinwall and Dave Boucher, "'You're Gonna Kill Me!': Dallas Police Body Cam Footage Reveals the Final Minutes of Tony Timpa's Life," *Dallas Morning News*, July 30, 2019, https://www.dallasnews.com/news/investigations/2019/07/31/you-re-gonna-kill-me-dallas-police-body-cam-footage-reveals-the-final-minutes-of-tony-timpa-s-life.

911 for help ended up dead."[24] The officers were still on duty and no disciplinary action had been taken at that time. In fact, DPD refused to release body-cam footage; that was only done after a three-year legal battle. A side-by-side comparison of the Timpa and Floyd cases is telling:

	George Floyd	Tony Timpa
Year	2020	2016
Circumstances leading to police encounter	Police called in response to passing counterfeit bill	Timpa called police and asked for help
Type of restraint	Knee on neck	Knee and hands on back/neck
Length of restraint	About eight minutes	About fourteen minutes
Officer demeanor during restraint	Calm and serious (hands in pocket)	Mocking and laughing
Officer reaction to unresponsiveness	None	Mocking, laughing, and "Is he dead?"
Legal response	All officers arrested and charged	Officers neither arrested nor charged and footage withheld for three years
Media/public response	Multiple funerals, congressional recognition, police reforms, name on everyone's lips, nationwide protests and riots	No one knew his name and few ever heard of his case

---

[24] Aspinwall and Boucher, "'You're Gonna Kill Me!': Dallas Police Body Cam Footage Reveals the Final Minutes of Tony Timpa's Life."

The George Floyd case was indeed tragic. However, it was not unique. Nor does it represent clear evidence of a particular pattern of police brutality regarding black men. No one took to Twitter demanding that Christian leaders prove their bona fides by speaking out on the Timpa case, and no one wrote articles in leading Christian publications about losing sleep over it. In fact, few—if any—of the people who mounted their moral high horses and took to the streets in protest over George Floyd even knew Tony Timpa's name. Why?

Because he was white, and his case did not advance the right narrative.

Tamir Rice

On November 22, 2014, Cleveland police received a call about someone in a park with a gun. One report notes that "Because of multiple layers in Cleveland's 911 system, crucial information from the initial call about 'a guy in here with a pistol' was never relayed to the responding police officers, including the caller's caveats that the gun was 'probably fake' and that the wielder was 'probably a juvenile.'"[25] No one knows if that information would have made a difference. What we do know is that "what the officers, Frank Garmback and his rookie partner, Tim Loehmann, did hear from a dispatcher was, 'We have a Code One,'" the department's highest level of urgency.[26] Upon arrival, the officers drove up to the gazebo where Rice was playing with his gun, and, as he walked toward them, Loehmann exited the car, weapon drawn, and shot the boy in the abdomen.

This case is tragic. However, despite the claim that "little black boys can't play with toy guns," or that only a black kid with a gun would be looked upon as a threat, the Tamir Rice case is not unique. In 2016 the *Washington Post* ran an article under the headline "In Two Years, Police

---

[25] Shaila Dewan and Richard A. Oppel Jr., "In Tamir Rice Case, Many Errors by Cleveland Police, Then a Fatal One," *New York Times*, January 22, 2015, https://www.nytimes.com/2015/01/23/us/in-tamir-rice-shooting-in-cleveland-many-errors-by-police-then-a-fatal-one.html.

[26] Ibid.

Killed 86 People Brandishing Guns That Look Real—but Aren't." Of those killed, eighty-one were men, five were women, fifty-four were white, and nineteen were black. Four of the eighty-six were under age seventeen. While none of this changes the tragedy of what happened to Tamir Rice, it does make it hard to argue that it was particularly or uniquely heinous and motivated by race.

Philando Castile

On July 6, 2016, thirty-two-year-old Philando Castile was shot dead in his car during a traffic stop. According to police transcripts, after being asked for his license and registration, Castile, who had a permit to carry a concealed weapon, told Officer Jeronimo Yanez, "Sir, I have to tell you, I have a … firearm on me."

Yanez replied, "Don't reach for it then," and Castile said, "I'm, I, I was reaching for…"

Yanez said, "Don't pull it out!"

Castile replied, "I'm not pulling it out," at which point, his girlfriend said, "He's not—" Yanez repeated, "Don't pull it out!" at which point the transcript simply reads, "(gunshots)."[27] Yanez fired seven times, hitting Castile with five shots. Castile's four-year-old daughter was in the back seat.

I remember this case vividly because it shook me, especially as I viewed it through the lens of history, social media, and my own personal anxiety. This wasn't the "racist" Deep South; this was *Minnesota*! Not to mention the fact that I have a license to carry and have had to disclose the fact that I was armed to an officer who had pulled me over. However, as I stepped back to look at this issue through a different lens, I had to admit that the Philando Castile case, though tragic, was also not unique.

---

[27] Transcript of Philando Castile traffic stop, Ramsey County website, July 6, 2016, https://www.ramseycounty.us/sites/default/files/County%20Attorney/Exhibit%201a%20-%20Traffic%20Stop%20Transcript.pdf.

That same summer, on June 25, Dylan Noble was killed by police in Fresno, California, under very similar circumstances. He was stopped by police, reached into his waistband, and was shot eleven times. Again, you don't know Dylan's name because he was white.

Nor are you likely to know the name of six-year-old Jeremy Mardis. In November 2015, he was killed when police in Louisiana opened fire on his father after he led them on a two-mile car chase. Jeremy, a first grader, was "shot several times in the head and torso and pronounced dead at the scene."[28]

Sariah Lane of Phoenix, Arizona, was just seventeen when she was shot and killed by police on April 20, 2017. "Her only mistake," according to news reports, "was taking a ride with her boyfriend in a car driven by a felon, 25-year-old Brandon Pequeno." As officers tried to arrest Pequeno, they thought he tried to reach for a gun. However, Pequeno didn't have one. "Three Mesa police officers unloaded 11 shots into the car, killing Pequeno and Lane, who was sitting in the backseat."[29]

Even worse: All three of the officers who opened fire on Lane sported long histories of officer-involved shootings. One had two, one had five, and one had seven.

Now, just try to imagine the outrage if either Pequeno or Lane had been black. Neither was.

Michael Brown

Rather than describe the Michael Brown case, I offer this succinct summary of the findings from the U.S. Department of Justice's investigation:

---

[28] Bryn Stole, "Authorities Try to Sort Out Details of Marshal-Involved Marksville Shooting That Left Child Dead, Father Wounded," *Acadiana Advocate*, November 10, 2015, https://www.theadvocate.com/acadiana/news/crime_police/article_f3269c39-5f7d-5a7c-99db-57f4ec309097.html.

[29] "Recent Police Shootings Raise Questions about Use of Deadly Force," Fox 10, October 30, 2017, https://www.fox10phoenix.com/news/recent-police-shootings-raise-questions-about-use-of-deadly-force.

There was no evidence to contradict [Officer Darren] Wilson's claim that Brown reached for his gun. The investigation concluded that Wilson did not shoot Brown in the back. That he did not shoot Brown as he was running away. That Brown did stop and turn toward Wilson. That in those next moments "several witnesses stated that Brown appeared to pose a physical threat to Wilson." That claims that Brown had his hands up "in an unambiguous sign of surrender" are not supported by the "physical and forensic evidence," and are sometimes, "materially inconsistent with that witness's own prior statements with no explanation, credible or otherwise, as to why those accounts changed over time."[30]

You may be inclined to think this summary came from the pen of some white, conservative, alt-right white supremacist. You would be wrong. It came from the pen of Ta-Nehisi Coates, one of the paragons of the Critical Social Justice movement.

Michael Brown never said, "Hands up, don't shoot!" That was a bald-faced lie told by one of the witnesses who later admitted as much. Don't miss the last line of Coates's recap: "[C]laims that Brown had his hands up 'in an unambiguous sign of surrender' are not supported by the 'physical and forensic evidence,' and are sometimes 'materially inconsistent with that witness's own prior statements with no explanation, credible or otherwise, as to why those accounts changed over time.'"

By comparison, "Hands up, don't shoot!" *was* uttered by Daniel Shaver. And it was caught on video! Shaver, a white man who had been waving a pellet gun out of a motel window, was by that time unarmed and attempting to comply with conflicting and confusing police commands when an officer told him, "If you do that again, we will shoot you." If you are wondering, "Do what again?" so was Daniel Shaver; the

---

[30] Ta-Nehisi Coates, "The Gangsters of Ferguson," *The Atlantic,* March 5, 2015, https://www.theatlantic.com/politics/archive/2015/03/The-Gangsters-Of-Ferguson/386893.

officer's commands were unclear and at times contradictory. Shaver, on his knees with his hands in the air, said, "Please do not shoot me."[31] But shoot him they did. Mesa (Arizona) Police Officer Philip Brailsford was charged with second-degree murder, but later acquitted. (Hence, Shaver's case dispels two myths: first, that police shootings of black suspects are unique, and second, that when police kill white people, they don't get away with it.)

Another aspect of the Michael Brown case that got a great deal of attention was his age. Much was made of the fact that Brown was nineteen when he was killed. Compare that to another case, as reported by MLive in Jackson, Mississippi: "A county sheriff's sergeant suffered 'significant injuries' ... during a traffic stop ... and fired his weapon, killing 17-year-old Deven Guilford of Mulliken."

Like Brown, Guilford was a teenaged male stopped by police. A struggle ensued. The teenager was shot to death. However, you didn't know this teenager's name and probably never heard of his case. Why? Because Guilford was white, so his story doesn't fit the narrative.

Breonna Taylor

Shortly after midnight on March 13, 2020, police bearing a no-knock warrant used a battering ram to enter the residence of Breonna Taylor in Louisville, Kentucky. According to the *New York Times*, "Ms. Taylor and her boyfriend, Kenneth Walker, had been in bed, but got up when they heard a loud banging at the door. After a brief exchange, Mr. Walker fired his gun. The police also fired several shots, striking Ms. Taylor."[32] This case captured the attention of the entire country as cries for "Justice for Breonna" became commonplace. LeBron James devoted

---

[31] CNN, "Unarmed Man Begs for Life, Shot by Police," YouTube, December 10, 2017, https://www.youtube.com/watch?v=7Ooa7wOKHhg.

[32] Richard A. Oppel Jr., Derrick Bryson Taylor, and Nicholas Bogel-Burroughs, "What to Know about Breonna Taylor's Death," *New York Times*, October 30, 2020, https://www.nytimes.com/article/breonna-taylor-police.html.

an entire postgame interview to raising awareness for and demanding justice in her case.[33] This is yet another tragic situation that is not unique.

In January 2016, twelve-year-old Ciara Meyer was shot and killed by Constable Clark Steele in Penn Township, Pennsylvania. The officer was serving an eviction notice on the girl's father, who produced a weapon. The officer fired at the man; the bullet passed through his arm and struck the girl. She later died from her wounds.[34]

In Taylor's case, it appears the first shots came from her boyfriend, and the police responded in kind. Meyer's father did not fire on police. However, once again, this twelve-year-old girl has not become a rallying point for social justice. No NFL players took a knee for her. No NBA stars used their access to the media to demand "Justice for Ciara."

Why? Because she was white, and her story does not advance the right narrative.

Anticipating Objections

I have had several conversations with people about these cases. Inevitably, those more inclined to view things through a CSJ lens will have one of several predictable objections. Two of them are nonsensical and do not deserve treatment here beyond exposing their nonsense and the underlying worldview on which it rests. The other two are worth our attention.

The first nonsensical idea is what I like to call the Mark Twain Objection. It was he who said, "There are three kinds of lies: Lies, damn lies, and statistics." This is the response represented by the three young black men in a Prager University video. When they heard the statistics on police

---

[33] Mallika Kallingal and Jill Martin, "LeBron James Uses Media Interview after First Scrimmage to 'Shed Light on Justice for Breonna,'" CNN, July 24, 2020, https://edition.cnn.com/2020/07/24/sport/lebron-james-on-justice-for-breonna-taylor/index.html.

[34] Barbara Miller, "Perry County DA: Investigation into Penn Township Shooting of 12-Year-Old Continues," PennLive, January 12, 2016, https://www.pennlive.com/news/2016/01/perry_county_da_investigation.html.

killings, their immediate response was, "Cap!" (an urban slang term meaning "bulls***"). Of course, this is a specious argument since the same people readily accept the 2.5-to-1 "statistic" without question.

The second nonsensical objection is the CSJ idea that objective scientific knowledge derived through data is "white" and therefore oppressive. (I'll discuss this in more detail later.) Again, these same people are happy to rely on the 2.5-to-1 statistic, as well as other statistical disparities, as long as it supports their claims that America suffers from systemic racism. There are, however, two other objections worth mentioning.

One is that the facts of these cases are not identical. The other is appealing to America's "racist past."

I am actually encouraged by the first objection as it puts the discussion on what I consider proper ground based on biblical principles. I am more than happy to argue the merits of each of these cases. In fact, I see that as real progress. Most people hear about one of these high-profile killings of a black person and immediately go into "the facts of the case are irrelevant" mode. To them, the number of black people killed by police is all that matters. Hence, if there are ten shootings of unarmed black men and nine of them are later deemed justified, that is irrelevant. The tally still comes up as "ten killed," the mantra remains "Justice for So-and-So," and the narrative marches on. So if someone disagrees with my assessment of the dissimilarities in these cases, then we are already on proper footing, and whenever and wherever true injustice (i.e., illegality) is found, we can join hands and advocate for justice when necessary.

The second objection, "consider America's racist history," is sometimes offered in isolation, but usually as a rebuttal once someone has been willing to look at the facts and agrees that the similarities in these cases are indeed probative.

The objection goes like this: "I see what you are saying, and I agree. However, you have to consider the history of racism in this country." This asserts that the only way to judge whether or not police killings of black people are acts of racism is to look at them through the lens of ... racism.

This is the major fault line that lies beneath the current discussion. More importantly, this is why those who do not accept, or at least understand, the underlying assumptions and presuppositions of Critical Social Justice end up scratching their heads in bewilderment as assertions of "racial injustice"—or worse yet, that "the police are hunting down and killing unarmed black men"—become increasingly prevalent.

It is imperative that we examine the worldview assumptions that underlie this division—and we will.

CHAPTER FOUR

A New Religion

W hen I was a new believer, two gentlemen knocked on my apartment door wanting to talk about religion. I was pleasantly surprised and eager for Christian fellowship. But something was "off" about
those two. I couldn't quite put my finger on it, but I knew it didn't feel
right. The next day I mentioned the exchange to two of my football
teammates, Brent Knapton and Max Moss. They had both grown up in
the church and were mentoring me, including buying me my first Bible
and teaching me how to study it. I knew if anybody could help me figure
out what was going on, they could.

When I described my visitors, Max and Brent looked at each other,
smiled, then turned to me and asked, "Mormons or Jehovah's Witnesses?"

I had no idea what they were talking about. "How am I supposed to
know?" I asked in all sincerity.

"Did they have name tags that identified them as 'Elder So-and-So'?"
Max asked.

I told him I hadn't seen any name tags. They looked at each other
again and said in unison, "They were Jehovah's Witnesses!" and pro-
ceeded to warn me about the cultic theology of the JWs. I was astonished!

I was also a bit disturbed. *How many cults are there? How will I know them? Am I a part of one?*

Those questions drove me deeper into what had already become an apologetics-oriented pursuit of Christian theology. I wanted to know what I believed, why I believed it, and to be able to defend it against legitimate objections. I also wanted to be sure that what I believed was rooted in Scripture and historic Christian orthodoxy.

That same passion has driven me to explore, analyze, and warn against yet another cult: the cult of antiracism.

My goal in this chapter is fourfold. First, I intend to lay out a picture of what I see as the theological underpinnings of the theology and worldview of Critical Social Justice. Second, I hope to help the reader see that this worldview stands in direct contradiction to the biblical worldview. Third, I will give examples that show the prevalence of this worldview within broader evangelicalism. Finally, I hope that this will all help the reader understand why identifying the elements of this worldview, far from being a tactic designed to "shut down conversation," is actually fundamental to having a genuine and God-honoring conversation about race at all.

The Religious Nature of Antiracism

At the epicenter of the coming evangelical catastrophe is a new religion—or, more specifically, a new cult. While some may consider the term "cult" unnecessarily offensive, it happens to be the most accurate term available to describe the current state of affairs. John McWhorter was the first observer I am aware of to refer to it as the "Cult of Antiracism." Others have used similar terms,[1] and I think they are right to do so.

---

[1] John McWhorter, "Atonement as Activism," *American Interest*, May 24, 2018, https://www.the-american-interest.com/2018/05/24/atonement-as-activism/; John McWhorter, "Antiracism, Our Flawed New Religion," Daily Beast, April 14, 2017, https://www.thedailybeast.com/antiracism-our-flawed-new-religion; James Lindsay, "Postmodern Religion and the Faith of Social Justice," Areo, December

The antiracist movement has many of the hallmarks of a cult, including staying close enough to the Bible to avoid immediate detection and hiding the fact that it has a new theology and a new glossary of terms that diverge ever-so-slightly from Christian orthodoxy. At least at first. In classic cult fashion, they borrow from the familiar and accepted, then infuse it with new meaning. This allows the cult to appeal to the faithful within the dominant, orthodox religions from which it draws its converts.

This new cult has created a new lexicon that has served as scaffolding to support what has become an entire body of divinity. In the same manner, this new body of divinity comes complete with its own cosmology (CT/CRT/I); original sin (racism); law (antiracism); gospel (racial reconciliation); martyrs (Saints Trayvon, Mike, George, Breonna, etc.); priests (oppressed minorities); means of atonement (reparations); new birth (wokeness); liturgy (lament); canon (CSJ social science); theologians (DiAngelo, Kendi, Brown, Crenshaw, MacIntosh, etc.); and catechism ("say their names"). We'll examine some of those topics in this chapter and a few later on.

In case you're wondering about its soteriology, there isn't one. Antiracism offers no salvation—only perpetual penance in an effort to battle an incurable disease. And all of it begins with pouring new meaning into well-known words.

Valparaiso University philosophy professor Aaron Preston's observations are helpful here. He describes practitioners of grievance studies as "resentful specialists in subversion who treat literature and philosophy, and indeed language itself, as tools to be used for political

---

18, 2018, https://areomagazine.com/2018/12/18/postmodern-religion-and-the-faith-of-social-justice/; Andrew Sullivan, "America's New Religions," *New York Magazine's Intelligencer,* December 7, 2018, https://nymag.com/intelligencer/2018/12/andrew-sullivan-americas-new-religions.html?utm_source=tw; Andrew Sullivan, "Is Intersectionality a Religion?" *New York Magazine,* March 10, 2017, https://nymag.com/intelligencer/2017/03/is-intersectionality-a-religion.html; Elizabeth C. Corey, "First Church of Intersectionality," *First Things,* August 2017, https://www.firstthings.com/article/2017/08/first-church-of-intersectionality; and many more.

purposes."[2] Ibram X. Kendi, one of the antiracist movement's leading voices, makes this clear in his bestselling book *How to be an Antiracist*, describing his parents' involvement with the Social Gospel and how it influenced him. "I cannot disconnect my parents' religious strivings to be Christian from my secular strivings to be an antiracist," he writes. "And the key act for both of us was defining our terms so that we could begin to describe the world and our place in it." He then draws a conclusion with which I could not agree more: "Definitions anchor us in principles."[3] (Unfortunately, in this case, "Everyone deceives his neighbor, and no one speaks the truth; they have taught their tongue to speak lies; they weary themselves committing iniquity" [Jeremiah 9:5]).

According to Kendi, "If we don't do the basic work of defining the kind of people we want to be in language that is stable and consistent, we can't work toward stable, consistent goals."[4] He then outlines that language as well as his goals in a book that has not only reached millions, but has served as a roadmap for many more who, although they do not know Kendi's name, have definitely been influenced by his definitions. He writes:

> To be an antiracist is to set lucid definitions of racism/antiracism, racist/antiracist policies, racist/antiracist ideas, racist/antiracist people. To be a racist is to constantly redefine "racist" in a way that exonerates one's changing policies, ideas, and personhood.[5]

It is important not to miss this. Kendi's journey has not been about actions; it has been about "arriving at basic definitions." His work is rooted in "setting lucid definitions."

---

[2] Aaron Preston, citing Richard Rorty, "Redefining Racism against Activist Lexicography," New Discourses, August 8, 2020, https://newdiscourses.com/2020/08/redefining-racism-against-activist-lexicography.

[3] Ibram X. Kendi, *How to Be an Antiracist* (New York, New York: Random House Publishing Group, Kindle Edition, 2019), 17.

[4] Ibid.

[5] Ibid.

Kendi and others are operating from a set of definitions that are neither new nor unique. They have been around since the days of the Frankfurt School, and in some cases, even earlier. However, today those words—or more specifically, the new meanings given to old words—have made their way into mainstream conscience and vocabulary, giving rise to a new religion where many now "trust in deceptive words to no avail" (Jeremiah 7:8). So let's examine the language and theology of the cult of antiracism.

We begin with its cosmology.

A New Cosmology: In the Beginning

On the first day, white people created whiteness.

Although many White people feel that being White has no meaning, this feeling is unique to White people and is a key part of what it means to be White; to see one's race as having no meaning is a privilege only Whites are afforded. To claim to be "just human" and thus outside of race is one of the most powerful and pervasive manifestations of Whiteness.[6]

Whiteness: a set of normative privileges granted to white-skinned individuals and groups which is "invisible" to those privileged by it.[7]

This statement is as critical to the cult of antiracism as Genesis 1:1 is to Christianity. Just as Christians cannot and do not conceive of anything in their worldview apart from the reality that there is a God who

---

[6] Robin DiAngelo and Özlem Sensoy, *Is Everyone Really Equal?: An Introduction to Key Concepts in Social Justice Education* (Multicultural Education Series) (New York, New York: Teachers College Press, Kindle Edition, 2012), 142–43.

[7] Neil Shenvi, "Antiracist Glossary," Neil Shenvi—Apologetics, https://shenvi-apologetics.com/an-antiracism-glossary-whiteness.

created the world, the cult of antiracism roots every aspect of its world-view in the assertion that everything begins with the creation of white-ness. More specifically, the creation of whiteness with the express purpose of establishing white people as the dominant, hegemonic oppres-sors and all non-white people as the objects of that oppression. This is the *sine qua non* of the antiracist metanarrative.

The foundation for this idea is laid in Critical Race Theory, then applied more broadly in other academic disciplines until it finally finds its way into the broader cultural context. "[T]he terms I am using are not 'theory-neutral descriptors' but theory-laden constructs inseparable from systems of injustice," wrote Robin DiAngelo in a 2011 article that was a precursor to her bestselling 2018 book *White Fragility*. She was discussing her use of the terms "white" and "whiteness." In other words, DiAngelo admits what many Christians either refuse to admit or simply don't know: that these terms carry the assumption of a worldview—particularly the worldview that lies at the foundation of CRT.

It doesn't take a trained theologian to see this. Let's look, for exam-ple, at the Encyclopedia Britannica's entry on Critical Race Theory:

> Critical race theory (CRT), the view that the law and legal insti-tutions are inherently racist and that race itself, instead of being biologically grounded and natural, is a socially constructed concept that is used by white people to further their economic and political interests at the expense of people of colour.[8]

This is CRT 101. Unfortunately, for many it has also become Chris-tianity 101. And sadly, pointing out the CRT roots is often dismissed as mere name-calling.

In February 2018, Jarvis Williams advanced these same ideas in a series of lectures in which he lambasted students and faculty with what could only be described as a CRT-laced tirade. "Whiteness is not about

---

[8] Tommy Curry, "Critical Race Theory," *Encyclopedia Britannica*, May 28, 2020, https://www.britannica.com/topic/critical-race-theory.

your biology, it's about ideology," Williams exclaimed. "It's a biological fiction, but a social fact. One aspect of whiteness was a way for Europeans who were different to homogenize themselves from these enslaved Africans." Williams would go on to state, "One reason we get slavery is because of the construct of whiteness."[9] In other words, according to a professor of New Testament Studies at the flagship seminary in the SBC, the cosmology of CRT is undisputed fact. White people created whiteness with the express purpose of oppressing and enslaving black people.

In a now-infamous tirade at the 2019 Sparrow Women Conference, Ekemini Uwan noted, "The reality is that whiteness is rooted in plunder, in theft, in enslavement of Africans, in genocide of Native Americans."[10] Both Williams's and Uwan's statements are indistinguishable from the ideology espoused by Robin DiAngelo, who wrote, "The idea of racial inferiority was created to justify unequal treatment." She said this to make the point that "belief in racial inferiority is not what triggered unequal treatment."[11] Imagine the theological and historical omniscience necessary to determine the priority of one of these sins over the other!

However, for the worldview to hold, one must accept the premise that the idea of inferiority was created *for the purpose* of justifying unequal treatment. As though unequal treatment, which was ubiquitous throughout the history of fallen humanity, needed a justification. One wonders what justification the Africans who sold my ancestors into slavery—probably after taking them as slaves of their own— needed in order to justify the unequal treatment of their fellow Africans. Did the Egyptians have to invent the concept of race in order to

---

[9] For the New Christian Intellectual, "Jarvis Williams on 'Whiteness' Pursuing Gospel Centered Racial Reconciliation," YouTube, August 29, 2019, https://www.youtube.com/watch?v=TAYy3nNdy4Y. The section I refer to begins forty-one minutes in and lasts approximately four and a half minutes.

[10] "Dallas Conference On-Stage Interview with Ekemini Uwan," Sparrow Women's Dallas Evangelical Conference, YouTube, https://www.youtube.com/watch?v=G9JQntpn71I.

[11] Robin J. DiAngelo, *White Fragility* (Boston, Massachusetts: Beacon Press, Kindle Edition, 2018), 16.

justify enslaving the Hebrews? Did the Babylonians? How about the Assyrians? The answer to these questions has to be "no" since race was invented 1) by white people and 2) for the express purpose of oppressing non-white people.

On the second day, white people created white privilege.

I think whites are carefully taught not to recognize white privilege, *as males are taught not to recognize male privilege.* So I have begun in an untutored way to ask what it is like to have white privilege. I have come to see white privilege as an invisible package of unearned assets that I can count on cashing in each day, but about which I was "meant" to remain oblivious. White privilege is like an invisible weightless knapsack of special provisions, maps, passports, codebooks, visas, clothes, tools, and blank checks.[12]

White Privilege: a series of unearned advantages that accrue to white people by virtue of their whiteness.
According to the cult of antiracism, whiteness was established in order to create, perpetuate, and preserve white privilege. It is also important to note that this doctrine is assumed to be wed to the concept of male privilege, and by extension to every other privilege associated with hegemony. In antiracist theology, white privilege is a ubiquitous term popularized in 1989 after the publication of Peggy McIntosh's now-famous paper "White Privilege: Unpacking the Invisible Knapsack." The paper is a classic example of grievance studies in that it was based entirely on assumptions, anecdotes, and personal observations,

---

[12] Peggy McIntosh, "White Privilege: Unpacking the Invisible Knapsack," https://www.racialequitytools.org/resourcefiles/mcintosh.pdf. This article is the gold standard and it does not have a single footnote! This proves DiAngelo's point about the assumptions in Whiteness Studies.

and completely devoid of scholarly research. Here is how McIntosh describes her "research":

> *I decided to try to work on myself* at least by identifying some of the daily effects of white privilege in my life. I have chosen *those conditions that I think in my case* attach somewhat more to skin-color privilege than to class, religion, ethnic status, or geographic location, though of course all these other factors are intricately intertwined. *As far as I can tell*, my African American coworkers, friends, and acquaintances with whom I come into daily or frequent contact in this particular time ... cannot count on *most of these conditions* (emphasis mine).[13]

Where else would phrases like "I decided to work on myself" or "as far as I can tell" be considered appropriate for academic research? They appear only in grievance studies. However, in the academic realm, this is a horse of a different color. According to Britannica, "Whiteness Studies begin with the premise that racism and white privilege exist in both traditional and modern forms, and rather than work to prove its existence, work to reveal it."[14] In other words, this is a foundational tenet of faith.

Nevertheless, McIntosh is the gold standard for teaching on white privilege both outside and inside the church. In one YouTube video, Matt Chandler, pastor of the Village Church in Flower Mound, Texas, former head of the Acts 29 network, and one of the leading representatives of the Young, Restless, and Reformed movement—in other words, not just some random evangelical—echoes McIntosh almost verbatim. "I have grown up with this invisible ... bag of privilege," he says in a direct-to-camera presentation. Then, as if to press McIntosh's analogy of "an invisible

---

[13] McIntosh, "White Privilege: Unpacking the Invisible Knapsack." This is as "clear" as it gets!

[14] Ibid.

package of unearned assets," he describes "a kind of invisible toolkit that I can reach in there at any given moment and have this kind privilege that a lot of other brothers and sisters don't have."[15]

These were not off-the-cuff remarks. The video, titled "How to Understand White Privilege," is very strategic. Chandler is clearly sympathetic to CRT's version of white privilege. Nor is he unique in this. Volumes could be filled with examples of mainstream evangelicals echoing this concept.

On the third day, white people created white supremacy.

> White supremacy is a historically based, institutionally per-petuated system of exploitation and oppression of continents, nations and peoples of color by white peoples and nations of the European continent; for the purpose of maintaining and defending a system of wealth, power and privilege.[16]

White Supremacy: any belief, behavior, or system that supports, promotes, or enhances white privilege.

It is important to note that white supremacy, as used by the Critical Social Justice movement, doesn't mean what it used to mean. "For many of us the term 'white supremacy' evokes strong images ranging from the Ku Klux Klan to the Nazi regime," notes Daniel Hill in his influential book *White Awake*. Then, in a classic attempt to promote the redefini-tion of terms that CRT requires in order to advance the antiracist world-view, he continues, "When we get past the emotional response to the

---

[15] The Village Church Resources, "How to Understand and Address White Privi-lege," YouTube, June 28, 2017, https://www.youtube.com/watch?v=pzUXZpMQlTQ.

[16] Center for the Study of Social Policy, "Race Equity Glossary of Terms," Edu-cate Not Indoctrinate, https://educatenotindoctrinate.org/glossaries/race-equity-glossary-of-terms.

term and consider its definition, we can see that it remains relevant."[17] In other words, the word doesn't mean what it used to mean, so we don't have to feel the way we used to about it. It also is far less provable in this context than someone's membership or status within the KKK.

This is perfectly in keeping with Sensoy and DiAngelo's *Is Everybody Really Equal?*, a mainstay in schools of education throughout the United States. "When we use the term White supremacy, we are not referring to extreme hate groups or 'bad racists,'" they write. "We use the term to capture the all-encompassing dimensions of White privilege, dominance, and assumed superiority in mainstream society."[18] And if you are going to take this ride and get on board with antiracist pursuits, you have to engage in the cognitive dissonance that comes when we attempt to ignore the definitions we know in an effort to apply the definitions we must use in order to adopt and apply this new worldview.

This is not your grandfather's version of white supremacy. It does not refer to the KKK or Neo-Nazis (except when it does). This version refers to the very air one breathes in a culture created by and for white people. "Race scholars use the term white supremacy to describe a sociopolitical economic system of domination based on racial categories that benefits those defined and perceived as white."[19] As a result, white supremacy is both ubiquitous and intractable. In a now infamous video, Southern Baptist Theological Seminary Provost Matthew Hall gives about as clear a summary of the antiracist doctrine of white supremacy as one can:

> Everything that you assumed or thought was normal in the world, or everything you thought was true about your tradition, your denomination, your own family, I'm going to pull the veil back, and what looked like *this beautiful narrative of*

---

[17] Daniel Hill, *White Awake* (Westmont, Illinois: InterVarsity Press, Kindle Edition, 2017), 52.

[18] DiAngelo and Sensoy, *Is Everyone Really Equal?*, 143.

[19] DiAngelo, *White Fragility*, 30.

faithfulness and orthodoxy, and of truth and righteousness and justice, I'm gonna peel that back and I'm going to show you the rotting corpse of white supremacy that's underneath the surface (emphasis mine).[20]

Note how closely Hall's definition of white supremacy mirrors the orthodox doctrine of total depravity. However, for Hall, this depravity is not shared by all humanity by virtue of having descended from Adam (Romans 5:12), but is limited to a certain spectrum of the melanin scale.

On the fourth day, white people created white complicity.

The white complicity claim maintains that all whites are complicit in systemic racial injustice; this sometimes takes the form of the mantra "all whites are racist." When white complicity takes the latter configuration, it implies not that all whites are racially prejudiced, but rather that all whites participate in and, often unwittingly, maintain the racist system of which they are part and from which they benefit.[21]

White Complicity: White people, through the practices of whiteness and by benefiting from white privilege, contribute to the maintenance of systemic racial injustice.[22]

In the 1978 movie *The Wiz*, Michael Jackson's character, the Scarecrow, is introduced with the song "You Can't Win," which sums up the concept of white complicity quite succinctly: "You can't win, you can't get even, and you can't get out of the game." For the antiracist, this is

[20] Trevor Loudon, "Critical Race Theory Promoted by Three Professors at Flagship Southern Baptist Seminary," YouTube, August 30, 2019, https://www.youtube.com/watch?v=M—gMO64r6U.

[21] Barbara Applebaum, *Being White, Being Good: White Complicity, White Moral Responsibility, and Social Justice Pedagogy* (Lanham, Maryland: Lexington Books, 2010), 140.

[22] Ibid., 2–3.

the equivalent of imputed guilt. Whereas Christians see Adam as the Federal Head of all mankind through whom the guilt of original sin is imputed to all of mankind, the cult of antiracism sees the inventors of whiteness as the Federal Head of all white people through whom guilt is imputed in the form of white complicity.

"Without confession to the sin of white racism, white supremacy, white privilege," contends *Sojourners* magazine founder Jim Wallis, "people who call themselves white Christians *will never be free* ... from the bondage of a lie, a myth, an ideology, and an idol."[23] This sentiment is an affront to the Gospel. "For the law of the Spirit of life *has set you free* in Christ Jesus from the law of sin and death" (Romans 8:2, italics mine). And again, "So if the Son *sets you free*, you will be free indeed" (John 8:36, italics mine). But this is the gospel of antiracism, where there is no freedom—at least, not for white people.

On the fifth day, white people created white equilibrium.

> White equilibrium is a cocoon of racial comfort, centrality, superiority, entitlement, racial apathy, and obliviousness, all rooted in an identity of being good people free of racism. Challenging this cocoon throws off our racial balance. Because being racially off balance is so rare, we have not had to build the capacity to sustain the discomfort. Thus, whites find these challenges unbearable and want them to stop.[24]

White Equilibrium: The belief system that allows white people to remain comfortably ignorant.

While the term "white equilibrium" is not as well-known as the others we have covered, it is no less important to the antiracist

---

[23] Jim Wallis, "On the 50th Anniversary of Dr. King's Assassination, Confessing the Church's Complicity in Racial Division," *Sojourners*, April 4, 2018, https://sojo.net/articles/50th-anniversary-dr-kings-assassination-confessing-churchs-complicity-racial-division.

[24] DiAngelo, *White Fragility*, 112.

cosmology. *The Social Justice Encyclopedia* is quite helpful here: it defines it as "occupying a position of privilege [which] allows a person to avoid having to deal with or even understand the experiences of oppression and marginalization, or indeed of bigotries like racism or even of the concept of race itself."[25] So even though you may not have heard the term, if you have spent any time discussing or studying the Critical Social Justice movement, you have definitely come across the concept.

Latasha Morrison's work gives us a glimpse into the influence these ideas have on contemporary evangelicalism. "In my work as a bridge builder," she writes, "I've seen how, time and time again, conversations about reconciliation stall when the topic of righting the wrongs comes up." Morrison goes on to explain, "Terms such as reparations, affirmative action, white privilege, and Black Lives Matter are nonstarters for so many folks, *in part because they disrupt the listener.* They remind him or her that making things right costs something, often power, position, or money."[26] Clearly, Morrison is referring to a disruption of equilibrium. This is important when interpreting objections to her work, which has become a mainstay in evangelical circles. One need not be trying to "shut down the conversation" or "uphold white supremacy" to object to material that is awash with Critical Social Justice ideology.

This is also a key to understanding what happened on the last day of creation for the antiracists.

On the sixth day, white people created white fragility.

Though white fragility is triggered by discomfort and anxiety, it is born of superiority and entitlement. White fragility is not

---

[25] James Lindsay, "White Equilibrium," New Discourses, January 13, 2020, https://newdiscourses.com/tftw-white-equilibrium.

[26] Latasha Morrison, *Be the Bridge* (New York, New York: Crown Publishing Group, Kindle Edition, 2019), 154.

weakness per se. In fact, it is a powerful means of white racial control and the protection of white advantage.[27]

White Fragility: the inability and unwillingness of white people to talk about race due to the grip that whiteness, white supremacy, white privilege, white complicity, and white equilibrium exert on them (knowingly or unknowingly).

Unless you have been hiding under a rock, you have been exposed to the term "white fragility." Not only has Robin DiAngelo's book by that title found an almost permanent place atop every bestseller list, but the term has also made its way into common vernacular and in many a CSJ sermon. White fragility also serves as a kind of Kafka trap. In other words, it is a denial of guilt that is seen as proof of guilt:

> The Claim: You have white privilege and are complicit in white supremacy and racism.
> The Response: That is not true! I (fill in rationale here).
> The Conclusion: That is just your white fragility fighting for equilibrium.

In the end, CSJ proponents believe white people can only respond appropriately to an accusation of racism by acknowledging, admitting, repenting of, and working to undo the racism. Anything other than that is evidence of white fragility. In fact, DiAngelo's book is replete with definitions of various forms of racism, including color-blind racism, aversive racism, cultural racism, and more. In the end, she defines racism in so many ways that the reader is left with no choice but to agree with her statement that our "racial socialization sets us up to repeat racist behavior, regardless of our intentions or self-image." Therefore, "We must continue to ask how our racism manifests, not if."[28]

---

[27] DiAngelo, *White Fragility*, 2.
[28] Ibid., 138.

Of course, all of this is related to the ultimate reality that grows out of the antiracist cosmology: the new original sin, which ironically, also happens to be the new unpardonable sin.

A New Original Sin: Racism

"I am a racist. If you think the worst thing somebody can call you is a racist then you're not thinking biblically.... I am going to struggle with racism and white supremacy until the day I die and get my glorified body and a completely renewed and sanctified mind because I am immersed in a culture where I benefit from racism all the time."[29]

What if I told you that statement was made by a leading evangelical? What if I told you he was the provost of the flagship seminary of the Southern Baptist Convention? What if I also told you that this statement was made in a public forum?[30]

You might think the scandal here is that the official confessed a grave sin, and nothing was done. You may be wondering, "Where was Dwight McKissic? Surely the man who wants the Founders removed from mugs and T-shirts as well as all buildings would have fired off a missive demanding the resignation of an admitted racist and white supremacist." However, you would be mistaken. The scandal here is not the sin this person admitted, but how an evangelical leader capitulated to the theology of the cult of antiracism and the complicity of the institution he represents.

You may think you know what racism is. However, you are almost certainly wrong—at least when it comes to the antiracist definition of

---

[29] For the New Christian Intellectual, "'I Am a Racist'—Mathew Hall, Provost at Southern Seminary," YouTube, July 31, 2019, https://www.youtube.com/watch?v=1IiKCYSevDU.

[30] To be fair, Hall has since gone on the record to repudiate CRT, and his statements were removed from Southern's website. However, the fact remains that he made such statements repeatedly, openly, and unambiguously. It is hard to imagine simply walking back erroneous statements with an apology as being acceptable on any other theological issue—especially one that has been repudiated by all six Southern Baptist seminary presidents.

racism. In fact, confusion and disagreement over this idea lie at the root of much of the disagreements among evangelicals about race, racism, and racial reconciliation. When most Christians speak of racism, we are referring to the traditional, historic definition like that offered by Merriam-Webster: "A belief that race is the primary determinant of human traits and capacities and that racial differences produce an inherent superiority of a particular race." Nor is Webster's definition unique. The Oxford English Dictionary defines racism as:

> A belief that one's own racial or ethnic group is superior, or that other such groups represent a threat to one's cultural identity, racial integrity, or economic well-being; (also) a belief that the members of different racial or ethnic groups possess specific characteristics, abilities, or qualities, which can be compared and evaluated. Hence: prejudice, discrimination, or antagonism directed against people of other racial or ethnic groups (or, more widely, of other nationalities), esp. based on such beliefs.[31]

However, it is important to note that for the antiracist, these definitions no longer suffice. In fact, there is a serious movement afoot to change the definitions found in English dictionaries to suit the theology of antiracism. But what is the definition of racism that CSJ is striving for? Robin DiAngelo's work is quite informative here:

> Given the dominant conceptualization of racism as individual acts of cruelty, it follows that only terrible people who consciously don't like people of color can enact racism. Though this conceptualization is misinformed, it is not benign. In fact, it functions beautifully to make it nearly impossible to engage in the necessary dialogue and self-reflection that can lead to

---

[31] Oxford English Dictionary's website, https://www-oed-com.dist.lib.usu.edu/view/Entry/157097?redirectedFrom=racism#eid.

change. Outrage at the suggestion of racism is often followed by righteous indignation about the manner in which the feedback was given.[32]

Note that DiAngelo sees this individualistic view of racism—the view we find in every reputable English dictionary—to be "misinformed." Consequently, notes Aaron Preston, "as this bit of specialized nomenclature has migrated beyond its native habitat in left-leaning academic circles in the humanities and social sciences, it has entered the vocabulary of the average English speaker without a single, clear meaning."[33] How then shall we understand the term?

The most popular antiracist curriculum among conservative evangelicals is Latasha Morrison's *Be the Bridge: Pursuing God's Heart for Racial Reconciliation.* In the accompanying curriculum, *Whiteness 101: Foundational Principles Every White Bridge Builder Needs to Understand*, Morrison defines racism as "a system of advantage based on race, involving cultural messages, misuse of power, and institutional bias, in addition to the racist beliefs and actions of individuals." It is important to note that this redefinition of racism, among other things, changes the location and therefore the nature of the sin. We are no longer dealing with the hearts of men; we are addressing institutions and structures. "For as long as America exists with its current institutions," writes DiAngelo, "it will also need to be in group therapy where our turn begins with: 'Hi. I'm America, and I'm racist.'"[34]

The implications of this statement are myriad. However, one bears mentioning here.

If DiAngelo and Morrison are right and 1) racism is corporate as opposed to individual, 2) racism is America's sin, and 3) racism is connected only to whiteness, then it follows that as a black man, I am not only exempt from racism, but I am also not an American. At least not in

---

[32] DiAngelo, *White Fragility*, 123.

[33] Preston, "Redefining 'Racism': Against Activist Lexicography."

[34] DiAngelo, *White Fragility*, 30.

any real sense. I am an ontological "other" who is a victim of America's sin, while not participating in it.

Imagine if we thought this way about other issues. If America goes to war, are black Americans not called to arms? If America is guilty of a crime or an atrocity, are black Americans absolved of that guilt as well? This may seem like an esoteric point. However, I assure you, it is as relevant as anything else discussed in this book. If America owes a debt and I am excluded from that debt, then the implication is that I am less than American. (The same is true if American Christianity is the subject, as it often is.)

In an antiracist handout for educators, DiAngelo gives the following list to help participants understand the concept:

> Racism exists today, in both traditional and modern forms.
> All members of this society have been socialized to participate in it.
> All white people benefit from racism, regardless of intentions; intentions are irrelevant.[35]

Much could be said about each of these points. However, my goal here is to help the reader see that these ideas are part of a system, a theology. Christians have been using these terms regularly of late, and in most cases, using them the same way the secular antiracists use them. Then, when called on it, the response (if the interlocutor is white) is some version of this: "That's your white fragility speaking." If the interlocutor is a "person of color," the accusation is: "That's your internalized racism." But in both instances, the ultimate accusation is: "You are just trying to 'shut down the conversation' about racial justice." Or "You just haven't done your homework (i.e., reading Ibram X. Kendi, Robin DiAngelo, Latasha Morrison, Michelle Alexander, Jemar Tisby, Daniel Hill, Richard Delgado,

---

[35] Robin J. DiAngelo, "Anti-Racism Handout," robindiangelo.com, June 2016, https://robindiangelo.com/wp-content/uploads/2016/06/Anti-racism-handout-1-page-2016.pdf.

Kimberlé Crenshaw, W.E.B. Du Bois, etc.), so you don't know any better."
According to Critical Social Justice, without social science, the Bible
doesn't make sense.

Systemic Sin

At the heart of the "woke" movement lies the idea that the sin of
racism is no longer to be understood as an individual sin. Instead, the
term now incorporates the idea of "institutional/structural racism" and
its implications. Hence, America has sinned, and *certain* Americans have
inherited that sin whether they know it or not. "Hurling the damning
label 'racist' at people and systems that don't deserve it in order to incite
revolutionary outrage is exactly the kind of subversive linguistic manip-
ulation prescribed in [the grievance studies] playbook," writes Aaron
Preston.[36] And leading evangelicals are following along. "[W]e have to
address racism as a corporate problem," wrote Criswell College President Barry Creamer for the *Dallas Morning News.* "In that light, we
have to make sure we're asking the right question." Then Cameron taps
his inner DiAngelo and states that the question is "not 'how do I fix
systemic racism in America?' But: 'In light of systemic racism's reality,
what actions on my part are right?'"[37]

In one of the approved canonical writings of the antiracism cult,
DiAngelo explains, "In the post–civil rights era, we have been taught that
racists are mean people who intentionally dislike others because of their
race; racists are immoral."[38] However, she explains that this antiquated
definition is no longer acceptable. For her and other leaders of the antiracist
cult, the definition of racism is much broader. Today's definition eschews
the individualistic proscriptions of the past, arguing instead that racism is

---

[36] Preston, "Redefining 'Racism': Against Activist Lexicography."

[37] Barry Creamer, "Our Faith and Ethics Must Challenge Our Norms on Race,"
Dallas Morning News, August 9, 2020, https://www.dallasnews.com/opinion/
commentary/2020/08/09/hi-im-america-and-im-racist.

[38] DiAngelo, *White Fragility,* 13.

this: "A far-reaching system that functions independently from the intentions or self-images of individual actors."[39] In other words, today we have "racism without racists."

This is why those inside and outside the cult of antiracism can use the same word while missing one another completely. What's worse, antiracists see the mention of individual guilt as evidence that one is not only an outsider, but … a racist. "Racism is a marriage of racist policies and racist ideas that produces and normalizes racial inequities,"[40] notes Ibram X. Kendi. Therefore, it follows that "institutional racism" and "structural racism" and "systemic racism" are redundant, when, according to the new definition, "Racism itself is institutional, structural, and systemic."[41] I appreciate Kendi's candor as it helps to identify the competing worldview more clearly. For example, he offers a concrete example of racism, as he defines it, that leaves no doubt as to the antiracist perspective.

First, Kendi defines the sin of racial inequity as being "when two or more racial groups are not standing on approximately equal footing."[42] He goes on to offer a concrete example: "71 percent of White families lived in owner-occupied homes in 2014, compared to 45 percent of Latinx families and 41 percent of Black families."[43] Having provided a definition and an example, Kendi closes the loop with something one almost never finds in CSJ literature or sermons: a solution. Or at least, a description of what the results will look like once the solution (antiracist policies) is applied: "An example of racial equity would be if there were relatively equitable percentages of all three racial groups living in owner-occupied homes in the forties, seventies, or, better, nineties."[44]

---

[39] DiAngelo, *White Fragility*, 20.

[40] Kendi, *How to Be an Antiracist*, 17.

[41] Ibid, 18.

[42] Ibid.

[43] Ibid.

[44] Ibid.

This is as clear as it gets! It is also critical to any analysis of the anti-racist worldview and its compatibility with biblical truth. How, for example, would we apply the Parable of the Talents in Matthew 25 to this kind of thinking? For the antiracist, the goal is equitable outcomes. A goal that, as we will see, is neither biblical, reasonable, nor achievable. In fact, at no time in the history of the world has the kind of equity Kendi seeks existed. But this also explains so many things we have seen, and will see as we go forward.

For example, this definition of racism explains why antiracists are not moved by the evidence in individual police shootings. For them, the only relevant fact is proportionality. If blacks are shot by police at a disproportionate rate, it is *de facto* racism. Moreover, any attempt to explain the disparity as anything other than racism is, according to DiAngelo, another form of racism called "aversive racism." This is why antiracists also cry foul when issues like out-of-wedlock birthrates, criminality, and cultural norms enter into the discussion. Furthermore, as we will see, it also explains why the mere reliance on things like facts, statistics, or the scientific method are actually seen as racist.[45] (That is, unless Kendi is using facts, statistics, and the scientific method to prove the existence of inequities.) In other words, if you do not accept this worldview, you are inevitably engaging in racism.

---

[45] The idea that the scientific method is inherently racist is a hallmark of CRT. In one of the seminal academic papers on the topic, Tara Yosso, one of the most-cited CRT academics, lists five key elements of the ideology. Among them, she identifies *"the challenge to dominant ideology.* CRT challenges White privilege and refutes the claims that educational institutions make toward objectivity, meritocracy, color-blindness, race neutrality and equal opportunity. CRT challenges notions of 'neutral' research or 'objective' researchers and exposes deficit-informed research that silences, ignores and distorts epistemologies of People of Color. CRT argues that these traditional claims act as a camouflage for the self-interest, power, and privilege of dominant groups in US society." See San Jose State University's "Critical Race Theory in Chicana/O Education," April 1, 2001, https://scholarworks.sjsu.edu/cgi/viewcontent.cgi?referer=https://duckduckgo.com/&httpsredir=1&article=1036&context=naccs. Also, a flier at the Smithsonian's Museum of African American History included the Scientific Method as "an element of whiteness." The document specified that this includes objective, rational, linear thinking; cause-and-effect relationships; and quantitative emphasis.

If you think this definition is limited to academics in grievance studies, you are sorely mistaken. For example, David Platt, in a momentous sermon delivered at Together for the Gospel in 2018, defined racism as "a system ... in which race, and specifically white and black skin colors, *profoundly affects people's economic, political, and social experiences.*" This is unmistakably taken from the antiracist lexicon. But lest you think it lets individuals off the hook, Jarvis Williams claims that "race and racial reconciliation are soteriological issues." Thus, not only are white Christians who fail to adopt antiracist theology and repent of racism in jeopardy of being alienated from God, but those who fail to elevate the preaching of the antiracist message to the same level as the preaching of the Gospel are apparently preaching another gospel—which, according to Williams, is no gospel at all. Ironically, it is the antiracists who have abandoned the Gospel since, in their view, there is no good news of grace. There is only law.

A New Law (the "Work" of Antiracism)

Albert Schweitzer once said, "A heavy guilt rests upon us for what the whites of all nations have done to the colored peoples. When we do good to them, it is not benevolence—it is atonement."[46] That sentiment lies at the heart of antiracism.

"What's the problem with being 'not racist'?" asks Kendi in *How to Be an Antiracist.* "It is a claim that signifies neutrality: 'I am not a racist, but neither am I aggressively against racism.' But there is no neutrality in the racism struggle. The opposite of 'racist' isn't 'not racist.' It is 'antiracist.'"[47]

In other words, antiracism means more than simply being "against racism." The new definition adds the dimension of activism. The antiracist, therefore, is one who "does the work" of exposing, combatting, and reversing the ubiquitous influences of racism in the past, present, and future. "You'll need to examine your own life and the lives of your

---

[46] David Lang, ed., *Assorted Quotations* (Altamonte Springs, Florida: OakTree Software, accordance electronic ed., 2001), paragraph 5139.

[47] Kendi, *How to Be an Antiracist*, 9.

ancestors so you can see whether you've participated in, perpetuated, or benefited from systems of racism," Morrison writes in *Be the Bridge*.[48]

That's right: it is not enough for white Christians to examine their hearts and lives to see whether they stand guilty (which they do); they must also examine the attitudes and actions of their ancestors—which, according to antiracist cosmology, includes all white people. And this is no small thing. In Morrison's theology, this is a cardinal doctrine. "That is the power of the unconfessed sin of white supremacy, racism, and resulting colorism: it leads to death, sometimes physical, sometimes metaphorical."[49]

It is one thing for me to suggest that antiracism is an expression of legalistic religion. It is another thing to see it in action. Kendi's proposed amendment to the United States Constitution makes the case better than I ever could:

> To fix the original sin of racism, Americans should pass an anti-racist amendment to the U.S. Constitution that enshrines two guiding anti-racist principals: Racial inequity is evidence of racist policy and the different racial groups are equals. The amendment would make unconstitutional racial inequity over a certain threshold, as well as racist ideas by public officials (with "racist ideas" and "public official" clearly defined). It would establish and permanently fund the Department of Anti-racism (DOA) comprised of formally trained experts on racism and no political appointees. The DOA would be responsible for preclearing all local, state and federal public policies to ensure they won't yield racial inequity, monitor those policies, investigate private racist policies when racial inequity surfaces, and monitor public officials for expressions of racist ideas. The DOA would be empowered with disciplinary tools to wield

---

[48] Morrison, *Be the Bridge*, 8.
[49] Ibid., 94.

over and against policymakers and public officials who do not voluntarily change their racist policy and ideas.[50]

As legendary economist Thomas Sowell (who is black) notes, "This conception of fairness requires that third parties must wield the power to control outcomes, overriding rules, standards, or the preferences of other people."[51] If one didn't know better, one might think Sowell's words in *The Quest for Cosmic Justice* were written in response to Kendi's amendment instead of two decades prior.

Four things are worth noting about Kendi's proposed amendment. First, he couches it in religious terms but gives it government-empowered teeth—thus removing all doubt that we are dealing with a legalistic religious movement. It is designed to "fix the original sin of racism." Second, because antiracism is rooted in law instead of gospel, Kendi's solution is legal rather than spiritual. Third, the amendment is rooted in the assumptions of CRT/I. It requires us to assume that "racial inequity is evidence of racist policy." Finally, the amendment must be enforced by a new priesthood, the Department of Antiracism. Why priesthood? Because the goal is fixing sin, the staffers' training is based in antiracism, and their power is meant to be wielded "against policymakers and public officials who do not voluntarily change their racist policy *and ideas*."

This is not just law-work; it is heart-work. This is inside-out, top-down transformation. This is the work of a new class of priests.

The words of Milton Friedman serve as a fitting caveat:

A society that puts equality—in the sense of equality of outcome—ahead of freedom will end up with neither equality nor freedom. The use of force to achieve equality will

---

[50] Ibram X. Kendi, "Pass an Anti-Racist Constitutional Amendment," *Politico*, 2019, https://www.politico.com/interactives/2019/how-to-fix-politics-in-america/inequality/pass-an-anti-racist-constitutional-amendment/.

[51] Thomas Sowell, *The Quest for Cosmic Justice* (New York, New York: Free Press, Kindle Edition, 1996), 12.

destroy freedom, and the force, introduced for good purposes, will end up in the hands of people who use it to
promote their own interests.[52]

---

[52] Sowell, *The Quest for Cosmic Justice*, 6–7.

CHAPTER FIVE

A New Priesthood

The cult of antiracism also has a priesthood. Like Israel's priesthood in the Old Testament, this one requires belonging to the proper tribe. In this case, however, the notion is flipped on its head. Instead of being required to be a Levite (read: white), this cult accepts priests based on their not being Levites. Hence, all oppressed minorities (people of color, women, LGBTQIA+,[1] non-citizens, the disabled, the obese, the poor, non-Christians, and anyone else with an accepted oppressed status) qualify for the priesthood in the cult of antiracism.

"Ethnic Gnosticism" is a term I coined several years ago to explain what I see as a dangerous and growing phenomenon in the culture that is creeping into the church. Gnosticism is derived from the Greek word *gnosis* (knowledge) and is based on the idea that truth can be accessed through special, mystical knowledge. The *International Standard Bible Encyclopedia* calls it "a heresy far more subtle and dangerous than any

---

[1] LGBTQIA+ stands for the usual Lesbian, Gay, Bisexual, Transgender, Queer, Intersex, and Allies. The plus serves in much the same way as "to an unknown God" covered the spiritual bases and avoided offense in Paul's day by acknowledging that of which one is currently unaware.

that had appeared during the early years of the church."[2] Ethnic Gnosticism, then, is the idea that people have special knowledge based solely on their ethnicity. This is a hallmark of both Critical Race Theory and its predecessor, Critical Theory. "CRT recognizes that the experiential knowledge of People of Color is legitimate, appropriate, and critical to understanding, analyzing and teaching about racial subordination," wrote University of California scholar Tara J. Yosso in *Race Ethnicity and Education*.[3] "Of course, the knowledge yielded by the standpoint of the proletariat stands on a higher scientific plane objectively," wrote Georg Lukács of the Frankfurt School. "It does after all apply a method that makes possible the solution of problems which the greatest thinkers of the bourgeois era have vainly struggled to find."[4]

It would be more accurate, though, in light of the broader assumptions of the Critical Social Justice movement to use the term "minority gnosticism," since the same argument is applied to all "oppressed minorities." In fact, it is their "oppressed" status that, according to CSJ, gives these groups their special knowledge. This is a central tenet of Critical Race Theory. "The voice-of-color thesis," writes Richard Delgado, "holds that because of their different histories and experiences with oppression, black, American Indian, Asian, and Latino writers and thinkers may be able to communicate to their white counterparts matters that the whites are unlikely to know." Thus, according to CRT, "Minority status ... brings with it a presumed competence to speak about race and racism."[5] This makes sense, since "Critical Race Theory builds on

---

[2] A.M. Renwick, "Gnosticism," edited by Geoffrey W. Bromiley, *The International Standard Bible Encyclopedia, Revised* (Grand Rapids, Michigan: William B. Eerdmans Publishing Company, 1979–1988), 484.

[3] Tara J. Yosso, "Whose Culture Has Capital? A Critical Race Theory Discussion of Community Cultural Wealth," *Race Ethnicity and Education* 8, no. 1 (August 23, 2006): 69–91, https://www.tandfonline.com/doi/pdf/10.1080/136133205200 0341006.

[4] Georg Lukács, *History, Class, and Consciousness*, Marxists.org, https://www.marxists.org/archive/lukacs/works/history/hcc07_1.htm.

[5] Richard Delgado, *Critical Race Theory* (Third Edition) (New York, New York: NYU Press, Kindle Edition, 2017), 11.

the insights of two previous movements, critical legal studies and radical feminism, to both of which it owes a large debt." Specifically, the debt CRT owes to radical feminism is the towering influence of *standpoint epistemology*, the hallmark of Ethnic Gnosticism.

"Each oppressed group," writes Sandra Harding in *The Feminist Standpoint Theory Reader*, "can learn to identify its distinctive opportunities to turn an oppressive feature of the group's conditions into a source of critical insight about how the dominant society thinks and is structured." Thus, she concludes, "standpoint theories map how a social and political disadvantage can be turned into an epistemological, scientific, and political advantage."[6] And, CRT would add, a political advantage. Standpoint theory posits that "there is a cognitive asymmetry between the standpoint of the oppressed and the standpoint of the privileged *that gives an advantage to the former over the latter*."[7]

Not a difference, mind you—an advantage. This advantage is based on Critical Theory, which was established by the late Italian philosopher Antonio Gramsci, the one-time leader of the Communist Party of Italy. This Marxist thread runs through all the grievance studies, such as radical feminism, queer studies, whiteness studies, etc. Delgado confirms this when he writes that CRT "also draws from certain European philosophers and theorists, such as Antonio Gramsci, Michel Foucault, and Jacques Derrida, as well as ... the Black Power and Chicano movements of the sixties and early seventies."[8]

The Three Facets of Ethnic Gnosticism

Ethnic Gnosticism has three basic manifestations. First, it assumes there is *a black perspective* all black people share (unless they are broken).

---

[6] Sandra Harding, *The Feminist Standpoint Theory Reader: Intellectual and Political Controversies* (New York, New York: Routledge, 2004), 7–8.

[7] José Medina, *The Epistemology of Resistance: Gender and Racial Oppression, Epistemic Injustice, and the Social Imagination* (Oxford, England: Oxford University Press, 2013), 197.

[8] Delgado, *Critical Race Theory*, 5.

Of course, no one will admit this since it is obviously racist. However, this is exactly what Ethnic Gnosticism advocates.

Second, it argues that white people's only access to this perspective comes from elevating and heeding black voices. Finally, it essentially argues that narrative is an alternative, and ultimately superior, truth. Again, most Christians will find this idea offensive, as well they should. Nevertheless, this is undeniably the perspective from which CRT and thus CSJ operate, and thus why they represent a fault line. Christians simply must reject this worldview.

Let's examine each of these assertions in turn.

A Singular Black Perspective

In an article published in *The Atlantic* in July 2020, Emma Green offers a poignant example of this:

> In 2018, a group of pastors led by John MacArthur, an influential white megachurch pastor in California, signed a statement decrying "social justice" and arguing against "postmodern ideologies derived from intersectionality, radical feminism, and critical race theory." It condemned "political or social activism" as not being "integral components of the gospel or primary to the mission of the church." This kind of sentiment is common among white evangelical leaders, several Black leaders who work in these spaces told me: White pastors aggressively enforce the boundaries of acceptable conversations on racism, weaponizing any position that bears even a whiff of progressive politics and slapping labels such as "social justice" and "cultural Marxism" on arguments about systemic injustice. Black leaders at predominately white organizations are careful to emphasize that caring about racism is a gospel issue.[9]

---

[9] Emma Green, "The Unofficial Racism Consultants to the White Evangelical World," *The Atlantic*, July 5, 2020, https://www.msn.com/en-us/news/us/the-unofficial-racism-consultants-to-the-white-evangelical-world/ar-BB16m2y9.

Several black leaders, including me, attended that conference. Notice how Green mentions none of us? For her, the statement repudiating social justice in the Church cannot be associated with black voices because it does not fit her narrative. The idea that white pastors "aggressively enforce" boundaries of conversations on racism and "weaponize" any they dislike by labeling them "social justice" and "cultural Marxism" is a convenient way to frame the discussion in an "us versus them" false dichotomy. That only works if disparate black "voices" are dismissed.

Perhaps the clearest and most widely publicized example of this aspect of Ethnic Gnosticism is what happened when Kentucky Attorney General Daniel Cameron announced in September 2020 the findings of the grand jury investigating the Breonna Taylor shooting. As I watched the press conference, I was struck by two things: 1) the providential reality that at that particular moment in time, God would have a black man serving as the highest ranking legal officer in the Commonwealth of Kentucky, and 2) the knowledge that Cameron's ethnicity would matter only if he announced murder charges against the officers in question. Otherwise, his blackness would be negated and dismissed as irrelevant, and he would be deemed "broken."

Cameron framed his words carefully and appropriately, striking a balance between his job as a prosecutor and his humanity:

> I want to once again publicly express my condolences. Every day, this family wakes up to the realization that someone they loved is no longer with them. There's nothing I can offer today to take away the grief and heartache this family is experiencing as a result of losing a child, a niece, a sister, and a friend. What I can provide today are the facts, which my office has worked long and hard to uncover, analyze, and scrutinize since accepting this case in mid-May. I urge everyone listening today to not lose sight of the fact that a life has been lost, a tragedy under any circumstances. The decision before my office as the special prosecutor in this case was not to decide if the loss of Ms. Taylor's life was a tragedy. The answer to

that question is unequivocally yes. There is no doubt that this is a gut-wrenching emotional case, and the pain that many people are feeling is understandable. I deeply care about the value and sanctity of human life. It deserves protection. And in this case, a human life was lost. We cannot forget that.

Cameron went on to dispel several myths about the Breonna Taylor case that are crucial not only because they matter to the case, but also because many Christian leaders have borne false witness in this matter and their sin was exposed in this press conference. (Lord willing, they will repent.) Here are some of those myths and the facts that dispelled them:

- Myth #1: The police were at the wrong house. (They weren't.)[10]
- Myth #2: The officers used a "no-knock" warrant. (They were specifically told to knock and announce their presence.)
- Myth #3: The officers did not announce themselves. (Eyewitnesses testified that the officers both knocked *and* announced.)
- Myth #4: The officers started the firefight. (Taylor's boyfriend, Kenneth Walker, admitted that he fired the first shot.)

---

[10] According to leaked documents, the warrant for Breonna Taylor's apartment was granted based on, among other things, 1) her possible involvement in a homicide after the body of an associate was found in a car Taylor rented in 2016, 2) the fact that a known drug dealer listed Taylor's address on his Chase Bank account, 3) the fact that Taylor twice bailed the dealer out of jail, 4) the fact that during recorded jailhouse phone calls between Taylor and the dealer, she collected drug money for him, 5) the dealer had packages delivered to Taylor's apartment, and 6) surveillance video and photos showed Taylor at the "trap house" with the dealer. "Breonna Taylor," Tatumreport.com, https://www.yumpu.com/en/document/read/63943132/breonna-taylor-summary-redacted1.

- Myth #5: One of the officers was shot by friendly fire. (The officers all fired .40-caliber rounds; the injured one was hit by a 9mm round, which is what Walker used.)
- Myth #6: The officers shot Breonna Taylor in her bed as she slept.[11] (Taylor was shot in the hall as she stood next to Walker, who opened fire.)

After Cameron delivered his remarks, several reporters asked telling questions: One inquired about the racial makeup of Cameron's investigative team. Another wanted to know the racial makeup of the grand jury. Why? Ethnic Gnosticism! The implication was that the officers weren't indicted because the grand jury lacked "*the* black perspective."

But what about the black attorney general standing at the podium who oversaw the whole thing? According to the press, he "turned his back on Black America"[12]; was "no different than the sell-out Negroes that sold our people into slavery"[13]; and "skinfolk but not ... kinfolk.... He does

[11] Marquise Francis, "'Sleeping While Black': Family Seeks Justice for Breonna Taylor, Killed in Her Bedroom by Police," Yahoo News, May 13, 2020, https://news.yahoo.com/asleep-while-black-family-seeks-justice-for-breonna-taylor-killed-in-her-bedroom-by-police-210858395.html; Elie Mystal, "Breonna Taylor Was Murdered for Sleeping While Black," *The Nation*, May 15, 2020, https://www.thenation.com/article/society/breonna-taylor-was-murdered-for-sleeping-while-black; Amina Elahi, "'Sleeping While Black': Louisville Police Kill Unarmed Black Woman," NPR, May 13, 2020, https://www.npr.org/2020/05/13/855705278/sleeping-while-black-louisville-police-kill-unarmed-black-woman; Bridget Read, "What We Know about the Killing of Breonna Taylor," *The Cut*, September 29, 2020, https://www.thecut.com/2020/09/breonna-taylor-louisville-shooting-police-what-we-know.html.

[12] Greg Moore, "Kentucky AG Daniel Cameron Turned His Back on America. Here's How to Fight Back," *Arizona Republic*, September 24, 2020, https://www.azcentral.com/story/opinion/op-ed/greg-moore/2020/09/24/daniel-cameron-turned-his-back-on-black-america/3515688001.

[13] Louis Casiano, "Women's March Co-Founder Tamika Mallory Says Kentucky Attorney General Daniel Cameron No Different Than 'Sell-Out Negroes,'" Fox News, September 25, 2020, https://www.foxnews.com/us/tamika-mallory-kentucky-negroes.

not speak for all of us."[14] This is straight out of the Ethnic Gnosticism handbook.

Cameron's presentation of the facts did nothing to dispel the narrative journalists and other social justice warriors want to tell about the Breonna Taylor case. MSNBC host Joy Reid, who is black, combined the first and third elements of Ethnic Gnosticism when she said, "According to the theory of the law that was voiced today by Attorney General Cameron, police have the perfect right to bust into your home in the middle of the night if you have any association that police are looking for, *even if they've already found them*. And they can shoot and *kill you in your bed* and walk away with no legal repercussions"[15] (italics mine). Note that Reid repeated two of the aforementioned dispelled myths as if they were facts, just moments after the AG presented evidence to the contrary. In a similar move, the *Arizona Republic* repeated two debunked myths, saying that Cameron's words did not excuse "the unconscionably light charges in the shooting death of Breonna Taylor, a Black woman *who was asleep in her home* when police burst in looking for drugs, *starting a firefight that killed her*"[16] (italics mine).

A Slate article goes to the heart of Ethnic Gnosticism's need to depict blacks who fail to hold to the singular black perspective as "broken": those who fail to toe the ethnic line are pandering to white Republicans. "Cameron's words, meant to justify the unsatisfying charges," the article states, "actually did more to explain his meteoric rise through the ranks of Republican politics."[17] In other words, *we all know what happened,*

---

[14] Thomas Catanacci, "He Is Not Kinfolk': MSNBC Guest Says Black Kentucky Attorney General Doesn't Represent Black People," The Daily Caller, September 23, 2020, https://dailycaller.com/2020/09/23/skinfolk-kinfolk-msnbc-guest-kentucky-attorney-general-daniel-cameron-doesnt-represent-black-people.

[15] Joy Reid, *The ReidOut*, MSNBC, September 23, 2020, https://archive.org/details/MSNBCW_20200923_230000_The_ReidOut.

[16] Moore, "Kentucky AG Daniel Cameron Turned His Back on America. Here's How to Fight Back."

[17] Joel Anderson, "The Usefulness of Daniel Cameron," Slate, September 25, 2020, https://slate.com/news-and-politics/2020/09/daniel-cameron-breonna-taylor-kentucky-attorney-general.html.

so anything that contradicts our *gnosis* is already wrong. Moreover, any black person who does not agree with our *gnosis* is broken, so our job is not to examine the evidence of the case, but the evidence of his life—since that is the only possible explanation.

All the while, white reporters interviewed these people without an ounce of pushback about the facts of the Taylor case that Cameron presented. Why? Not only because it wasn't politically expedient, but because they are good antiracists who know that they (according to CRT) are operating from an inferior and incomplete perspective.

White People Cannot "See" without Black Voices

Ethnic Gnosticism argues that white people's only access to the singular black perspective comes from elevating and listening to black voices. This is why I refer to it as "the new priesthood." Of course, as the previous discussion shows, this only includes black voices that speak "the singular black truth" rooted in "the experience of black oppression."

Evangelicalism is echoing the same sentiment. Everywhere you turn, another prominent voice is calling for the recognition and elevation of black voices, sometimes even in ways that clearly advocate the principles of Ethnic Gnosticism. "Whiteness. Has. Caused. Blind. Ness. Of. Heart. Whiteness. Has. Caused. Blind. Ness. Of. HEART!"[18] chanted *Woke Church* author Eric Mason (citing Ephesians 4:18). "The Bible can't tell us what its like to be black in America, or how to address systemic discrimination in housing or education," tweeted *Veggie Tales* creator Phil Vischer. "We need to listen to voices who study the issues and have had the experience."[19]

Note two things about Vischer's tweet. First, he uses the phrase "listen to voices." Not to people or experts, but "voices." Second, we

---

[18] Woke Preacher Clips, "Eric Mason: 'Whiteness Has Caused Blindness of Heart!'," YouTube, September 23, 2020, https://www.youtube.com/watch?v=O-O6Ufo3GH8.

[19] Phil Vischer (@philvischer), Twitter, June 9, 2020, https://twitter.com/phil-vischer/status/1270468029093216257?s=20.

need to listen to "voices" who 1) study and 2) have had *the experience.*
This is connected to the first principle of Ethnic Gnosticism. For example, Vischer doesn't recommend listening to, say, Thomas Sowell's
"voice" or John McWhorter's "voice," since they do not have *the experience.* How do I know? Because Vischer, who made a viral video on
systemic racism, specifically refers here to addressing "systemic discrimination." Hence, he has already couched the discussion in CT/CRT terms.

There is a great deal of theoretical and philosophical support for this
sentiment. Sensoy and DiAngelo, for example, deal extensively with this
idea in *Is Everyone Really Equal?* After questioning whether true objectivity is "desirable, or even possible,"[20] they explain:

> The term used to describe this way of thinking about knowl-
> edge is that knowledge is socially constructed. When we refer
> to knowledge as socially constructed, we mean that knowledge
> is reflective of the values and interests of those who produce it.
> This term captures the understanding that all content and all
> means of knowing are connected to a social context.[21]

This is why critical theorists believe that 1) the quest for objectivity is
tantamount to a quest for white supremacy, and 2) we must value voices
from "social contexts" outside of the racial hegemony to experience what
critical theorists refer to as "other ways of knowing." This is crucial to CSJ
since "[critical] scholars argue that a key element of social injustice involves
the claim that particular knowledge is objective and universal."[22]

Not to belabor the point, but it is important for me to make this
connection. People accuse those of us who oppose CSJ of calling those
with whom we disagree names or using broad generalizations to

---

[20] Robin DiAngelo and Özlem Sensoy, *Is Everyone Really Equal?: An Introduction to Key Concepts in Social Justice Education* (Multicultural Education Series)
(New York, New York: Teacher's College Press, 2012), 7.

[21] Ibid.

[22] Ibid.

demonize them. I do not deny that that has happened. However, as bad as that is, there is something worse, and that is promoting ideologies that are antithetical to the Gospel. Ethnic Gnosticism is dangerous, at least in part because it is rooted in neo-Marxism and Critical Theory. In a book poetically titled *Rhodes Must Fall: The Struggle to Decolonise the Racist Heart of Empire*, Kehinde Andrews makes the connection even clearer when he writes, "The neglect of Black knowledge by society is no accident but a direct result of racism." Read carefully as Andrews unpacks what he means by "Black knowledge": "Black Studies redresses this marginalisation by focusing on those *knowledges* produced at the margins and aims to create knowledge that can have a liberatory impact."[23] Having introduced the idea of other "knowledges," he then ties the idea back to CT/CRT/I with all its trimmings:

> As Malcolm X argued, "truth is on the side of the oppressed," and the standpoint of Blackness provides a unique understanding of society. Black Studies is part of the wider movement to decolonise knowledge and to debunk the racist assumptions of the taken-for-granted Eurocentric truth regimes. This has never been a battle that was just academic— knowledge shapes the world. Eurocentric knowledge created the racist social order we experience.[24]

This reads like Andrews opened up a CRT thesaurus and went to town! He made all the connections, and in doing so, perfectly illustrates my point. These ideas are rooted in a *worldview*. And that worldview has crept into the Church.

In his book *Removing the Stain of Racism from the Southern Baptist Convention*, Southern Baptist Theological Seminary professor Jarvis

---

[23] Kehinde Andrews in *Rhodes Must Fall: The Struggle to Decolonise the Racist Heart of Empire* (London, United Kingdom: Zed Books, Kindle Edition, 2018).

[24] Ibid.

Williams urges white Christians to "be quick to listen and slow to speak on race when they do not understand,"[25] because in his view, "white supremacy and racism are complicated issues." He goes on to explain what the proper "understanding" of these issues requires:

> These issues relate to concepts such as racialization, critical race theory, mass incarceration, economic inequality, educational inequality, and other forms of systemic injustice. Speaking ignorantly about these issues is inappropriate. Southern Baptists, especially white Southern Baptists with privilege and without personal experience of the challenges associated with being a black or brown person in the U.S., should spend more time listening to their black and brown brothers and sisters instead of trying to speak to, at, about, or for them.[26]

Note how Williams shifts from the idea that these are "complicated issues" to appealing to the "personal experience of the challenges associated with being a black or brown person." This is classic Ethnic Ggnosticism. White people don't understand because of their "privilege" (read: hegemony, oppression, etc.), and black people *do* understand because of their personal experience (with hegemony, oppression, etc.). In a May 2020 sermon, pastor and former International Mission Board President David Platt bowed to these forces when he said, "I want to sacrifice more of my preferences as a white pastor ... I need to grow ... I do not want to speak from the Bible on issues that are popular among white followers of Christ.... *And I know, as a white pastor, I have blind spots, so I am part of the problem.*"[27]

---

[25] Jarvis J. Williams and Kevin Jones, *Removing the Stain of Racism from the Southern Baptist Convention* (Nashville, Tennessee: B&H Publishing Group, Kindle Edition, 2017), 99.

[26] Ibid.

[27] McLean Bible Church, "Praying and Working for Justice: Racialization," YouTube, May 27, 2020, https://www.youtube.com/watch?v=UUs5mQ0WBP8.

If black people know racism, and white people cannot know racism (and are racist by default as a result of their white privilege), then the only acceptable response is for white people to sit down, shut up, and listen to what black people have to say on the matter.

That is exactly what the *Be the Bridge* curriculum and Facebook group—one of the most recommended resources on race among contemporary evangelicals—is about. Thabiti Anyabwile, arguably the leading CSJ voice in the broader evangelical sphere, has endorsed, recommended, and promoted *Be the Bridge* many times. Here is a picture of what it looks like when the Church accepts the premises of Ethnic Gnosticism (from the rules for white members of the *Be the Bridge* Facebook group):

> Don't "whitesplain." Do not explain racism to a POC. Do not explain how the microaggression they just experienced was actually just someone being nice. Do not explain how a particular injustice is more about class than race. It's an easy trap to fall into, but you can avoid it by maintaining a posture of active listening.
>
> Don't equate impact with intent. Yes, we all know your heart was in the right place and you meant well. But your words or behavior had a negative impact on those around you, and that's what matters. Apologize and do better next time.
>
> Don't demand proof of a POC's lived experience or try to counter their narrative with the experience of another POC. The experiences and opinions of POC are as diverse as its people. We can believe their stories. But keep in mind: just because one POC doesn't feel oppressed, that doesn't mean systemic, institutional racism isn't real.
>
> Do not chastise POCs (or dismiss their message) because they express their grief, fear, or anger in ways you deem "inappropriate." Understand that historically, we white people have silenced voices of dissent and lament with our

cultural idol of "niceness." Provide space for POCs to wail, cuss, or even yell at you. Jesus didn't hold back when he saw hypocrisy and oppression; POCs shouldn't have to either.

Don't get defensive when you are called out for any of the above. When a POC tells you that your words/tone/behavior are racist/oppressive/triggering, you stop. Don't try to explain yourself (see #6.) Don't become passive-aggressive or sarcastic. Don't leave in a huff. (It may be helpful, however, to inconspicuously step outside/go to the restroom and take a deep breath.) Remain cognizant of the dynamics of white fragility, and take note of how it usually shows up in you.

Allow me to give one final example of this kind of thinking within the Church. In a recent tweet, Anthony Bradley, a well-known conservative Reformed evangelical scholar, makes a poignant practical application of the foundation Williams previously laid out for Southern Baptists:

> [B]lack people in America have relied on God's word to help them survive white people. When you're white & in the dominant culture, you've never needed the Old Testament covenant-keeping Redemptive God. Yours became a Christianity of moralism.... Evangelicals will be confused by the black church because they've never needed the God who acts through miracles to redeem them from something that's not their fault. So of course they will eventually question the reliability & veracity of text. Life's been pretty easy. One of the privileges of being white in America is never needing God to stop a society from trying to destroy you & your family. So the Bible is a book for evangelicalism, disciple-making, & teaching morals. Not a book for personal AND social, cosmic survival.... As such, Great Commission Christianity doesn't know what to do with [the] Old Testament. They have to make Jesus (& Paul) appear in the OT

in order for the text to have meaning. *The traditional black church is far more Trinitarian about the whole counsel of God than evangelicals* (italics mine).[28]

Note the separation he makes between evangelicals/Great Commission Christianity and black people/the traditional black church. Also note the clear connection between those categories and the ability to know and experience God rightly. Finally, note how all of this is rooted in experience and narrative.

Narrative Trumps Truth

The third and final plank in the Ethnic Gnosticism platform is the idea that narrative is an alternative and ultimately superior truth. One of CRT's hallmarks is storytelling—particularly, as its architects define it, *legal storytelling* and *counterstorytelling*. Legal storytelling is "using stories, parables, and first-person accounts to understand and analyze racial issues,"[29] while counterstorytelling is "writing that aims to cast doubt on the validity of accepted premises or myths, especially ones held by the majority."[30] The practice "has enjoyed considerable vogue, and has spread to other disciplines."[31]

Essentially, CRT uses storytelling as an alternative truth. As the old legal adage goes, "If the law is on your side, pound the law; if the facts are on your side, pound the facts; if neither is on your side, pound the table."

---

[28] Anthony Bradley (@drantbradley), "This is simple: black people in America have relied on God's word to help them survive white people. When you're white & in the dominant culture, you've never needed the Old Testament covenant-keeping Redemptive God. Yours became a Christianity of moralism & your kids walked," Twitter, February 4, 2019, 9:46 a.m., https://twitter.com/drantbradley/status/1092434184130490369.

[29] Delgado, *Critical Race Theory*, 178.

[30] Ibid., 171.

[31] Ibid., 53.

CRT would change the last part of that to "if neither is on your side, 1) assume it is because of racism, and 2) tell a story or counterstory."

Storytelling and the Racism of American Policing

Perhaps the biggest problem with storytelling and counterstorytelling is that those stories so often are proven wrong—or worse, just plain false. We have all heard stories about racist police stops. I have even told one or two myself. There is no doubt that many black Americans have had run-ins with cops who are on power trips, having a bad day, or really were racist. I have described my own such run-ins elsewhere. But what about when they're not? What about when the officer was professional, courteous, even lenient, but the storyteller gives a different account? Shouldn't this give us pause? Three examples help demonstrate my point.

Example #1: The Liar

In April 2018, Reverend Jerrod Moultrie, the president of a South Carolina chapter of the NAACP, was pulled over by police. In a now-deleted Facebook post, Moultrie wrote, "Tonight I was racially profiled by Timmonsville Officer [Chris Miles] cause I was driving a Mercedes Benz and going home in a nice neighborhood."[32]

Moultrie then took things a step further.

Timmonsville Police Chief Billy Brown said Moultrie contacted him the next morning to accuse Miles of racial profiling and mistreating him during the stop. According to Moultrie's statement to the chief, the officer not only accused him of having drugs in his car, but did so in front of Moultrie's wife and grandchild.[33] The chief's documents state that the officer "asked [Moultrie's wife and grandchild] not to move because the

---

[32] Camila Molina, "SC NAACP Leader Says He Was Racially Profiled. Body Cam Footage Tells a Different Story," *News & Observer*, May 15, 2018, https://www.newsobserver.com/news/local/article211166024.html#storylink=cpy.

[33] Larry Elder, "Who's Doing the 'Racial Profiling'?," *The Tribune-Democrat*, June 11, 2018, https://www.tribdem.com/news/editorials/larry-elder-who-s-doing-the-racial-profiling/article_ad3915b0-6b3a-11e8-ab22-8bc873585ac7.html.

officer looked as if he might shoot them or something. He also made mention that the officer continued to ask him about his neighborhood. Why was he in that neighborhood? And (threatened) to put him in jail in reference to something dealing with the registration to the vehicle."[34]

When the chief investigated, Miles's body camera footage told a different tale: Moultrie failed to signal a turn and had the wrong tags on his new Mercedes-Benz. The body cam footage shows that Miles was courteous, professional, and extremely helpful, telling Moultrie where to go to get the proper tags. (After his lie was revealed, Moultrie removed the Facebook post.)

Example #2: The Misinformed

In February 2015, actress Taraji P. Henson accused police in Glendale, California, of racially profiling her son during a visit to the University of Southern California. Henson was so upset by the incident that she vowed to send her son across the country to Howard University rather than allow him to stay in Southern California. "I'm not paying $50K so I can't sleep at night wondering is this the night my son is getting racially profiled on campus," she told *Uptown Magazine*.

Then the Glendale Police Department released the body cam footage showing the stop was initiated when Henson's son drove through a yellow light while a pedestrian was crossing the street.[35] He also handed the officer an expired insurance card, to which the officer responded, "That's alright," and then, "OK, good job," when the young man produced the proper document. The officer smelled marijuana, which Henson admitted having in his possession without a permit, along with Ritalin that wasn't prescribed to him. In an act that can only be described as extremely lenient, the officer said, "I'm going to give you a citation for the marijuana. I'm not going to give you a citation for running that yellow because that will actually put a moving violation on your license."

---

[34] Elder, "Who's Doing the 'Racial Profiling'?."

[35] "Police Release Video of Actress Taraji P. Henson's Son Marcell Being Stopped in Glendale," *Los Angeles Times*, March 27, 2015, https://www.latimes.com/83163502-132.html.

He barely even mentioned the Ritalin—a highly addictive drug in the same class as OxyContin, opium, and fentanyl—other than to say, "If you have Ritalin on you and you're not supposed to, don't do it. That's a big violation, and I wouldn't want to do it."

To her credit, Henson recanted after the video was released. "A mother's job is not easy and neither is a police officer's," she wrote in an Instagram post. "Sometimes as humans we overreact without gathering all of the facts.... As a mother in this case I overreacted and for that I apologize. Thank you to that officer for being kind to my son."[36]

Example #3: The Sincerely Wrong

On April 27, 2018, Dawn Hilton-Williams was driving through Brunswick County, Virginia, on her way home to South Carolina after watching her daughter play in a tennis tournament. She was pulled over by a Brunswick County Sheriff's deputy for going seventy miles per hour in a zone where the speed limit was fifty-five. Afterward, she made an emotional cell phone video that she later posted to Facebook, describing what she called "a racist police stop."[37] Hilton-Williams talked about being afraid because she was "in a rural little town." She panned the camera around, showing the long stretch of rural highway, and said, "This is where we got lynched." The video was filled with angst, tears, and passion.

After receiving numerous calls from people who had seen the Facebook video, Brunswick County Sheriff Brian Roberts decided to review the body-cam footage. It shows a by-the-book traffic stop, with the deputy even saying, "please," "thank you," and "ma'am." However, when the officer presents the ticket, Hilton-Williams tells him, "I'm not going to sign that ticket. I don't have to sign that." The officer reiterates that her signature is not an admission of guilt, but acknowledgment of her understanding that she must either pay a fine or appear in court. He then tells her that if she doesn't sign, he will be forced to arrest her,

---

[36] Taraji P. Henson (@tarajiphenson), Instagram, March 27, 2015, https://www.instagram.com/p/0v0KjQOuFM/?taken-by=tarajiphenson.

[37] Planetvance, "Dawn Hilton-Williams Traffic Stop in Virginia on 4/27/2018," YouTube, May 10, 2018, https://www.youtube.com/watch?v=RbrWFpLLLxk.

impound her vehicle, and take her before the magistrate. It is textbook de-escalation with a motorist, and Hilton-Williams agrees to sign.

But after the body-cam footage was released, instead of admitting that she had completely misrepresented the stop, Hilton-Williams maintained her assertion that it was racism, even claiming the cop ticketed her "for going 5 miles over the speed limit." (She was fifteen over.) Her assertion was not based on the facts of the case (she had those wrong), what the officer did or said, or even how he said it (which she misrepresented). Instead, it is based solely on black people suffering racism and trauma throughout history. In Hilton-Williams's mind, she was victimized, and in a classic case of Ethnic Gnosticism, she believes all black people understand that. "Why do only African Americans and people of color know what I'm going through right now?" she asks in her video. She then claims, "Everybody I know who is African American has been through this at least one time." She went on to name several victims of recent police shootings and suggested that her fear arose from the very real possibility of joining them—even though that possibility was improbable under the circumstances.

How many of the pastors who put BLM blackouts on their social media profiles, wrote heartfelt apologies for their "Silence is Violence" missteps, or pledged to "elevate black voices" did so after "listening to the countless stories of our African American brothers and sisters" that told of being pulled over in a racist stop?

I am weary of hearing testimony after testimony of white pastors who threw reason and Scripture out the window because of narratives. How many of those narratives were like the three mentioned above? How many were lies? How many were exaggerations? And how many were the genuine expression of fear and trauma that, though sincere, directly contradicted the facts? The answer is, we don't know.

The rate of police killings of black Americans has fallen by 70 percent over the course of my lifetime.[38] Yet every time I turn around, it

[38] Kameron J. Sheats et al., "Violence-Related Disparities Experienced by Black Youth and Young Adults: Opportunities for Prevention," *American Journal of Preventative Medicine* 55, no. 4 (October 2018): 462–69, doi:10.1016/j. amepre.2018.05.017.

seems there is a headline about police hunting and killing unarmed black men and motorists testifying of profiling, threats of violence, and intense fear of police brutality.

The fear, as in the case of this woman who was pulled over for speeding on a rural highway, is real. When the officer responded firmly to Hilton-Williams's refusal to sign her ticket, I believe she really was afraid. She really did think about police shootings that had taken place over the previous years. She also thought about countless stories she had heard about police racism and brutality.

But what she *thought* wasn't based on reality.

In a recent man-on-the-street interview conducted by Prager University, three young black men were asked how many unarmed black men the police killed in 2019. "About a thousand," said one. "At least a thousand," said the second. The third estimated, "Fourteen hundred." When asked how many unarmed white men were killed by police that same year, their answers ranged from four to fourteen. The young men were astonished to learn that only nineteen white men and nine black men had been killed by police in 2019, according to the *Washington Post* database, the most reliable and up-to-date source available. When asked what they thought about the data, they responded, "Cap."[39]

These young men are not unique. I have seen several similar videos where people of all ages and ethnicities estimate police shootings of unarmed black men range from several hundred to a thousand or more.

But why are those numbers so out of touch with reality? As we are about to explore, it's because those ideas contain a kernel of truth.

The Alternative to Ethnic Gnosticism

As Christians, we are called to "Rejoice with those who rejoice, weep with those who weep" (Romans 12:15). And again in Job, we read, "Did not I weep for him whose day was hard? Was not my soul grieved for the

---

[39] Prager U, "Are the Police Targeting Unarmed Blacks?" YouTube, July 15, 2020, https://www.youtube.com/watch?v=GYUQ8_Sf6Kc.

needy" (Job 30:25)? We are also told to "Remember those who are in prison, as though in prison with them, and those who are mistreated, since you also are in the body" (Hebrews 13:3). May the Lord grant us grace to take such admonitions seriously.

But the Bible also admonishes us to do things that fly in the face of Ethnic Gnosticism and its assumptions. The very idea of dividing people up by ethnicity, then declaring some of them wicked oppressors and others the oppressed, is inconsistent with the biblical doctrine of universal guilt:

> What then? Are we Jews any better off? No, not at all. For we have already charged that all, both Jews and Greeks, are under sin, as it is written: "None is righteous, no, not one; no one understands; no one seeks for God. All have turned aside; together they have become worthless; no one does good, not even one." "Their throat is an open grave; they use their tongues to deceive." "The venom of asps is under their lips." "Their mouth is full of curses and bitterness." "Their feet are swift to shed blood; in their paths are ruin and misery, and the way of peace they have not known." "There is no fear of God before their eyes." (Romans 3:9–18)

This is not the state of white men; it is the state of *all* men. As such, the idea that there is special knowledge or revelation available to some and hidden from others by virtue of their race or position in the oppressor/oppressed scheme is unthinkable—and unbiblical.

If it doesn't come from the Bible, where is it coming from?

CHAPTER SIX

A New Canon

In a September 2020 article for *Commentary*, Executive Editor Abe Greenwald wrote, "The revolutionaries have deemed American customs, culture, habits, and ideas racist. And instead of Mao's *Little Red Book* to guide them in the ways of the proletariat, they have Robin DiAngelo's *White Fragility*, which shows them all the hidden places where racism is to be found and rooted out."[1]

In the wake of George Floyd's death and the riots that followed, there were more than protests going on: there was also a frenzy of research. "Everyday Americans swapped Black Lives Matter reading lists and strove, however misguidedly, to broaden their conception of racial inequity," Greenwald noted.[2] Not to be outdone, in an article titled "The Antiracist Curriculum White Evangelicals Need,"[3] *Christianity Today* observed that

---

[1] Abe Greenwald, "Yes, This Is a Revolution," *Commentary*, September 2020, https://www.commentarymagazine.com/articles/abe-greenwald/yes-this-is-a-revolution/.

[2] Ibid.

[3] "The Anti-Racist Curriculum White Evangelicals Need," *Christianity Today*, June 19, 2020, https://www.christianitytoday.com/partners/intervarsity-press/antiracist-curriculum-white-evangelicals-need.html.

"[M]any white people in America have begun to ask 'where do I start?'"—
and listed books, articles, films, and social media platforms editors believe
will help move white people toward antiracism.

If you find this odd, you probably haven't had a conversation with
a Christian millennial recently. If you have, it probably involved you
trying to have a biblically based theological discussion about current
issues and the millennial rolling his eyes and telling you to "do your
homework" to get a more informed, *nuanced* approach. That person
may even have rattled off a list of sociology, political science, and history
books you need to read, plus a few by Christian authors who, having
read the aforementioned books, now see the issues through new lenses
that either don't include, completely misinterpret, or misapply the Bible
in an effort to achieve their goal.

The *Christianity Today* list is, in many ways, a public version of that
conversation. Therefore, it is instructive for us here. It includes:

Books

*Be the Bridge: Pursuing God's Heart for Racial Reconcilia-
tion* by Latasha Morrison
*Rediscipling the White Church: From Cheap Diversity to
True Solidarity* by David W. Swanson
I'm Still Here: Black Dignity in a World Made for Whiteness
by Austin Channing Brown
*The Color of Compromise: The Truth about the American
Church's Complicity in Racism* by Jemar Tisby
*White Awake: An Honest Look at What It Means to Be
White* by Daniel Hill
The Souls of Black Folk by W.E.B. Du Bois
Men We Reaped by Jesmyn Ward
Beyond Colorblind: Redeeming Our Ethnic Journey by
Sarah Shin

Articles

"Letter from a Birmingham Jail" by Reverend Dr. Martin Luther King Jr.
"The Case for Reparations" by Ta-Nehisi Coates
"Walking While Black" by Garnette Cadogan

Feature Films

Just Mercy
13th

Social Media

"I'm Sorry. I'm Listening. I'm Learning." by Osheta Moore
"We don't want triumphalism. We want change!" by Danté Stewart

Children's Resources

God's Very Good Idea: A True Story of God's Delightfully Different Family by Trillia Newbell
Brown Girl Dreaming by Jacqueline Woodson
The Hate U Give by Angie Thomas

I Agree with Reading Broadly

Before I address the glaring problems with the idea of an antiracist curriculum for white evangelicals, allow me to be clear about one thing: I do not share the sentiment of those who believe that reading beyond the Bible is unwarranted, unwise, unfruitful, or unfaithful. In fact, I have had many encounters with Christians who find my penchant for broad reading quite troubling. This is especially true in some of the homeschool circles in which I run, but I believe that it is important for Christians to be well-informed. In fact, one of the reasons we are so committed to home education is the flexibility it gives us in terms of curricular choices. For that reason, we either encourage or require our kids to read Adolf Hitler's *Mein Kampf*; Charles Darwin's *The Origin of Species by the Means of Natural Selection: Or, the Survival of Favoured Races in the Struggle for Life*; *The Autobiography of Malcolm X*, which exposes them to the ideas of the Nation of Islam; *The Souls of Black Folk* (which made the *Christianity Today* list and was written by W.E.B. Du Bois, an avowed Communist who praised the Soviet Union, eventually renounced his American citizenship, and left the country); the essays of Ralph Ellison; the poetry of Langston Hughes (for whom one of my grandchildren is named); *The Chronicles of Narnia*; *The Lord of the Rings*; and several books on Greek mythology—all of which many in the fundamentalist wing of the homeschool movement also consider taboo.

This desire to reach beyond the familiar is due in large part to the influence of my ethnic heritage. I resonate with writers and thinkers like Ellison and Du Bois, whose work champions this cause. "So in Macon County, Alabama, I read Marx, Freud, T. S. Eliot, Pound, Gertrude Stein and Hemingway," opined Ellison with more than a hint of irony. "Books which seldom, if ever, mentioned Negroes were to release me from whatever 'segregated' idea I might have had of my human possibilities.... It requires real poverty of the imagination to think that this can come to a Negro only through the example of other Negroes, especially after the performance of the slaves in re-creating themselves, in good part, out of the images and myths of the Old Testament Jews."[4] Nor was Ellison writing in an historical vacuum. "I sit with Shakespeare and he winces not," wrote Du Bois in *The Souls of Black Folk*, a piece that undoubtedly

---

[4] Ralph Ellison, *The Collected Essays of Ralph Ellison* (New York, New York: Random House Publishing Group, Kindle Edition, 2003), 164.

influenced Ellison. "Across the color line I move arm in arm with Balzac and Dumas ... I summon Aristotle and Aurelius and what soul I will, and they come all graciously with no scorn nor condescension."[5] Of course, today's Critical Theorists would accuse both Ellison and Du Bois of "internalized racism" as they hypocritically insist on reading these black giants while they simultaneously scorn and eschew the works of Western literature to which they both pay homage.

On a personal note, I spend nearly as much time reading books with which I disagree as those which affirm my positions. Nor is my reading limited to theology. I read history, political science, sociology, and a host of other topics. For instance, on one speaking tour in the U.K. a few years back, I had a lot of time on the train, so I was able to read Ta-Nehisi Coates's *Between the World and Me* on one part of the journey and *Hillbilly Elegy* on another. And I was able to identify with and profit from both. So my objection to the *Christianity Today* list is not based on the grounds that I believe Christians should limit themselves to reading in an echo chamber. On the contrary, I have read, watched, or listened to most of the resources on their list and much more from the perspective they represent. Moreover, there is nothing on the list that I would consider *verboten*. Nevertheless, I see in this list yet another fault line.

But before we explore it in detail, allow me to offer two case studies.

Case Study #1: John Onwuchekwa

John Onwuchekwa, or John O., is a pastor whose name and platform have risen to the highest highs of Big Eva. He has published two books with 9Marks and has been platformed at some of the biggest and most significant events in evangelicalism in recent years. He also serves as a council member for the Gospel Coalition. John O. made waves in the summer of 2020 when he announced that his church, after receiving

---

[5] W.E.B. Du Bois, *The Souls of Black Folk* (Digireads.com Publishing, Kindle Edition, 2016), 36.

$175,000 from the SBC to refurbish its facilities, was leaving the South-ern Baptist Convention over what he saw as its failure to make sufficient strides in the area of racial justice. Many criticized him over the statement explaining the church's decision and the sermon his church chose to air on the day it was announced. There was significant pushback against those who saw in both evidence of a theological drift. Then in early September, John O. joined Jemar Tisby (author of a *New York Times* bestseller that makes most of the reading lists) on the *Pass the Mic* pod-cast.[6] Tisby is one of the leading evangelical voices in the Critical Social Justice movement: his book appears on numerous antiracist reading lists, and he is a contributor to the Gospel Coalition.[7]

Responding to John O.'s comments there could fill an entire chapter, but I will focus on just one concerning the Bible. He said, "You start to read books outside of the Bible and they help you understand what's being said in the Bible." So far, so good. However, anticipating the orthodox response to what he *means* by this, John O. adds, "That's sacrilegious to some folks," which of course is patently false. No one, outside of a few extremist cults, has ever had a problem with the idea that books outside of the Bible "help you understand the Bible." Obvi-ously, he is referring to something more. "It's like this," he continues, *"unless you had science, the Bible would not make sense."*

That is as significant a statement as he could possibly have made. In a single sentence, John O. impugned the sufficiency of Scripture, a fact that he makes clear as he explains further: "Archeology is a science. If we did not have archeology, much of your Bible would not make sense.... The problem is when we start to talk about social sciences and history, now all of a sudden, those are out of bounds."[8] And there it is!

---

[6] Jemar Tisby has become one of the leading voices in the Critical Social Justice movement. His book *The Color of Compromise* is a tour de force of CRT/I ideol-ogy, complete with a call for reparations.

[7] A search for Tisby's name on the TGC website results in forty hits, https://www.thegospelcoalition.org/?s=Jemar+Tisby.

[8] John Onwuchekwa on *Pass the Mic* podcast with Jemar Tisby, as cited by Woke Preacher Clips (@WokePreacherTV), ".@JawnO on @PasstheMic explaining his

John O.'s point—shared by many, if not most of the authors on *Christianity Today's* reading list, and evinced by the list's very existence, is that you really don't get what the Bible is trying to say about social justice until you read social science and history. I would add that by "read social science and history," those in the CSJ camp inevitably mean Tisby and not Sowell, DiAngelo and not McWhorter, Kendi and not Lindsey, Alexander and not Steele. In other words, when he and others say "social science and history," they mean books written from, informed by, or in service to the perspective of CT, CRT, and Intersectionality.

My point here is not that John O. and I are on different sides of the social justice discussion; we certainly are. It is that he is outside the bounds of Scripture, theology, and Church history. The social sciences may be useful tools, but they are far from *necessary*. "All Scripture is breathed out by God and profitable for teaching, for reproof, for correction, and for training in righteousness, that the man of God may be complete, equipped for every good work" (2 Timothy 3:16–17). In no area does God require me to walk in a level of righteousness for which the Scriptures do not equip me—including any and all aspects of justice.

"His divine power has granted to us all things that pertain to life and godliness, through the knowledge of him who called us to his own glory and excellence, by which he has granted to us his precious and very great promises, so that through them you may become partakers of the divine nature, having escaped from the corruption that is in the world because of sinful desire" (2 Peter 1:3–4). What could possibly be beyond the scope of "all things that pertain to life and godliness"? Moreover, what could a social science text give me that would be better or more sufficient than partaking in "the divine nature" or "having escaped the corruption that is in the world because of sinful desire"?

---

church's exit from SBC: One of the early moments that made him want to jump ship was when churches pulled funds from ERLC because Russell Moore said 'Donald Trump is not a nice guy... he's not decent with manners,'" Twitter, September 7, 2020, 11:15 a.m., https://twitter.com/WokePreacherTV/status/1302988874139013121.

Christians have understood this from the beginning. The orthodox understanding of the nature and sufficiency of Scripture, as outlined in historic confessions, makes it clear that what John O. proposes is beyond the pale. According to chapter one, paragraph one of both the Westminster Confession (Presbyterian) and the Second London Baptist Confession:

> The Authority of the Holy Scripture for which it ought to be believed dependeth not upon the testimony of any man, or Church; but wholly upon God (who is truth it self) the Author thereof; therefore it is to be received, because it is the Word of God. (WCF, 1.1., 2LBC 1.1)[9]

In other words, the Bible neither needs nor finds authority outside of itself. The Belgic Confession puts an even finer point on the matter:

> We believe that those Holy Scriptures fully contain the will of God, and that whatsoever man ought to believe, unto salvation, is sufficiently taught therein. For, since the whole manner of worship, which God requires of us, is written in them at large, it is unlawful for any one, though an apostle, to teach otherwise than we are now taught in the Holy Scriptures: nay, though it were an angel from heaven, as the apostle Paul saith. For, since it is forbidden, to add unto or take away anything from the word of God, it doth thereby evidently appear, that the doctrine thereof is most perfect and complete in all respects. *Neither do we consider of equal value any writing of men, however holy these men may have been, with those divine Scriptures, nor ought we to consider custom, or the great multitude, or antiquity, or succession of times and persons, or councils, decrees or statutes, as of equal value*

---

[9] David Lang, ed., "The 1677/1689 London Baptist Confession of Faith," *Creeds, Confessions and Catechisms* (Altamonte Springs, Florida: OakTree Software, Inc., 2006), paragraph 4718.

*with the truth of God, for the truth is above all; for all men
are of themselves liars, and more vain than vanity itself.*
Therefore, we reject with all our hearts, whatsoever doth not
agree with this infallible rule, which the apostles have taught
us, saying, Try the spirits whether they are of God. Likewise,
if there come any unto you, and bring not this doctrine,
receive him not into your house (italics mine).[10]

The assertion that "unless you had science, the Bible would not make
sense" flies in the face of the teaching of the Bible as well as the historic
understanding of that teaching in reference to the sufficiency of the Bible.
In this matter, I hope John O.'s statements were the result of a momentary
lapse. If not, his understanding of the Bible is heretical, and his eisegetical
reading of Critical Social Justice into the text is rooted in his heretical
view of Scripture. If that is the case, he is currently on a trajectory that
will leave him and those who follow him shipwrecked.

And this is why these fault lines are so critical. Eventually, they shift,
and when they do, the results are catastrophic.

Case Study #2: David Platt

At the 2018 Together for the Gospel Conference, David Platt, then
head of the Southern Baptist Convention's International Mission Board,
delivered a message from Amos 5, then repented in tears for his white
privilege, silence, and inaction. Those inclined toward CSJ found it
inspiring. But to others, Platt's message represented a fault line. It was
an exercise in eisegesis.[11] In other words, instead of being faithful to the

---

[10] Lang, "The Belgic Confession of Faith," *Creeds, Confessions and Catechisms*,
paragraph 457.

[11] Stanley Grenz, David Guretzki, and Cherith Fee Nordling, *Pocket Dictionary
of Theological Terms* (Downers Grove, Illinois: InterVarsity Press, 1999), 49.
Eisegesis: Literally, "drawing meaning out of" and "reading meaning into,"
respectively. Exegesis is the process of seeking to understand what a text means or
communicates on its own. *Eisegesis* is generally a derogatory term used to

text of Amos 5, he read foreign ideas into the text to make the Bible serve his agenda. "[T]the most aggravating aspect of Platt's message," wrote one blogger, "was his flagrant misuse of Amos 5."[12]

One pastor summed it up well:

> MLK: "Men should NOT be judged by the color of their skin."
>
> T4G: "Pastors should be judged by the color of their congregations."[13]

A *Christianity Today* writer tried to reduce the criticism to some kind of white fragility,[14] but that was both inaccurate and disingenuous. In fact, many of those who agreed with Platt's sentiment acknowledged that his sermon fell short of exegetical standards. At least two high-level evangelical leaders (one closely associated with the conference) said as much to me personally. (Neither, of course, would go on record.)

Moreover, the message fell short of Platt's own standard: He has a Ph.D. in preaching and served as a professor of preaching and apologetics at New Orleans Baptist Theological Seminary. So if anybody knows better than to misuse Scripture like that, it is David Platt. The obvious question then is why someone of his caliber could preach a sermon that

---

designate the practice of imposing a preconceived or foreign meaning onto a text, even if that meaning could not have been originally intended at the time of its writing.

[12] "David Platt on Racism and Why Your Church Is So White," Bible Thumping Wingnut Network, April 16, 2018, https://biblethumpingwingnut. com/2018/04/16/david-platt.

[13] Jim Osman (@jimcosman2), "MLK: 'Men should NOT be judged by the color of their skin.' T4G: 'Pastors should be judged by the color of their congregations.' #T4G18 #MLK50Conference," Twitter, April 13, 2018, 11:04 p.m., https://twitter.com/jimcosman2/status/984990869462761472.

[14] John C. Richards Jr. and Daniel Yang, "Preaching on Racism from the 'White' Pulpit: Reflections on David Platt's Talk at T4G," *Christianity Today*, April 12, 2018, https://www.christianitytoday.com/edstetzer/2018/april/preaching-on-racism-platt.html. This article never used the term "white fragility," but it definitely fit DiAngelo's description of it.

led one preaching professor to tell me privately, "If he had done that in my class, I would have given him a D"?

The answer is simple: David Platt loves Jesus, loves people, and is passionate about reconciliation. I know this because I know and love David Platt. I also know he started reading and being influenced by the woke canon. Consequently, he began to reach beyond the Bible to find God's truth regarding race.

How did he get to that point? According to an article on the Gospel Coalition's website,[15] 9Marks Founder Mark Dever suggested Platt read *Divided by Faith: Evangelical Religion and the Problem of Race in America* by Michael Emerson and Christian Smith—a book Dever has publicly praised, saying, "This won't be the most exciting book you read this year, but it may have the most exciting results in your life."[16]

Platt's message was dripping with the book's influence, especially his emphasis on the concept of America's being "racialized," which is the book's main theme. Ironically, the book does not make *Christianity Today's* list. However, it is arguably the most frequently referenced and recommended race resource among evangelicalism's "Big Three," also known as the Gospel Coalition, 9Marks, and Together for the Gospel.

My point here is not whether *Divided by Faith* has merit. I think it does. My point is this: If someone like David Platt can go off the rails and start reading things into Scripture during a sermon delivered at one of the largest and most influential conferences in evangelicalism due to the influence of a sociology text, what do we think is going to happen when we create a new canon in the form of an "antiracist curriculum" for white evangelicals? Especially when that canon consists of literature from the realm of history, political science, and sociology that is not based in biblical exegesis.

---

[15] David Daniels, "Why David Platt and Ligon Duncan Repented for Racial Blindness," Gospel Coalition, August 20, 2018, https://www.thegospelcoalition. org/article/david-platt-ligon-duncan-racial-blindness.

[16] Mark Dever, "Book Review: Divided by Faith," ERLC, November 29, 2017, https://erlc.com/resource-library/book-reviews/book-review-divided-by-faith.

The Fault beneath the List

Back to my point about *Christianity Today*'s list being one of evangelicalism's dangerous fault lines: Some of you may be wondering why I commend broad reading on one hand, then offer a warning about this new "curriculum" on the grounds that it will lead people astray. Isn't that a contradiction? I don't believe so.

First, I am not taking issue with the idea of a list. I actually think it is a good idea to have a list of recommended resources for people to read on topics like this. Many such lists have helped me. The sheer volume of resources on topics like this makes it impossible for anyone to read or even know about *everything* available. Lists can help broaden and narrow the field. For instance, seeing the same resource on multiple lists is a good sign that it is significant. Also, seeing new resources that you haven't seen before can also be helpful.

Second, I am not taking issues with the particular books on the list. Others have torn *Christianity Today's* list apart based on the authors' politics, faith, or lack thereof; I find that tactic counterproductive. Remember, I reject a narrow approach to literature and culture and am in favor of reading broadly. Some of the resources that I have found helpful in bolstering my own understanding of issues come from writers with whom I disagree; for example, Douglas Murray is a practicing homosexual, but his book *The Madness of Crowds* is one of the best things I have ever read on the current cultural crisis. James Lindsay and John McWhorter are both atheists, but both have been invaluable assets in my quest to become better equipped to address issues like CRT and CSJ (remember, I got the term "Critical Social Justice" from Lindsay). So far be it from me to suggest that we should tear apart the *CT* reading list based on the authors' backgrounds alone, or even the content they proffer.

I am taking issue with what this list represents: what it *means*. I am taking issue with the presuppositions behind it. Specifically, 1) its underlying assumption that the Bible is not sufficient to address issues of race and/or justice and 2) its stated assumptions about the very nature of both race and justice. "[W]e are only talking in a circle when we say that we advocate justice, unless we specify just what conception of justice we have in mind,"[17] writes Thomas Sowell in *The Quest for Cosmic Justice*. "This is especially so today, when so many advocate what they call 'social justice'—often with great passion, but with no definition. All justice is inherently social. Can someone on a desert island be either just or unjust?"

The Sufficiency of Scripture in Matters of Race and Justice

The general theme of the current CSJ movement within evangelicalism is a covert attack on the sufficiency of Scripture. People are not coming right out and saying that the Bible is not enough. Instead, high-profile pastors get up and speak about the ways in which modern sociology texts have done for them what the revelation of Scripture has been unable to do. My dear friend Paul Washer put it well when he noted, "Five years ago, I was amazed as I saw the young, restless, and Reformed crowd at conferences talking about their latest encounters with Spurgeon, Calvin, Kuyper, and Machen ... now they're all talking about Christian Smith, Jemar Tisby, and Robin DiAngelo."

Granted, most of the men mentioned above believe firmly in the sufficiency of Scripture and have done so for decades. I am not talking about the liberal, openly social gospel/liberation theology wing of the CSJ movement. (At least not in this chapter.) In fact, many of the men to whom I am referring here have been on the front line of the battle against liberalism, mysticism, and pragmatism for many years. That is why the allusion to an unofficial new canon is so disturbing.

"I have spent much of my life in a haze of relative cluelessness about and culpable indifference to many of the concerns that are addressed in this book,"[18] writes Ligon Duncan, chancellor of the Reformed Theological

---

[17] Thomas Sowell, *The Quest for Cosmic Justice* (New York, New York: Free Press, Kindle Edition, 2001), 3.

[18] Eric Mason, *Woke Church* (Chicago, Illinois: Moody Publishers, Kindle Edition, 2018), 15.

Seminary, in his forward to Eric Mason's book *Woke Church*. Unfortunately, "the concerns that are addressed in this book" are not exegetical. Far from being rooted in groundbreaking exposition of the biblical text, Mason's book is part of this new canon. Nor is Duncan's an isolated voice. The internet has been teeming with similar confessions in recent years. How can this be possible in light of what we know about the Bible?

Please hear me well. I am not saying that men should not come to understand more of God's revelation as they grow. On the contrary, we must always be reforming. *Semper reformanda* was and is the cry of the Reformation. However, the CRT crowd in evangelicalism are not men who have been challenged on their *interpretation of Scripture*—they are proclaiming that *sources outside of Scripture* have brought them to a new, better, and more complete understanding of God's truth on race.

At least three realities should give us pause when men who have been studying and teaching the Bible for many decades proclaim that they have come to some life-altering revelation *that has not been derived from Scripture.*

First, the Bible is the Word of God. Paul says, "All Scripture is breathed out by God." In other words, the Bible is not merely the words and speculations of men. Nor is it dependent upon the words or ideas of men for its authority. Unlike the texts in the new antiracist canon, the Bible carries the authority of God Himself.

Second, the Bible is "profitable for teaching, for reproof, for correction, for training in righteousness" (2 Timothy 3:17). In other words, since race is undoubtably a "righteousness" issue, the Bible is profitable for teaching those who are ignorant about race, rebuking those who are in sin concerning race, correcting those who are in error about race, and training everyone who is pursuing righteousness in regard to race. To put a finer point on it, there is not a book in the world that is better suited to address men on the issue of race than the Bible. That is not to say that there is no help to be found in other books. It is, however, to say that they are not essential.

Third, the Bible is sufficient. The Bible is the only canon through and by which "the man of God may be complete, equipped for every good work" (2 Timothy 3:17). This includes the work of race relations of any and every kind. It is the Bible—not sociology, psychology, or political science—that offers sufficient answers not only on race, but on every ethical issue man has faced, or will ever face.

This, of course, is at odds with secular theories like Critical Theory, Intersectionality, Critical Race Theory, and Critical Social Justice. This is why the idea of a new canon that is "desired to make one wise" (Genesis 3:6) for so-called "racial justice" is a problem for Bible-believing Christians.

The Concept of Antiracism Is Inherently Flawed

What must we do to be antiracist? *Christianity Today*'s answer is nothing less than a full-throated recitation of the ideology of Critical Race Theory. "This question, of course, can mean many things. It can mean, 'Where do I start to understand the history of police brutality in America?' or 'Where do I start to deal with the fact that I have lived a segregated life?' or 'Where do I start to understand systemic racism?'" the author writes. In two short sentences, the piece makes it clear that the proposed curriculum is designed to promote Critical Social Justice. Let's look at the three assumptions in turn.

First, "Where do I start to understand the history of police brutality in America?" As we've already discussed, this is a red herring. The idea that America has a race-based police brutality problem is simply not true. We have already seen that the overall statistics on police shootings, the best-known cases, and an honest look at crime rates convincingly rebut the idea that police are "hunting and killing black men in the streets." Also, notice the move away from the human heart right into the public/political sphere. This, by the way, is why CSJ proponents tend to down-play the sufficiency of Scripture: to them, racism is not a heart issue or personal sin; it is a "systemic" problem. Therefore, reform is the solution, not repentance.

"Where do I start to deal with the fact that I have lived a segregated life?" This question is ironic for Americans like me who have had the opportunity to live in other parts of the world. When my family and I arrived in Zambia, we were struck by how monolithic the culture is. As Americans, we are used to seeing people from every tribe, tongue, and nation wherever we go. Moreover, we are used to the fact that every one of those people has the right and privilege of calling themselves Americans. But most of the world is monolithic. Zambians are not only people who were born in Zambia, they are *black people* who were born in Zambia. We have a dear friend whose parents immigrated to Zambia from India. Although he was born in Zambia, he is not considered Zambian simply because he is not black and his parents immigrated from abroad. Say what you will about race problems in the United States, I have *never* had anyone tell me I cannot be considered American because of the color of my skin!

However, there is a deeper issue here: that of what D.A. Carson calls "cherished pluralism,"[19] which goes beyond the *fact* of pluralism to argue for the *superiority* of pluralism. "[W]hen the reality, empirical pluralism, has become 'a value in itself, even a priority': it is cherished." For example, consider the following scenario: Two pastors meet at a conference. Eventually, they get around to the questions every pastor asks fellow pastors these days, "How many ya running?"

That used to be where the conversation stalled out—the size of the congregation. However, now there is a second, more important question: "How diverse is your church?" We don't just want to know how many people are there; we want to know what color they are. Whereas in years gone by that would have included all ethnicities, today we just want to know the black-white makeup (because in this climate, other minorities simply don't matter). In the past, the pastor with the biggest church was the winner;

---

[19] D.A. Carson, *The Gagging of God* (Grand Rapids, Michigan: Zondervan Academic, Kindle Edition, 1996), 18.

today, it is the one with the best black-white split. In this climate, the pastor with the inferior black-white split not only pastors the inferior church, but he is actually considered the inferior pastor—or, more precisely, the inferior person. (Hence, this question gets to the heart of another flaw in our thinking regarding race.) But *Christianity Today* saves the worst question for last.

"Where do I start to understand systemic racism?" This is the crux of the matter. This is why we need a curriculum in the first place. The idea, you see, is that the Bible may help you with a number of things, but it simply cannot help you even begin to understand systemic racism. That is because "systemic racism" is a moving target.

Christianity Today makes the point succinctly by stating, "In an effort to incline hearts toward understanding, minds toward wisdom, and hands toward doing justice, CT Creative Studio has compiled a resource list specifically oriented toward coming alongside our white brothers and sisters in the work of becoming and living as anti-racists."

As we saw earlier, the term "antiracist" is loaded. It has a very specific meaning—part of which includes the idea of works-based righteousness. White people are not called to look to God for forgiveness. They are not told that Christ's blood is sufficient. No, they are told that they must do the unending work of antiracism. And this work must be done regardless of their own actions since the issue at hand is a matter of communal, generational guilt based on ethnicity.[20]

This flies in the face of the clear teaching of Scripture. The Bible makes it clear that God forgives sin. Consider the following passages:

And no longer shall each one teach his neighbor and each his brother, saying, "Know the LORD," for they shall all know me, from the least of them to the greatest, declares the

---

[20] Latasha Morrison, *Be the Bridge* (New York, New York: Crown Publishing Group, Kindle Edition, 2019), 79. Morrison's work, one of the mainstays of every evangelical antiracist canon, is replete with references to generational guilt. It is promoted throughout evangelical circles as a "go-to" resource for racial reconciliation in the Church.

LORD. "For I will forgive their iniquity, and I will remember their sin no more." (Jeremiah 31:34; cf. Hebrews 8:12; 10:17)

And sin, once forgiven, is removed far from us, "As far as the east is from the west, so far does he remove our transgressions from us." (Psalm 103:12)

Who is a God like you, pardoning iniquity and passing over transgression for the remnant of his inheritance? He does not retain his anger forever, because he delights in steadfast love. (Micah 7:18)

"I, I am he who blots out your transgressions for my own sake, and I will not remember your sins." (Isaiah 43:25)

The idea that we need a new canon to be able to decipher what the Bible says, or more specifically, what it means regarding race, is quite troubling. This attack on the sufficiency of Scripture should serve as a call to arms.

CHAPTER SEVEN

The Ground Is Moving

F ault lines, where most earthquakes occur, are cracks in the earth's surface where tectonic plates meet and slide past each other. Usually, they are moving too slowly for us to notice, but when stress builds up, they'll suddenly slip, causing an earthquake.

People don't live on fault lines because they like the destruction earthquakes bring. They do it because the beauty above is real and tangible; the danger beneath lies out of sight and out of mind...until the ground starts shaking. Few places on earth can match the picturesque scenery, the ideal weather, or the rich, fertile soil of the San Francisco Bay Area; that's why millions call it home. But when earthquakes hit, people wonder why anyone would choose to live in a place where such devastation is likely.

The same can be said of the current fault lines in evangelicalism. Catch a glimpse of a Christian community unstained by racism, classism, sexism, or injustice, and you can see why many are willing to risk everything for the sake of a movement that offers such hope. But what if the movement that purports to have the answers to all these problems is built on a fault line destined to distort the Gospel, cause even deeper divisions, and wreak havoc?

Those who have seen the devastation of an earthquake know the solution for those living on fault lines is to move to safer ground, or at least build structures that can withstand the coming catastrophe. Evangelicalism does have a fault line—and my goal is to show my brothers and sisters being tossed to and fro by the winds of sociological doctrine how to get to safety.

We are right to pursue justice, peace, and unity (Micah 6:8; Romans 12:18; John 17:20–21). That is not the fault line. The fault lies in believing that such a vision can be attained by affiliating with, using the terminology of, or doing anything other than opposing in the most forceful terms the ideology that lies at the root of the social justice movement.[1]

A Lack of Clarity and Charity

I am a debater; I always have been. But in the current climate, debate is becoming a lost art—partly because of a general decline in the study of logic and rhetoric, but mostly because of the general feminization of culture and its consequent disdain for open verbal combat.

Gone are the days of Luther and Erasmus slugging it out over the question of original sin. Today both men would be accused of being petty (for daring to split hairs over such theological minutia), mean-spirited (for daring to speak so forcefully in favor of their own position and against the other's), and downright un-Christlike (for throwing around the word "heresy"). I have often said, "The Eleventh Commandment is, 'Thou shalt be nice' … and we don't believe the other ten."

---

[1] I will differentiate between the concept of biblical justice and that of social justice in later chapters. For now, allow me to say that my argument is simply that Christians are obligated to "do justice"; social justice is a specific set of ideas that stands in stark opposition to the biblical concept of justice.

One of the negative results of this is no longer being able to deal with ideas without attacking the people who hold them. Disagreements quickly deteriorate into arguments and worse. Consequently, taking a position on an issue carries the automatic assumption that one is utterly opposed not only to the opposing view, but to all who hold it. Therefore, we don't debate ideas at all, but go straight for personal attacks and character assassination. And this debate is no different.

To the anti–Critical Social Justice camp, those on the side of CSJ are all Cultural Marxists. Conversely, to the social justice camp, those who oppose their cause are all racists (even fellow black people like me who, according to their definition of racism, can't be racists ... but I digress). The result is a standstill—a demilitarized zone that exists, not because hostilities have ceased, but because we all tacitly believe there is no solution.

Meanwhile, well-meaning Christian laypeople find themselves at a loss. Which side do they choose? There are "big names" on both sides, so who's right?

The Dallas Statement

In June 2018, I had the sobering privilege of spending a day with fifteen men who would eventually become the driving force behind the Dallas Statement on Social Justice and the Gospel. I was hesitant to attend, but since one of my heroes, John MacArthur, called the meeting, I thought I should be there. What came out of that meeting would, in my estimation, prove to be a pivotal piece of the puzzle in the contemporary discussion of race, ethnicity, and justice inside and outside the Church.

My initial hesitation had nothing to do with a lack of desire to engage the issue, but it was meant to address issues arising from the CSJ movement in the United States, and I was living in Zambia. Also, I didn't want my participation to hinder the work.

I had already raised the ire of many on the CSJ front through articles and speaking engagements. Moreover, I knew that my signature, along with that of every other black signatory, would be viewed as tokenism— cover for the "racists" in the Church who allegedly didn't want to discuss social justice—despite the fact that nearly half the attendees stated openly that I had introduced them to the dangers of the social justice movement either directly or indirectly.[2] Ironically, I am still frequently either eliminated from the discussion or cited as a token or pawn by those who advocate CSJ within the Church. This makes it much easier to dismiss the Dallas Statement as the product of a group of white supremacists who are "tone deaf" on racial justice.

In the end, I chose to help shape and sign the statement because I believed the potential benefits far outweighed the inevitable costs. My goal then, as now, was to bring both clarity and unity. I knew that we would produce an imperfect document. I also knew some would be waiting anxiously, not to receive it, but to parse it. However, I also knew others saw the coming catastrophe and hoped someone would speak up. We all knew unity could never be achieved without clarity.

Documents like the Dallas Statement are never meant to be a final word. The Bible is the final word. Nor did we believe our statement would be beyond reproach. Tom Ascol, the principle architect of the first draft of the Dallas Statement, captured this sentiment perfectly when he wrote:

> The statement makes no claim of any ecclesiastical authority. It is issued for the purpose of calling attention to and clarifying concerns. We have spoken on these issues with no disrespect or loss of love for our brothers and sisters who disagree with what we have written. Rather, *our hope is that this*

---

[2] Tom Ascol, Tom Buck, Josh Buice, James White, and other drafters of the Dallas Statement have been very open about this fact both in public and in private.

*statement might actually provoke the kind of brotherly dia-
logue* that can promote unity in the gospel of our Lord Jesus
whom we all love and trust.

But that is not what happened. In fact, there has been very little
formal pushback or dialogue. Most of our friends at 9Marks, the Ethics
and Religious Liberty Commission, the Gospel Coalition, Together for
the Gospel, the Southern Baptist Convention, and the Presbyterian
Church of America—all of whom had historically embraced us as ministry partners and been willing to critique us as brothers—didn't write
a single word one way or the other.

Tim Keller did offer a comment. When asked about the Dallas Statement, his response said more about his philosophical presuppositions
than it did about the document. "[T]he statement can't be judged based
upon whether or not the words are right," he said, "but by the consequences those words might eventually bring about."

By contrast, when John MacArthur, the lighting rod with whom
most people associate the Dallas Statement, decided to hold services at
his church in Southern California last summer in defiance of Governor
Gavin Newsom's orders to keep churches from meeting during the coronavirus pandemic, 9Marks fired off a missive addressing MacArthur's
decision from a biblical, theological, and historical perspective. But the
Dallas Statement didn't warrant a drop of ink. Did these groups fail to
address the statement because it was correct? If so, why didn't they join
us in signing it? Was it because, as more than one of the leaders of the
aforementioned ministries stated, "The group lacked any names with
gravitas,"[3] therefore implying the statement was insignificant? If

---

[3] More than one key leader in those organizations said the major problem with
the Dallas Statement was not its content, but the fact that we failed to get up-front
participation from people with significant reputations. This, of course, is tragic.
For men to say outright that they are not willing to affix their signature to a document with which they agree simply because they (or those more powerful than
they) were not asked to help shape it is disingenuous at best.

MacArthur, who called the meeting, lacks "gravitas," then there's no need to warn people to be cautious about following his lead.

No, there was a much bigger issue at play—a fault line everybody knew was there and that nobody wanted to acknowledge.

Faults and Fractures within the Evangelical Movement

None of these groups or leaders would openly identify with CRT/I or CSJ. In fact, they all swear up and down that they *do not* hold to such ideas. However, they regularly use CRT/I categories in defining racial justice/injustice. They embrace the key CRT idea that racism is "normal." They continually speak of and refer to cases like George Floyd in terms of racial injustice. They define the disagreement in terms of their having a different view of the "importance" of race, but they continue to express an ideology that decides this importance based on presuppositions regarding disparities.

Before taking the Dallas Statement public, we shared it with several people with a view toward gaining both support and honest, helpful critique. Members of several of these organizations pleaded with us not to publish it—not because they disagreed, but because they thought it would be "unhelpful."

Silencing Dissent

Dozens of pastors, professors, and concerned Christians have told me they find themselves at a loss to explain the upheaval they are experiencing. One private message I received from a leader in a well-known international ministry captured this tension very well:

> *Hello Pastor Baucham, I am writing to you as a heartbroken gospel sharer.... I would like to get your help regarding one of the largest missions organizations on earth that is*

becoming consumed with the racial identity and reconcilia-
tion "conversation." Indoctrination is a more accurate term.
Literally thousands of Jesus-loving staff are becoming dis-
tressed and heartbroken over this sudden departure from the
Gospel in this organization....

He went on to say that the "ministry is being taken over presently by a very progressive group who keeps pushing radical speakers on us and, again, the staff are grieving and wondering what happened so suddenly?"

Three issues he presents resonate with others I have received. First, there is the sense of helplessness and discouragement. Godly men and women find themselves in a position that feels completely beyond their control or even understanding, and they are looking for help.

Second, there is a sense that these changes have happened suddenly. Of course, those of us who have been watching know that these changes were not sudden. The fault lines that are shifting today have been there for a long time.

Finally, there is a sense of urgency over preserving the Gospel. It is ironic that both sides of this fault line claim to be 1) passionately pursuing the Gospel and 2) afraid that the other side represents compromise that will undermine it. This is the foundation of both my greatest fear and my greatest hope in this debate. While I am aware that there are extremes at play that threaten to obscure the Gospel, I am convinced that much of what we are seeing today is disagreement between well-meaning brothers and sisters who are arguing around the margins but holding fast to the center—to the Gospel. However, I must admit that hope is fading fast.

The crux of this brother's message was that he wanted to suggest me "as an alternative speaker to the indoctrination that is occurring." Then, in what has to be the most disturbing part of his note, he admits, "I do not think they will say yes, but I do feel that they might feel deep conviction from the Holy Spirit if they say no because they will be reminded that they are 'preaching' a one-sided message." This is a very important piece of the puzzle. This man wanted to respond to the onslaught of racial/social justice by inviting a black man to speak to the organization. He hoped my minority status would blunt criticism that is virtually certain to come when one dares to disagree with the "conversation." In fact, he asked that I never mention his name, "as we feel it is not presently safe to disagree with certain ministry leaders ... due to the forcefulness of their current direction."

Here, dear reader, is the heart of the matter. The environment within evangelicalism is so hostile that it has a chilling effect. In this environment, dissent is not only unwelcome, but condemned. Consequently, many godly, thoughtful, well-meaning, justice-loving brethren are being silenced. As a result, the fault lines continue to shift, and the catastrophe gets ever closer.

I have received dozens of similar messages from people who are at a loss to explain the sudden shift beneath their feet. From seminary professors who have been warned or reprimanded for addressing racial/ethnic issues (from the "wrong" perspective), to pastors and church staff who have had decades of faithful ministry called into question, to faculty members at Christian universities who prepare lectures with one eye on the truth they intend to convey and the other on potentially career-ending statements they must avoid, the fault lines are everywhere.

Surviving the Coming Catastrophe

I wish I could say that this book is meant to help us avoid the impending catastrophe. However, it is not. This catastrophe is unavoidable. These fault lines are so deeply entrenched, and the rules of engagement so perilously complex, that the question is not if but when the catastrophe will strike. In fact, the ground is already shaking. Relationships are being ruined, reputations are being tarnished, careers are being destroyed, and entire denominations are in danger of being derailed.

If we are to survive this catastrophe, we must understand it. We must understand what the fault lines are. We must also know where they lie.

The clearest evidence of the coming collapse we have seen in recent years came at the Southern Baptist Convention's 2019 annual meeting. I write this not because I anticipate a particularly Southern Baptist audience for this book, but because the size, scope, and influence of the SBC makes these events both relevant and ominous. If it can happen in the SBC, it can happen anywhere.

Every year, representatives of the forty-seven thousand churches, called messengers, show up to elect officers, hear reports, and conduct the business of the SBC. Chief among their responsibilities is voting on resolutions. It is worth noting that—since the SBC is technically not a denomination but a voluntary association of confessing, free churches—the resolutions are not binding. Nevertheless, they represent the collective voice of the Convention and have great influence among the churches.

In 2019, there was very little pre-Convention buzz about Resolution #9 on Critical Race Theory and Intersectionality (see Appendix B). Many wondered how such a resolution made its way to the Convention. Others thought it would never make it out of the committee. But Resolution 9 was as strategic as any the SBC has seen in decades. To the casual observer, it may seem like a lot of "inside baseball," so allow me to explain why this was a critical cultural moment, and why it was inevitable that Resolution 9 would eventually pass.

First, Resolution 9 was a response to the Dallas Statement. Southern Baptist churches, like all others nationwide, were reeling from divisions over social justice, with the evangelical movement's upper echelons dividing into clearly delineated sides. The most prominent events in the country featured messages and/or panel discussions either defending or opposing the growing social justice movement.

Second, leaders of many SBC entities pleaded with and warned their personnel not to sign the Dallas Statement. One former Southern Seminary professor went public about the warnings he says he and other faculty and staff received concerning it. He is one of only three professors from SBC seminaries who signed the statement—and for his pains, this one believes it led to a series of events that culminated in his firing.[4]

Finally, the SBC had to pass Resolution 9 because its first draft forced the hand of Convention leaders. Once it was submitted, there were basically three options: the resolution could have been sent to the floor as it was, it could have been allowed to die in committee, or it could be amended. The Committee on Resolutions chose the latter (see Appendix C), and there is clear evidence why.

Political Maneuvering

There are a few other procedural issues worth mentioning. First, Resolution 9 almost passed without any debate or discussion from the floor—but not because there was none to be had; there was. (Several attendees, including two of the original drafters and signers of the Dallas Statement, were still standing by microphones waiting for their turn to speak when the resolution was sent to the floor for the vote.)

No, the debate was muted because SBC President J.D. Greear, an outspoken proponent of all things social justice, waited until there were only a few minutes left in the session, then tried to package resolutions 9–13 to be voted on as a block! Several messengers erupted at the mere thought. Eventually, a motion was made and seconded, but the vote did not pass. Resolution 9 had to stand on its own merits.

A second and perhaps more deceptive issue is the fact that the Committee on Resolutions had its fingerprints scrubbed from the final document. Because they gutted and rewrote Resolution 9, it still bears the name of the original author, even though it ended up being a

---

[4] One former Southern Seminary professor confirmed the warnings he and other faculty and staff received concerning it. Conversations That Matter, "Downgrade at Southern Seminary: Critical Theory & Al Mohler (Part III)," YouTube, May 25, 2020, https://m.youtube.com/watch?v=Z4Wc3nGPGyY.

grotesque misrepresentation of what he submitted originally. Hence, anyone looking at the historical record, unless they dig beneath the surface, will have no idea who actually wrote Resolution 9, or the implications thereof.[5]

The original Resolution 9 on Critical Race Theory and Intersectionality was submitted by Stephen Feinstein, pastor of Sovereign Way Christian Church in Hesperia, California, who also serves as a chaplain in the U.S. Army Reserves. What happened to Feinstein's resolution was nothing short of scandalous, but the scandal went largely unnoticed. I fully expect to see book-level treatments, Masters theses, and doctoral dissertations analyzing the origins, background, political maneuverings, and theological implications of the Resolution 9 controversy. Space does not allow for such a treatment here, but even a cursory look at the matter reveals issues that should concern not only Southern Baptists, but any Christian concerned about the current trajectory of evangelicalism.

Comparing a few key passages from the two resolutions is revealing. I want the reader to see that this was a deliberate act of duplicity. If the original text of Resolution 9 had been sent to the floor, there would be no cover for the SJW. Seminary presidents would have to explain, among other things, why material Resolution 9 condemned was being taught in their classrooms. And others would have asked, "If this is the way the Convention feels, why hasn't a single high-level SBC leader signed the Dallas Statement?"

There is a clear difference in the tone of the motivation behind the two versions of Resolution 9:

---

[5] Tom Ascol, "Resolution 9 and the Southern Baptist Convention 2019," from the Founders Ministry blog, June 15, 2019, https://founders.org/2019/06/15/resolution-9-and-the-southern-baptist-convention-2019/. Tom is a long-time Southern Baptist and regular attendee at the convention. He offers very helpful insights into the inner workings of the convention that shed light on the particular rules, traditions, and maneuvers that led to the final passage of Resolution 9 and its implications.

Original Resolution	Final Resolution
WHEREAS, the rhetoric of critical race theory and intersectionality found in some Southern Baptist institutions and leaders is causing unnecessary and unbiblical division among the body of Christ and is tarnishing the reputation of the Southern Baptist Convention as a whole, inviting charges of theological liberalism, egalitarianism, and Marxism....	WHEREAS, Concerns have been raised by some evangelicals over the use of frameworks such as critical race theory and intersectionality....

Similarly,

Original Resolution	Final Resolution
WHEREAS, both critical race theory and intersectionality as ideologies have infiltrated some Southern Baptist churches and institutions— institutions funded by the Cooperative Program....	WHEREAS, Evangelical scholars who affirm the authority and sufficiency of Scripture have employed selective insights from critical race theory and intersectionality to understand multi-faceted social dynamics....

It is worth noting that two of the individuals to whom Feinstein alluded in the original draft were members of the committee that gutted and transformed his resolution. Committee Chairman Curtis Woods and member Walter Strickland have been promoting CRT and Intersectionality through their positions as professors at Southern and

Southeastern Seminaries, respectively, as well as through other events both within and outside the SBC.[6 7 8]

Remember, the messengers on the floor of the Convention only vote on the final resolution. They never saw the "concerns [that] have been raised by some evangelicals ..." nor would they know that those concerns were related directly to the actions of the man arguing for the completely gutted and revised version of the resolution.

Having identified the players, it is clear that the perpetrators of this "infiltration" are identifying themselves as "evangelical scholars who affirm the authority and sufficiency of Scripture." Ironically, as we will see, Resolution 9 itself denies the sufficiency of the Scripture it claims to uphold.

Another area of departure between the resolutions is evident in their assessment of the nature of CRT:

Original Resolution	Final Resolution
WHEREAS, critical race theory and intersectionality are founded upon unbiblical presuppositions descended from Marxist theories and categories, and therefore are inherently opposed to the Scriptures as the true center of Christian union....	WHEREAS, Critical race theory is a set of analytical tools that explain how race has and continues to function in society, and intersectionality is the study of how different personal characteristics overlap and inform one's experience....

[6] "A Southern Baptist Seminary Professor Promotes Liberation Theology," Enemies Within the Church, August 9, 2019, https://enemieswithinthechurch.com/2019/08/09/a-southern-baptist-seminary-professor-promotes-liberation-theology/.

[7] Strickland's pro-liberation theology curriculum can be found at https://drive.google.com/file/d/1m-2DQuN5bTDWwU3IeDGg-1l5gmW5yVnU/view.

[8] Strickland's interview with the Jude 3 Project, in which he praises James Cone and other heretical liberation theology exponents, can be seen at Jude 3 Project, "The Balanced Scholar: The Life and Work of J. Deotis Roberts | Walter Strickland," YouTube, October 14, 2016, https://www.youtube.com/watch?v=vxqW-HQ8Fuc.

This is the crux of the matter: The million-dollar question is whether CRT is a worldview or merely an analytical tool. In other words, are there worldview assumptions that must be accepted in order to apply the tool? If there are, then the authors of the final resolution are either naive or downright subversive.

According to the founders of CRT, the "movement is a collection of activists and scholars engaged in studying and transforming the relationship among race, racism, and power." Based on those assumptions, CRT "questions the very foundations of the liberal order, including equality theory, legal reasoning, Enlightenment rationalism, and neutral principles of constitutional law."[9] Moreover, the movement itself asserts that, "Unlike some academic disciplines, critical race theory contains an activist dimension. It tries not only to understand our social situation but to change it, setting out not only to ascertain how society organizes itself along racial lines and hierarchies but to transform it for the better."[10]

How, then, can CRT be viewed or used as "a set of analytical tools that explain how race has and continues to function in society"? Tools don't explain; worldviews do. And CRT is a worldview based on clear, unambiguous assumptions:

> CRT recognizes that *racism is engrained in the fabric and system of the American society.* The individual racist need not exist to note that institutional racism is pervasive in the dominant culture. *This is the analytical lens that CRT uses in examining existing power structures.* CRT identifies that these power structures are based on white privilege and white supremacy, which perpetuates the marginalization of people of color (italics mine).[11]

---

[9] Richard Delgado, *Critical Race Theory* (Third Edition) (New York, New York, New York University Press, Kindle Edition), 3.

[10] Ibid., 8.

[11] "What is Critical Race Theory?" UCLA School of Public Affairs, Critical Race Studies, https://spacrs.wordpress.com/what-is-critical-race-theory.

These terms are discussed in greater detail elsewhere in this book. However, a few basic assumptions are worth noting. First, racism is engrained in the fabric and system of American society. Second, that racism has been redefined so as to no longer require the existence of individual racists. Third, CRT exists to examine power structures which are assumed *a priori*. Fourth, these power structures are identified based on the assumed definitions and existence of white privilege and white supremacy.

The distinction between the two drafts is made even clearer when addressing the ways in which CRT and Intersectionality can or should be used:

Original Resolution	Final Resolution
WHEREAS, critical race theory and intersectionality are founded upon unbiblical presuppositions descended from Marxist theories and categories, and therefore are inherently opposed to the Scriptures as the true center of Christian union....	WHEREAS, Critical race theory and intersectionality alone are insufficient to diagnose and redress the root causes of the social ills that they identify, which result from sin, yet these analytical tools can aid in evaluating a variety of human experiences....

The statement, "Critical race theory and intersectionality alone are insufficient to diagnose and redress the root causes of the social ills that they identify," may sound innocuous. However, it is anything but. Perhaps an illustration will help make the point.

One of my sons used to have a terrible time with his throat. He was constantly coughing, hacking, and grunting. We tried everything! We had him gargle, coat his throat, drink more water, and change his diet. Then we took him to see a doctor. The doctor said, "He has asthma." I said, "OK, but what does that have to do with stuff getting stuck in his throat?" The doctor explained that asthma narrowed all his respiratory passages, including his throat. I was doubtful. We got an inhaler. Within a few days, all my son's symptoms were gone! Turns out we were analyzing his problem based on faulty assumptions. And that is exactly what is wrong with CRT/I.

Again, a little background goes a long way here. The term "Intersectionality" was coined by Kimberlé Crenshaw. She developed the idea under the tutelage of her mentor, Derrick Bell, the founder of Critical Race Theory. The two concepts are linked inexorably not only by the relationship between their founders, but by their Marxist underpinnings and goals. According to Resolution 9, CRT and Intersectionality identify social ills and "aid in evaluating a variety of human experiences." Many have noted that, like many of the ideas in Critical Social Justice, Intersectionality possesses a kernel of truth. A complex web of intersections shape and influence one's experience of the world. But what are the underlying assumptions intersectional theorists use for their assessment and analysis? Another side-by-side comparison will shed light on that question:

Original Resolution	Final Resolution
WHEREAS, critical race theory divides humanity into groups of oppressors and oppressed, and is used to encourage biblical, transcendental truth claims to be considered suspect when communicated from groups labeled as oppressors....	WHEREAS, Critical race theory and intersectionality have been appropriated by individuals with worldviews that are contrary to the Christian faith, resulting in ideologies and methods that contradict Scripture....

This one takes the cake! To say that CRT/I "have been appropriated by individuals with worldviews that are contrary to the Christian faith" is like saying heat has been appropriated by the sun. Intersectionality, according to its founder, is inseparable from feminist ideology and identity politics. In fact, the title of the seminal article outlining the concept is "Intersectionality, Identity Politics, and Violence against

Women of Color."[12] In addition to identity politics and feminist theory, Intersectionality is rooted in the Marxist assumption of Oppressor/Oppressed categories. "Intersectionality means the examination of race, sex, class, national origin, and sexual orientation and how their combination plays out in various settings. These categories—and still others—can be separate disadvantaging factors... *or an intersection of recognized sites of oppression.*"[13]

The *Encyclopedia of Diversity and Social Justice* puts an even finer point on the matter:

> Our experiences of the social world are shaped by our ethnicity, race, social class, gender identity, sexual orientation, and numerous other facets of social stratification. Some social locations afford privilege (e.g., being white) while others are oppressive (e.g., being poor). These various aspects of social inequality do not operate independently of each other; they interact to create interrelated systems of oppression and domination. The concept of intersectionality refers to how these various aspects of social location "intersect" to mutually constitute individuals' lived experiences.[14]

Again, note the clear Critical Theory categorizations. The language of oppressor/oppressed and the underlying Marxist worldview are inseparable from the analytical tools of CRT and Intersectionality.

Curtis Woods's dissertation "The Literary Reception of the Spirituality of Phillis Wheatley (1753–1784): An Afrosensitive Reading" gives us several clues as to what he considers to be an appropriate use of CRT/I

---

[12] Kimberlé Crenshaw, *Mapping the Margins: Intersectionality, Identity Politics and Violence against Women of Color,* https://www.racialequitytools.org/resourcefiles/mapping-margins.pdf.

[13] Delgado, *Critical Race Theory,* 58.

[14] Sherwood Thompson, *Encyclopedia of Diversity and Social Justice* (Lanham, Maryland: Rowman & Littlefield Publishers, Kindle Edition, 2014), 435.

as analytical tools. Perhaps the most poignant is his glowing praise of Ibram X. Kendi: According to Woods, "Kendi's work is phenomenal because he deftly incorporates critical race theory, theology, anthropology, sociology, and philosophy in narrating the history of racist ideas in America."[15] In case you are unfamiliar with Kendi's work, he is a seminal figure in the secular Critical Social Justice movement whose work is anything but biblical.

Much more could and needs to be said about this. What happened at the SBC is far more significant than most people realize—more significant than I could possibly communicate in a single chapter. The overwhelming majority of people who raised their ballots in support of Resolution 9 did so not because they agreed with or even understood the matter at hand, but because they trusted the Committee on Resolutions. It also passed because a black professor from the flagship seminary in the SBC stood there and defended the resolution using hot-button language like "the Gospel of Jesus Christ" and "the sufficiency of Scripture" in order to obscure the fact that the resolution he helped write compromised both.

In the end, there were several factors that led the SBC to pass the resolution—including that among all the voices that spoke to the issue, one was conspicuously absent. Dr. Albert Mohler, the most respected theologian and cultural apologist in the SBC, who has repeatedly repudiated CRT, didn't say a word. Nor could he. For Mohler to oppose Woods from the floor would not only have been professionally awkward, but it would most certainly have been seized upon by race baiters in the SBC—an opportunity to accuse Mohler of publicly opposing Woods only because he is black, and

---

[15] Curtis Anthony Woods, "The Literary Reception of the Spirituality of Phillis Wheatley (1753–1784): An Afrosensitive Reading, A Dissertation Presented to the Faculty of the Southern Baptist Theological Seminary" (Louisville, Kentucky: Southern Baptist Theological Seminary, May 2018), 91, https://repository.sbts.edu/bitstream/handle/10392/5714/Woods_sbts_0207D_10471.pdf?sequence=1&isAllowed=y.

opposing CRT/I because he is a "racist" who want to "shut down the conversation" about racial justice, or to please the "white supremacist faction" within the SBC.[16]

---

[16] As this book was on its way to press, the Council of Seminary Presidents of the Southern Baptist Convention released a statement on November 30, 2020, that is nothing short of a complete repudiation of CRT as well as Resolution 9. While the organization condemns "racism in any form," the seminaries agree that "affirmation of Critical Race Theory, Intersectionality and any version of Critical Theory is incompatible with the Baptist Faith & Message." The issue was addressed at several convention meetings late in the year. This is a complete reversal of the language adopted in Resolution 9 in 2019. See George Schroeder, "Seminary Presidents Reaffirm BFM, Declare CRT Incompatible," SBC News, November 30, 2020, https://www.baptistpress.com/resource-library/news/seminary-presidents-reaffirm-bfm-declare-crt-incompatible/.

CHAPTER EIGHT

The Damage

There is a reason San Francisco's Transamerica Pyramid suffered no significant damage in the 7.1-magnitude 1989 Loma Prieta earthquake in Central California. Its pyramid shape and "earthquake-friendly" foundation make it about as quake-resistant a high-rise building as you'll find.[1]

Not all earthquake damage is created equal. Some buildings are better suited to withstand the trauma. One of the deadliest disasters in recent history was the 7.0 earthquake that struck Haiti in 2010, taking hundreds of thousands of lives as it toppled more than 100,000 structures. Similar magnitude, but totally different outcome than Loma Prieta. Why? "At the time, Haiti had no quake-resistant building codes or in-depth understanding of its vulnerability,"[2] the *Miami-Herald* tells us. In

---

[1] Jeff White, "Five Reasons Buildings Fail in an Earthquake—and How to Avoid Them," *Healthcare Design*, https://studylib.net/doc/18074210/five-reasons-buildings-fail-in-an-earthquake.

[2] Jacqueline Charles, "Haiti's 2010 Earthquake Killed Hundreds of Thousands. The Next One Could Be Worse," *Miami Herald*, January 12, 2020, https://www.miamiherald.com/news/nation-world/world/americas/haiti/article237830414.html#storylink=cpy.

other words, paying more attention to infrastructure and preparation would have spared many lives.

For those whose worldview considers power, oppression, and hegemony to be the basis for all human relationships, my story is only important if it affirms said oppression. For them, what I am sharing is a textbook (literally) example of internalized oppression. I am not exaggerating. The following list of examples of internalized oppression is from Özlem Sensoy and Robin DiAngelo's book *Is Everyone Really Equal?*, one of the most influential college textbooks currently being used to train future educators:

- Seeking the approval of and spending most of your time with members of the dominant group
- Behaving in ways that please the dominant group and do not challenge the legitimacy of its position
- Silently enduring microaggressions from the dominant group in order to avoid penalty
- Believing that your struggles with social institutions (such as education, employment, or health care) are the result of your (or your group's) inadequacy, rather than the result of unequally distributed resources between dominant and minoritized groups
- Harshly criticizing members of your group who do not assimilate to dominant norms ("Pull up your pants!" "Speak English!")[3]

One of the greatest tragedies of the Critical Social Justice movement is how it promotes devastation by encouraging people and communities of color to avoid "adopting the dominant culture" by eschewing real data.

---

[3] Robin DiAngelo and Özlem Sensoy, *Is Everyone Really Equal?: An Introduction to Key Concepts in Social Justice Education* (Multicultural Education Series) (New York, New York: Teachers College Press, Kindle Edition, 2011), 49–50.

As Thomas Sowell points out in *Discrimination and Disparities*, the CSJ crowd "proclaim that statistical disparities show biased treatment—and that this conclusion must be believed without visible corroborating evidence ... unless sheer insistent repetition is regarded as evidence."[4]

This kind of thinking and argumentation lies at the very heart of Critical Race Theory and the Critical Social Justice movement. According to CRT:

> Racial inequality emerges from the social, economic, and legal differences that white people create between "races" to maintain elite white interests in labour markets and politics, giving rise to poverty and criminality in many minority communities.[5]

Let's examine this claim line by line. First, the subject is "racial inequality." What does that mean? Whatever it is, it "emerges from the social, economic, and legal differences that white people create between races." And these differences are created for a sinister purpose: "to maintain elite white interests in markets and politics." Now we get to the definition of racial inequality. It is what this evil white creation gives rise to: "poverty and criminality in minority communities."

When you combine this concept with the idea that attributing inequality to anything other than racism is—well, racist—you are left with no alternative than to "do the work of antiracism."

There are four glaring problems with this scenario. First, this idea is an example of circular, question-begging logic at its worst. Second, accepting this argument requires repudiating entire swaths of research on alternate causes of racial inequalities. Third, it leads to the condemnation of biblical truth and a well-established preaching tradition—a black

---

[4] Thomas Sowell, *Discrimination and Disparities* (New York, New York: Basic Books, Kindle Edition, 2018), 163.

[5] Tommy Curry, "Critical Race Theory," *Encyclopedia Britannica*, https://www.britannica.com/topic/critical-race-theory.

preaching tradition. And fourth, it feeds into a victimology mindset that teaches disadvantaged people that their only hope is the benevolence, good will, and eventual revolutionary political action of well-meaning white saviors. For the rest of the chapter, I will address each one of these points

> so that we may no longer be children, tossed to and fro by the waves and carried about by every wind of doctrine, by human cunning, by craftiness in deceitful schemes. Rather, speaking the truth in love, we are to grow up in every way into him who is the head, into Christ, from whom the whole body, joined and held together by every joint with which it is equipped, when each part is working properly, makes the body grow so that it builds itself up in love. (Ephesians 4:14–16)

Circular, Question-Begging Logic

According to research by the Cato Institute, 62 percent of Americans say the political climate these days prevents them from saying things they believe because others might find them offensive. And this is not limited to one side of the political spectrum. "Majorities of Democrats (52 percent), independents (59 percent) and Republicans (77 percent)," according to the report, "all agree they have political opinions they are afraid to share."[6]

One is that systemic/structural racism is not the only, or even the primary, explanation for inequities. If you have engaged in such conversations lately, you have learned there is no such thing as brotherly disagreement on this issue. On these matters, there is right and there is wrong. More accurately, there is the CRT view on the one hand, and some version of white fragility, "privilege-preserving epistemic pushback,"[7] or

---

[6] Emily Ekins, "New Poll: 62% Say the Political Climate Prevents Them from Sharing Political Views," Cato Institute, July 22, 2020, https://www.cato.org/blog/poll-62-americans-say-they-have-political-views-theyre-afraid-share.

[7] Alison Bailey, "Tracking Privilege: Preserving Epistemic Pushback in Feminist and Critical Race Philosophy Classes," *Hypatia* 32, no. 4 (September 2017): 876–92.

some other modern CSJ disorder on the other. This is where the circular reasoning comes in.

The argument goes something like this: Systemic racism is the cause of disparities. If you doubt that, it is because you are a racist who wants to protect your power and keep those disparities in place. This has to be true because, if you were not racist, you would know that the cause of disparities is … racism. The news is replete with examples of people who have lost their jobs over this madness.

Kurt Beathard was the offensive coordinator for the Illinois State University football team. That is, until he found a BLM flyer on his office door and replaced it with a flyer of his own stating, "All Lives Matter to Our Lord and Savior Jesus Christ." Beathard was fired within weeks.[8] Professor Stephen Hsu was forced to resign from his position as vice president of research and innovation at Michigan State University over alleged "scientific racism." His actual crime? Interviewing an expert on police shootings who debunked the CRT myths surrounding them. (Apparently, merely associating with someone who questions the narrative is tantamount to "scientific racism.")[9] Portland State University professor Bruce Gilley was subjected to international scrutiny and scorn after starting a "Critiques of BLM" reading group. And the list goes on!

The CSJ view is considered both unfalsifiable and unassailable. Facing off with a true believer is a reminder that "a brother offended is more unyielding than a strong city, and quarreling is like the bars of a castle" (Proverbs 18:19). If you do find someone willing to engage on the topic, you will eventually get to the question-begging spiral. I have had many of these conversations, and they all lead in the same direction: at the heart of every malady is an historic wrong.

---

[8] Jason King, "The Kurt Beathard Story Exemplifies BLM's Successful Attack on Christianity and Football," Outkick, https://www.outkick.com/the-kurt-beathard-story-exemplifies-blms-successful-attack-on-christianity-and-football.

[9] Brittany Slaughter, "Scholar Forced to Resign Over Study That Found Police Shootings Not Biased against Blacks," College Fix, June 30, 2020, https://www.thecollegefix.com/scholar-forced-to-resign-over-study-that-found-police-shootings-not-biased-against-blacks.

Take an imaginary discussion about a young man in trouble with the law who was eventually expelled from school:

Could his history of drug use be a contributing factor?

Not his fault … Racist policies flooded the inner city with drugs.

How about his record of poor academic performance and absence from school?

Inequities created inferior schools that minorities are unmotivated to attend.

Could the lack of a father in his home have anything to do with it?

That is a byproduct of slavery and an excuse used to blame the victim.

In the end, the answer to everything is racism. Not only is this kind of reasoning logically flawed, but it also flies in the face of a substantial body of sociological research and the historic preaching and understanding of the black church.

Repudiating the Research

In his book *Human Diversity,* Charles Murray sheds light on the orthodoxy in social science. "The core doctrine of the orthodoxy in the social sciences is a particular understanding of human equality," he notes. "I don't mean equality in the sense of America's traditional ideal—all are equal in the eyes of God, have equal inherent dignity, and should be treated equally under the law—but equality in the sense of sameness."[10] Murray calls this "the sameness premise." The premise holds that in "a properly run society, people of all human groupings will have similar life outcomes."[11] While this premise sounds good, Murray demonstrates convincingly, using copious data, that it is false. "The political expression of the orthodoxy," he adds, "had its origins

---

[10] Charles Murray, *Human Diversity* (New York, New York: Grand Central Publishing, Kindle Edition, 2020), 2.

[11] Ibid.

in the mid-1960s with the legal triumphs of the civil rights movement and the rise of feminism."[12] Nor is this coincidental.

"The crucial question," writes Thomas Sowell, "is not whether evils exist but whether the evils of the past or present are automatically the cause of major economic, educational and other social disparities today." In Sowell's view, the fundamental problem is the assumption that "disparities are automatically somebody's fault, so that our choices are either to blame society or to 'blame the victim.'... Yet," he asks, "whose fault are demographic differences, geographic differences, birth order differences or cultural differences that evolved over the centuries before any of us were born?"[13] Nor is Sowell alone in his perspective.

"Many vocal advocates for racial equality have been loath to consider the possibility that problematic patterns of behavior could be an important factor contributing to our persisting disadvantaged status," writes Brown University economics professor Glenn Loury in a Manhattan Institute essay called "Culture, Causation, and Responsibility." "Some observers on the right of American politics ... take the position that discrimination against blacks is no longer an important determinant of unequal social outcomes. I have long tried to chart a middle course—acknowledging antiblack biases that should be remedied while insisting on addressing and reversing the patterns of behavior that impede black people from seizing newly opened opportunities to prosper."[14]

Both Loury and Sowell chart a course that is not only sensible, but is also aligned with the historic view of the black church in America. Neither argue that America is free of racism, but both argue that there are other issues that must be addressed regardless of racism.

---

[12] Murray, *Human Diversity*, 2.

[13] Sowell, *Discrimination and Disparities*, 117.

[14] Glenn Loury, "Why Does Racial Inequality Persist? Culture, Causation, and Responsibility," Manhattan Institute, May 7, 2019, https://www.manhattan-institute.org/racial-inequality-in-america-post-jim-crow-segregation.

Bashing the Black Pulpit

There are certainly black churches that are rife with Marxist liberation theology, CRT, Intersectionality, and the social gospel. With all the churches that exist in a country the size of the United States, this should come as no surprise. However, if you assume that this means the pulpits in black churches don't address personal responsibility, you are wrong. White liberals like Robin DiAngelo, Jim Wallis, and Daniel Hill may chafe at the idea of black responsibility, but black pastors do not. The internet is filled with clips of black pastors getting standing ovations as they passionately admonish their young members to "pull up your pants, get an education, stop dropping babies all over the place, learn to speak proper English, get all that gold out of your mouth...." They and their members know that, regardless of what is going on outside the black community, culture matters. The black family matters. Education matters. Decisions and choices matter. And above all, God's Word matters.

I am not suggesting that evangelical proponents of CSJ do not know this—at least not the ones on the conservative end of the spectrum. My point here is that the fault line is shifting. There is a growing shift toward extremes. Today, any preacher who intends to make a statement to a black audience or about the black community from a biblical text that addresses personal responsibility will have to spend the lion's share of his message doing so much apologizing and explaining that the force of his admonitions will die the death of a thousand qualifications. Gone are the days when a preacher can assume his audience will give him the benefit of the doubt.

I have come to the conclusion that such qualifications do more harm than good. Preachers who spend more time trying to be helpful than they do trying to be truthful are doing a disservice to those to whom they preach. There is a place for nuance, but the clear admonitions of Scripture are not it.

Thomas Sowell is one of the most significant intellectuals of our day. His words are useful here:

Disagreements about social issues in general seem to be not only inevitable but even beneficial, when opposing sides are forced to confront contrary arguments that might not have been considered before, and examine empirical evidence not confronted before. Neither side may have taken all the factors into consideration, but having to cope with each other's different views may bring out considerations that neither side gave much thought to at the outset.[15]

With this in mind, I want to address four areas where this is particularly true: fatherlessness, education, crime, and abortion.

The Importance of Fathers

In a speech delivered at the Morehouse Conference on African American Fathers two decades ago, William Raspberry said,

> Are black fathers necessary? You know, I'm old and I'm tired, and there are some things that I just don't want to debate anymore. One of them is whether African American children need fathers. Another is whether marriage matters. Does marriage matter? You bet it does. Are black fathers necessary? Damn straight we are.

Morehouse College is one of the historically black colleges and universities (HBCU) that falls to the far left on both the political and theological spectrum. I have a dear friend who went to seminary at Morehouse back in the 1990s who summed it up well when he said, somewhat tongue-in-cheek, "I think maybe one of my professors was actually a Christian." I say this only to highlight the significance of the aforementioned statement and the conference where it was made. This was not a

---

[15] Sowell, *Discrimination and Disparities*, vii.

white supremacist speaking at some kind of alt-right rally. This was a black man speaking at Morehouse!

Morehouse administrators later wrote that they "believe that among the most urgent problems facing the African American community, and the entire nation, is the reality that 70 percent of African American children are born to unmarried mothers, and that at least 80 percent of all African American children can now expect to spend at least a signifi-cant part of their childhood years living apart from their fathers."[16] This has long been a concern among black religious, political, and community leaders and continues to be so to this day. However, the rise of CSJ and CRT has led to a sea change. Today it is neither popular, nor in many cases acceptable, to address the need for moral change in the black community.

In June 2008, then-Senator Barack Obama gave a Father's Day mes-sage at the Apostolic Church of God in Chicago that today would be considered classic verbal violence on most university campuses.

"[I]f we are honest with ourselves," he said, "we'll admit that way too many fathers also are … missing from too many lives and too many homes." He went on to say that fathers "have abandoned their respon-sibilities, acting like boys instead of men. And the foundations of our families are weaker because of it."[17] Then, in a moment Obama probably wishes he could erase, he took off his CRT hat and made a statement that would definitely require a trigger warning:

> We know the statistics—that children who grow up without
> a father are five times more likely to live in poverty and com-
> mit crime; nine times more likely to drop out of schools and
> twenty times more likely to end up in prison. They are more
> likely to have behavioral problems, or run away from home,

---

[16] "Turning the Corner on Father Absence in Black America: A Statement from the Morehouse Conference on African American Fathers," Morehouse College, fall 1998.

[17] "Obama's Father's Day Remarks," *New York Times*, June 15, 2008, https://www.nytimes.com/2008/06/15/us/politics/15text-obama.html.

or become teenage parents themselves. And the foundations
of our community are weaker because of it.[18]

This speech was given from the pulpit of a black church, and there
was not a hint of surprise, controversy, unease, or disagreement. Why?
Because this has been common fare since time immemorial! This is
"speaking the truth in love" (Ephesians 4:13).

Nor is this just a black thing. "The science tells us that the number
one predictor of economic mobility for poor kids in America is the share
of two-parent families in their neighborhood,"[19] wrote University of
Virginia sociology professor W. Bradford Wilcox, a leading researcher
on the importance and impact of marriage and family. That well-known
fact is why Obama told his Father's Day audience that two-parent families are "what keeps [children's] foundation strong. It's what keeps the
foundation of our country strong."[20] And the future president didn't stop
there. He went on to address another issue that is often deemed verboten
by the antiracist crowd: the need for high standards and a commitment
to education in the black community.

Education and High Standards

In typical Obama-speaking-at-a-black-church fashion, the then-
senator took aim at the all-too-prevalent culture of underachievement.
You know, the rampant truancy, failure to do homework, and the general
indifference to learning, all in the name of the poisonous notion that
pursuing academic excellence is a manifestation of "acting white." It's
one of those things black people are only allowed to talk about when
white people are not listening. Evidently, Obama forgot he was being

---

[18] "Obama's Father's Day Remarks."

[19] W. Bradford Wilcox, "First Family, Then Freedom: Replying to Thomas D.
Klingenstein, 'Preserving the American Way of Life,'" American Mind, June 11,
2020, https://americanmind.org/features/preserving-the-american-way-of-life/
first-family-then-freedom/.

[20] "Obama's Father's Day Remarks."

recorded, because he encouraged fathers to set "an example of excellence for our children," noting that, "if we want to set high expectations for them, we've got to set high expectations for ourselves." He went even further, stating, "It's great if you have a job; it's even better if you have a college degree."[21] Is he wrong? Was the church wrong for applauding? Are myriad black pastors around the country wrong for saying the exact same thing Sunday after Sunday? Of course not!

This is part of the legacy of Black America. We are a proud people who have always seen the need to strive for education. Noted historian Robert Higgs, commenting on the astonishing feat of achieving black literacy in post-slavery black America, noted, "For a large population to transform itself from virtually unlettered to more than half literate in 50 years ranks as an accomplishment seldom witnessed in human history."[22] This led to levels of economic advancement that were also unprecedented.

It is unfortunate that this part of black history is often glossed over due to its inconsistency with the current victimology narrative. However, the facts are undeniable. "The conventional attitudes of blacks toward marriage, parenting, school, and work a century ago," writes Jason Riley in *False Black Power?*, "aided and abetted [an] unprecedented black economic advancement and complicate liberal claims that black antisocial behavior in the twenty-first century is a 'legacy' of slavery and Jim Crow."[23]

It is important not to miss Riley's point. Those attempting to blame fatherlessness, crime, and a lack of black achievement today on the legacy of slavery must account for the fact that one hundred years after slavery ended, blacks, according to many measures, were actually doing better than they have in the sixty years since the Civil Rights Act. Sowell notes, "As of 1960, two-thirds of all black American children were living with both parents. That declined over the years, until only one-third were

---

[21] "Obama's Father's Day Remarks."

[22] Jason L. Riley, *False Black Power?* (New Threats to Freedom Series) (West Conshohocken, Pennsylvania: Templeton Press, Kindle Edition, 2017), 48.

[23] Ibid., 53–54.

living with both parents in 1995." This was more pronounced among families in poverty, where "85 percent of the children had no father present."[24] How then, given the fact that the trajectory worsened *after* 1960, can slavery and Jim Crow be the cause?

Obama's Father's Day speech struck a similar tone in that he located the problem and the solution not outside the black family, but inside. "They see when you are inconsiderate at home; or when you are distant; or when you are thinking only of yourself," he warned. Then, in a move that would make DiAngelo and Kendi cringe, he connected behavior in the black family to pathologies in the black community, noting, "It's no surprise when we see that behavior in our schools or on our streets."[25] No surprise? Why? Because it is what systemic racism has produced? No—because the way we live in our families matters! Again, according to the gurus of antiracism, this is not to be done. This is what Robin DiAngelo calls "aversive racism."

But Obama wasn't done. Next he turned his attention to another taboo issue in the current CSJ debate: crime. And when he did, he once again echoed the sentiments and findings of others who have studied the matter, including the Morehouse Conference.

Crime

[C]ontrolling for race, neighborhood characteristics, and mother's education and cognitive ability, boys raised in single parent homes are twice as likely to commit a crime leading to incarceration. A child growing up without both parents also faces a greater risk that he or she will be a victim of a crime, especially child abuse.[26]

---

[24] Sowell, *Discrimination and Disparities*, 180.

[25] "Obama's Father's Day Remarks."

[26] "Turning the Corner on Father Absence in Black America."

This statement from the Morehouse Conference is consistent with Wilcox's more recent research which found that "the rule of law is strongest in communities where stable married families dominate the local landscape."[27] This connection between stable families and the rule of law is something most of us know intuitively. It doesn't mean that we have a simplistic understanding of racism or deny it exists. It just means that we understand the importance of the family as it relates to the community at large.

Again, from Obama's Father's Day speech:

> Yes, we need more cops on the street. Yes, we need fewer guns in the hands of people who shouldn't have them. Yes, we need more money for our schools, and more outstanding teachers in the classroom, and more afterschool programs for our children. Yes, we need more jobs and more job training and more opportunity in our communities. But we also need families to raise our children. *We need fathers to realize that responsibility does not end at conception. We need them to realize that what makes you a man is not the ability to have a child—it's the courage to raise one.*

And just when it seemed he couldn't get more politically incorrect, Obama took a bite of another forbidden fruit and said, "It's up to us to tell our sons those songs on the radio may glorify violence, but in my house we give glory to achievement, self-respect, and hard work."[28] Then he moved on to the *sine qua non* of racial politics: homicide rates.

I started this book addressing the deaths of black men because it is the touchstone of the current debate. At the end of the day, it is not income inequality, incarceration, or education that causes the greatest stir; it is those deaths. Whenever we hear people talking about "the discussion about race," or "issues of racial justice," it usually comes on

---

[27] Wilcox, "First Family, Then Freedom."

[28] "Obama's Father's Day Remarks."

the heels of a high-profile police killings like Michael Brown, Philando Castile, or George Floyd. But when Obama stated that "homicide is a leading cause of death for black Americans of all ages,"[29] he wasn't using hyperbole. Nor was he alluding to the killing of "unarmed black men" by police. He was referring to black-on-black murder.

According to the *American Journal of Preventative Medicine*, "[I]n 2000, for people aged 10–34 years, homicide rates were more than 11 times higher for blacks than the rate for whites." And that number has not improved. "In 2015, homicide rate for blacks aged 10–34 years was 13 times the rate for whites."[30] And almost all of those murders happen not at the hands of the police or white people, but other blacks—usually young black men. This is why sermons in black churches have frequently and forcefully addressed violence. Nor has the church been alone in its concern. "Far from ignoring the issue of crime by blacks against other blacks," writes James Forman in *Locking Up Our Own*, "African American officials and their constituents have been consumed by it."[31]

Feeding the Victim Mentality

If we say we have no sin, we deceive ourselves, and the truth is not in us. If we confess our sins, he is faithful and just to forgive us our sins and to cleanse us from all unrighteousness. If we say we have not sinned, we make him a liar, and his word is not in us. (1 John 1:8–10)

---

[29] Kameron J. Sheats et al., "Violence-Related Disparities Experienced by Black Youth and Young Adults: Opportunities for Prevention," *American Journal of Preventative Medicine* 55, no. 4 (October 2018): 462–69, doi:10.1016/j. amepre.2018.05.017.

[30] Ibid.

[31] James Forman Jr., *Locking Up Our Own* (New York, New York: Farrar, Straus and Giroux, Kindle Edition, 2017), 11.

If the first false claim is "Police are hunting and killing unarmed black men," the second is that "white people are hunting and killing unarmed black men." The Black Lives Matter movement gained traction and prominence after the Michael Brown case, but it traces its origins back to the killing of Trayvon Martin. These two cases are often conflated not only by BLM, but by evangelical SJWs as well.

"So when I watch a video like George Floyd's," wrote Christian pastor and rapper Shai Linne, "it represents for me the fresh reopening of a deep wound and the reliving of layers of trauma that get exponentially compounded each time a well-meaning white friend says, 'All lives matter.'" [32] For Linne, this is about "the systemic factors that contributed to the George Floyd situation,"[33] which is why he contends that though all lives matter, "in this country, black lives have been treated like they don't matter for centuries and present inequities in criminal justice, income, housing, health care, education, etc. show that all lives don't actually matter like they should."[34] So for him and others in the evangelical CSJ movement, it is impossible to separate these cases.

I disagree. Not only should we separate these issues, but if we are intent on addressing the underlying questions, we *must* separate them.

The Trayvon Martin and Ahmaud Arbery cases were not so-called "state-sanctioned killings." I reject that categorization altogether in the post–Civil Rights era. It damages our understanding of history to lump modern police killings with cases like that of Medgar Evers and Emmett Till. There was a time of state-sanctioned killings of blacks. Thank God we do not live in that time now! We live in a time when such cases would be unthinkable, and anyone who argues otherwise is hard pressed to prove that their assertion is anything more than hyperbole.

The Martin and Arbery cases involved civilians, and thus belong to a discussion about the broader issue of intraracial violence. This is a

[32] Shai Linne, "George Floyd and Me," Gospel Coalition, June 8, 2020, https://www.thegospelcoalition.org/article/george-floyd-and-me.

[33] Ibid.

[34] Ibid.

discussion the CSJ movement does not want to have since the facts not only disprove their narrative, but obliterate it. According to federal Bureau of Justice Statistics, in interracial violence involving blacks and whites, white perpetrators account for 15 percent of the cases while black perpetrators account for 85 percent.[35] In other words, far from there being an epidemic of whites "hunting down innocent, unarmed black men," when it comes to interracial violence, black people are overwhelmingly more likely to victimize white people than the other way around.

This is also true when it comes to crimes against the police, as mentioned earlier. A police officer is 18.5 times more likely to be killed by a black assailant than an unarmed black man is to be killed by a cop.[36] And before you accuse me of "victim blaming" or "promoting negative stereotypes about black criminality," remember, my point in raising these statistics is to expose and warn against the flippant use of univariate analysis in order to "prove" racism. I no more accept the notion that these stats prove something endemic to black people than I accept the notion that disparities in police killings prove racial injustice in policing. Both stats require more honest, robust analysis and a rejection of CRT/I presuppositions.

A History of Accountability and Action

Current cries about "over-policing" of black communities and the need to "defund the police" are inconsistent with the facts on the ground. According to recent Gallup polls, most black Americans (81 percent) want police to spend the same amount of or more time in their area as before protests broke out in 2020.[37] This resonates with my own experi-

---

[35] "Race/Ethnicity," Bureau of Justice Statistics, https://www.bjs.gov/index.cfm?ty=tp&tid=922.

[36] Heather Mac Donald, *The War on Cops* (New York, New York: Encounter Books, Kindle Edition, 2016), 79.

[37] "Black Americans Want Police to Retain Local Presence," Gallup, August 5, 2020, https://news.gallup.com/poll/316571/black-americans-police-retain-local-presence.aspx.

ence growing up in a high-crime area. I remember days when I had to walk through territory that was unfamiliar or unwelcoming. I always had my head on a swivel, looking for gangbangers who might want to jam me up. Like all young black men in my neighborhood, I had nightmares about being caught in the wrong place at the wrong time and being asked, "What set you claimin'?" However, on one occasion I had no fear of this, and that was when there was a heavy police presence. Ironically, though I feared the police, I still had a sense that when 5-0 was roaming the hood, I was safe.

This complicated relationship with the police is something worth exploring. "I have tried to recover a portion of African American social, political, and intellectual history," writes James Forman, "a story that gets ignored or elided when we fail to appreciate the role that blacks have played in shaping criminal justice policy over the past forty years."[38] In his book *Locking Up Our Own*, Forman weaves a narrative supported by historical and data analyses and demonstrates the little-known or -appreciated fact that blacks have not only viewed crime as a major issue, but have also played a significant role in shaping the modern legal response to that problem.

African Americans performed this role as citizens, voters, mayors, legislators, prosecutors, police officers, police chiefs, corrections officials, and community activists. Their influence grew as a result of attaining political power, especially after the passage of the Voting Rights Act of 1965. And to a significant extent, the new black leaders and their constituents supported tough-on-crime measures.[39]

Forman's work helps dispel one of the most persistent myths of our day concerning crime and punishment: the idea that disparate penalties for crack and powder cocaine represent *de facto* evidence of racism in the criminal justice system. In fact, "the racial-conspiracy hypothesis," writes Barry Latzer, "has never been established in historical scholarship

---

[38] Forman, *Locking Up Our Own*, 10.

[39] Ibid.

and remains the redoubt of a few ideologues."[40] Latzer's work takes dead aim at the claims of Michelle Alexander, whose popular book *The New Jim Crow* is a favorite on antiracist reading lists in spite of its several glaring problems, some of which Forman raises.[41]

Forman's work, as well as my personal experience growing up in South Central Los Angles, show that, "in the years preceding and during our punishment binge, black communities were devastated by historically unprecedented levels of crime and violence." This increase was largely driven by the fact that during the heroin epidemic, "homicides doubled and tripled in D.C. and many other American cities throughout the 1960s," which is important to keep in mind when considering the crack versus powder cocaine disparity. The crack epidemic came two decades after the heroin epidemic and dwarfed it in terms of impact. Crack was "a terrifying drug whose addictive qualities and violent marketplace caused some contemporaries to label it 'the

---

[40] Barry Latzer, "Michelle Alexander Is Wrong about Mass Incarceration," *National Review*, April 4, 2019, https://www.nationalreview.com/magazine/2019/04/22/michelle-alexander-is-wrong-about-mass-incarceration.

[41] See Michael VanderHeijden, "Faculty Publications: Critique of the New Jim Crow," Lillian Goldman Law Library blog, April 17, 2012. VanderHeijden shares an example of a common critique of Alexander's work. He writes, "Prof. Forman questions the usefulness of the analogy which, he argues, leads to a distorted view of mass incarceration by: failing to consider black attitudes toward crime and punishment; focusing on the War on Drugs and neglecting violent crime; and drawing attention away from the harms that mass incarceration has on the most disadvantaged groups. He also warns that in seeking to find parallels between the Old Jim Crow and mass incarceration, scholars risk overlooking other terrible aspects of the Old Jim Crow." See also Mac Donald, *The War on Cops*, 212. Mac Donald writes, quoting President Obama, "The 'real reason our prison population is so high' is that we have 'locked up more and more nonviolent drug offenders than ever before, for longer than ever before.'" This assertion, which drew applause from the audience, is the most ubiquitous fallacy of the deincarceration movement. It gained widespread currency in 2010 with Michelle Alexander's book *The New Jim Crow*. See also R.L. Stephens II, "Mass Incarceration Is Not the New Jim Crow," at http://www.orchestratedpulse.com/2015/04/mass-incarceration-not-new-jim-crow/. For a review from the left, see also "The New Jim Crow Discredited, Advocates Demand Revision," libcom.org, February 3, 2013, https://libcom.org/news/new-jim-crow-discredited-advocates-demand-revision-03022013.

worst thing to hit us since slavery.'"[42] This is why Latzer challenges Alexander's assessment of the problem:

> The notion that the buildup of the criminal-justice system, which began in the 1970s but gained steam over the next three decades, was part of a plot to undo the civil-rights movement rather than a response to the massive crime and drug wave that afflicted this country not only is dubious revisionist history, but it overlooks the strong support of black leadership for an expansion of the criminal-justice system.[43]

Any analysis of the difference in penalties must take these facts into consideration. The historical context simply does not lend itself to the kind of simplistic analyses and assertions of the CSJ crowd. In a March 2019 op-ed published in *National Review,* Alexander acknowledged the fact that violent crime "accounts ... for 54 percent of [black inmates] in prison." Latzer celebrates the fact that Alexander "now concedes that mass incarceration cannot be addressed without doing something about violent crime," which he argues (and I agree) "is a big improvement over her *New Jim Crow* claim that drug prosecutions were the heart of the problem.[44] Forman's analysis of the issue is both nuanced and sobering. Again, from *Locking Up Our Own*:

> As they confronted this devastating crime wave, black officials exhibited a complicated and sometimes overlapping mix of impulses. Some displayed tremendous hostility toward perpetrators of crime, describing them as a "cancer" that had to be cut away from the rest of the black community. Others

---

[42] Forman, *Locking Up Our Own*, 10.

[43] Barry Latzer, "Michelle Alexander Is Wrong about Mass Incarceration," *National Review*, April 4, 2019, https://www.nationalreview.com/magazine/2019/04/22/michelle-alexander-is-wrong-about-mass-incarceration/.

[44] Ibid.

pushed for harsher penalties but acknowledged that these measures would not solve the crisis at hand. Some even expressed sympathy for the plight of criminal defendants, who they knew were disproportionately black. But that sympathy was rarely sufficient to overcome the claims of black crime victims, who often argued that a punitive approach was necessary to protect the African American community—including many of its most impoverished members—from the ravages of crime.[45]

As someone who survived this historic moment, I can attest to the fact that the situation on the ground was harrowing. There were days when I feared the police, but I feared the drug dealers more. I knew there was racism. I also knew that the crack epidemic was devastating. I knew it turned people into zombies who would sell their bodies, or the bodies of their children, for a rock. I knew that a "crackhead" would kill you if he thought he could find money in your pockets with which to get high. And I knew the drug behind this rampant addiction was the catalyst for the regular barrage of drive-by shootings that caused my streets to run red with blood.

My cousin Jarmal was not killed by the police; he was shot by another drug dealer while selling crack. I learned what freebasing cocaine was by walking in on my father while he was doing it.[46] I also stood over my father's hospital bed after he had taken five bullets in a crack-related incident, then preached at his funeral several years later, after his prolonged crack use had so compromised his heart that it simply failed him. Yes, crack was a monster ... a demon. It squandered fortunes, demolished families, shipwrecked some lives, and ended others. In the end, the response was not perfect, but it was understandable.

---

[45] Forman, *Locking Up Our Own*, 10–11.

[46] Freebasing, according to addictiongroup.org, is a method in which the user puts the base form of the drug in a glass pipe and heats it until it boils. Then he or she inhales the vapors for a faster, more intense high. See https://www.addiction-group.org/drugs/illegal/freebasing.

But crack is not the only demon plaguing black America. Nor is it the worst. There is another that takes and destroys even more lives.

Abortion: The Unspoken Epidemic in Black America

"The question of 'life' is the question of the twentieth century," said Jesse Jackson in a 1978 speech that is uncharacteristic of his later stance. "Race and poverty are dimensions of the life question, but discussions about abortion have brought the issue into focus in a much sharper way." He concluded with a point that he has belied by his actions, but which nonetheless remains true: "How we will respect and understand the nature of life itself is the overriding moral issue, not of the black race, but of the human race."[47] I could not agree more! That is why I believe the abortion question belongs at the center of any discussion about race and justice.

Kermit Gosnell and Why We Don't Know His Name

Kermit Gosnell is one of America's most prolific and least-known serial killers. That is because his crimes took place at the intersection of a series of political realities that rendered them inconvenient for those who would normally make much of a man whose victims numbered in the thousands.

First, Gosnell was an abortionist in impoverished West Philadelphia. This meant those in the media, who are overwhelmingly pro-abortion, were reluctant to call his crimes "murder." Second, Gosnell's victims were predominantly black. This was inconvenient because, to the CSJ movement, the primary social justice issue is not the taking of human life through abortion, but abortion's *availability* to women. Third, Gosnell is black. Therefore, the pro-abortion lobby viewed him as a saint

---

[47] Jesse Jackson, "How We Respect Life Is the Overriding Moral Issue," Right to Life News, January 1977, http://groups.csail.mit.edu/mac/users/rauch/nvp/consistent/jackson.html.

providing a vital service for a systemically and intersectionally oppressed, underrepresented minority. Never mind the fact that his facility was a vile maze of unsanitary equipment, bags and jars of discarded fetal body parts, cat feces, and rat droppings that went uninspected for decades at a time. The Philadelphia community he preyed upon didn't make a peep until federal agents raided his clinic in February 2010 looking for prescription drugs he was allegedly selling in the neighborhood—not investigating the death of an immigrant woman who died under his care or any of the many obvious health code violations agents discovered. (Nor did those things seem to concern his legal team; when they were mentioned at his 2013 trial, his attorney sniffed, "If you want Mayo Clinic standards, then you go to the Mayo Clinic.... It fits their needs, this racist, elitist prosecution, to make this a homicide.")[48]

Until then, the small band of pro-life protestors who preached and prayed outside the clinic were viewed as the problem—not Gosnell.

Make no mistake about it: Kermit Gosnell was a murderer. He regularly performed abortions long after the legal limit of twenty-four weeks and killed babies who were born alive in his clinic by snipping their spinal cords with scissors. He was eventually tried and "convicted of murdering three babies born alive, and found guilty of involuntary manslaughter in the overdose death of an adult patient"[49] who was given too much anesthesia. And if you haven't heard about his case, it may be because the media refused to even cover his trial until their absence in the courtroom was made known.

But why? There are protests and riots in the streets, prominent pastors take to Twitter demanding outrage, and Big Eva publishes *Liturgies of Lament* and public lamentation services (led by ministers who in most cases have never led a liturgical service of any kind) over cases that often

---

[48] Joseph A. Slobodzian, "FBI Agent Recounts Raid on Gosnell Abortion Clinic," *Philadelphia Inquirer*, March 19, 2013, https://www.bjs.gov/index. cfm?ty=tp&tid=922.

[49] "Doctor Kermit Gosnell Found Guilty of Murdering Infants in Late-Term Abortions," Fox News, May 13, 2013, https://www.foxnews.com/us/ doctor-kermit-gosnell-found-guilty-of-murdering-infants-in-late-term-abortions.

turn out to be justified police homicides. However, most do not know Gosnell's name. Nor is his an isolated case.

An Unreported Genocide

Planned Parenthood Founder Margaret Sanger started what became known as the Negro Project in order to reduce the black population through birth control.[50] Sanger was a Malthusian eugenicist who believed black and brown people were inherently inferior. Her first achievement among the black community came in 1923 when she opened a clinic in Harlem, where she "hired African American doctors, nurses, and an all-black advisory council to help her clients feel more at ease—and more inclined to listen to her birth control propaganda."[51] She also relied on black clergy to advance her message.[52] Today that message is the accepted norm among a vast majority of the black population.

Fifteen and a half million black babies have been aborted since 1973. That means abortion is not only the leading cause of death among black Americans, but it has taken more black lives than heart disease, cancer, accidents, violent crime, and AIDS combined.[53] Though black women make up less than 13 percent of the population, they account for 35 percent of all abortions. In major cities like New York, Philadelphia, and Los Angeles, more black babies are aborted than born.[54] The fact that nearly 80 percent of Planned Parenthood's abortion clinics are in minor-

---

[50] "Margaret Sanger Started What She Called 'the Negro Project' to Reduce the African American Population by Pushing Birth Control," Culture of Life Studies Program, http://www.sangervideo.com/negroproject.html.

[51] Ibid.

[52] Tanya L. Green, "The Negro Project: Margaret Sanger's Eugenic Plan for Black America," BlackGenocide.org, http://www.blackgenocide.org/negro.html.

[53] Ibid.

[54] Carole Novielli, "Tragic Report: More Black Babies Are Aborted in New York City Than Are Born," NRL News, February 16, 2020, https://www.national-righttolifenews.org/2020/02/tragic-report-more-black-babies-are-aborted-in-new-york-city-than-are-born.

ity neighborhoods often raises a "chicken or the egg" debate as to whether Sanger's eugenics dream or black people's penchant for self-destruction is to blame. In either case, the fact remains that black women are killing their unborn children at alarming rates. This is an issue of paramount concern, or at least it should be.

Much of the discussion about abortion in the black community tends to ignore one simple fact:

According to a recent Gallup poll, from 2001 to 2007, 31 percent of black Americans thought abortion was morally acceptable. From 2017 to 2020, that number rose to 46 percent. Over that same time period, non-black voters' approval of it went up from 41 percent to 43 percent. There was also an eight-point jump in the number of blacks who believe abortion should be legal under any circumstance (from 24 percent to 32 percent). By comparison, non-black Americans only saw a two-point change (up from 25 percent to 27 percent).

What jumped out at me when I saw these statistics was not only the dramatic change, but the fact that in both instances, blacks went from having the most conservative views on the issue to having the most liberal. In other words, from 2001 to 2007, blacks were less inclined to support abortion than the average American (by ten points!). What changed?

It is impossible to say for sure. However, I would venture to say that the election of the most pro-abortion president in the history of the United States in 2008 and 2012 had something to do with it.

Barack Obama garnered 95 percent of the black vote in 2008 and 93 percent in 2012. I wrote articles beginning in 2007 excoriating him for his tragic record on abortion. As a state senator, Obama openly and vigorously opposed the Illinois Born-Alive Infant Protection Act, which would require medical personnel to save the lives of babies born alive during abortions as opposed to leaving them to die, which was the normal practice at the time. He was the only Illinois state senator to actually speak in opposition to the bill when it was debated in 2002.[55] (A federal

---

[55] Robert P. George, "Obama and Infanticide," *Public Discourse*, October 16, 2008, https://www.thepublicdiscourse.com/2008/10/282.

version of the bill passed both houses of Congress without a single dissenting vote, which is practically unheard of—making his opposition to it even more glaring.)

The only thing I found more disturbing than this was the reaction I got when raising the issue with black Christians, many of whom are either flat-out pro-choice or only reluctantly pro-life. Either the Gallup poll which found a 46-percent approval rate for abortion among blacks is a gross underestimation, or I have been engaging in conversations with the wrong black people.

Racism is real, and it is alive and well in America. I have said as much from many pulpits on many occasions. Remember, my target here is the notion that "inequity *must* equal injustice." It is this notion that undermines efforts to bring law and the Gospel to bear in the lives of those categorized as oppressed, as well as those categorized as oppressors. I can and do look injustice in the eye and call it what it is. It is my duty as a herald of God's Word. In this case, however, the injustice I see is the false witness-bearing, Marxist ideology-promoting, Gospel-perverting ideology of Critical Race Theory and its offshoots.

In the next chapter, we will explore some of the ways those offshoots have begun to manifest themselves.

CHAPTER NINE

Aftershock

Aftershocks occur in rocks located near the epicenter or along the fault that harbored the principal quake. Although the intensity associated with most aftershocks is small compared with that of the principal earthquake, many are large enough to hamper rescue efforts by further destabilizing buildings and other structures and can be stressful for local residents coping with the damage and loss of life wrought by the principal quake.[1]

On July 28, 1976, a 7.1-magnitude event struck the city of Luanxian, China. I say "event" because it was not an earthquake; it was an aftershock. The initial earthquake that struck the nearby city of Tangshan was a 7.5-magnitude. In other words, the initial earthquake was so severe that the aftershock was greater than some of the most catastrophic earthquakes in history. By comparison, the San Fernando quake of 1971 was a 6.6. The 1989 Loma Prieta quake was a 7.1, and the infamous

---

[1] John P. Rafferty, "Aftershock," *Encyclopedia Britannica*, https://www.britannica.com/science/aftershock-geology.

1994 Northridge earthquake was a 6.7. All three are among the ten deadliest earthquakes in U.S. history, but are of a lower magnitude than the Luanxian aftershock.[2]

The moral of this story is, "Don't underestimate the catastrophic potential of aftershocks."

Strange Bedfellows

One of the unintended consequences of the Critical Social Justice movement is that Christians who adopt its underlying ideologies will not be able to avoid the damage it creates. "The idea that evangelicals can adopt the analysis of contemporary critical theory with respect to race and sex, but not with respect to sexuality, gender identity, or religion is naïve—at best," writes apologist Neil Shenvi. Shenvi holds a Ph.D. in chemistry, but it doesn't take that level of scientific acumen to understand the inevitable link between the aspects of Critical Social Justice that evangelicals are eager to embrace and those they want to avoid, because as Shenvi notes, "these views all share the same root: a particular understanding of oppression."[3]

A quick glance at the website of any social justice organization will make this clear. Back in 2007, *Social Work Today* offered a list of the "Top Five Social Justice Issues of Our Day,"[4] which included: celebrating diversity, child welfare, healthcare reform, poverty and economic injustice, and affordable housing. Maryville University's list includes: climate change, racial equity, LGBTQ+ rights, and affordable healthcare. If you check Yeshiva University's list, you also will find: voting rights, climate

---

[2] Betsy Mason, "The 10 Deadliest Earthquakes in U.S. History," Wired, November 21, 2000, https://www.wired.com/2008/11/gallery-deadly-earthquake.

[3] Neil Shenvi, "Short Review of Adams' Teachings for Diversity and Social Justice," Neil Shenvi—Apologetics blog, https://shenviapologetics.com/short-review-of-adams-teachings-for-diversity-and-social-justice.

[4] "The Top 5 Social Justice Issues Facing Social Workers Today," *Social Work Today*, March/April 2007, https://www.socialworktoday.com/archive/marapr2007p24.shtml.

justice, healthcare, refugee crisis, racial justice, income gaps, gun violence, hunger and food insecurity, and equity. All of these pale in comparison to the Education for Justice list, which includes a whopping thirty-seven issues! (And yes, I'm going to list all of them):

Consumerism	Human Trafficking	Mental Health	Sexual Abuse Crisis in the Church
Climate Change	Hunger	Migration	Signs of the Times
Death Penalty	Immigration	Natural Disasters	Terrorism
Economic Justice	Inequality	Pastoral Circle	Torture
Education	Integral Ecology	Global Poverty	U.S. Elections
Gender Equality	Interfaith	U.S. Poverty	War
Genocide	Intergenerational Justice	Racial Justice	Water
Healthcare	Sustainable Development	Refugees	
Homelessness	Land Grabbing	Restorative Justice	
Human Rights	Liberation Theology	Racism	

By the way, if you think this list is exhaustive, it's not. It ignores several other hot-button social justice issues like veganism, ableism, beauty standards, animal testing, body positivity, and COVID-19, which all have significant followings. And while these things may seem random or unrelated, I assure you, that is not the case. They all stem from the same critical worldview. Scratch the surface of each one of these issues and you will find:

1. Hegemony: there is a group of people who possess illegitimate power and create structures to maintain it
2. Oppressor/Oppressed Paradigm: the hegemonic overlords have systems in place to preserve their power and oppress the minority

3. Gnostic Priests: people whose experience of oppression gives them insight that is unavailable to their oppressors

4. Enlightened Saviors: the people from the oppressor class who are exempt from their participation in the oppression and serve as representatives and saviors of the oppressed in order to shepherd them through the revolutionary process of usurping the hegemony (for a not-so-small fee)

Then there is the interconnectedness of the issues themselves.

Julie Cappiello's article "Here's How Veganism Is Undeniably Linked to Other Social Justice Issues" (posted at MercyForAnimals.org) is a prime example of the interconnectivity in the Critical Social Justice movement. Cappiello connects veganism to environmental justice, racial equality, immigration, and workers' rights in ways that are pretty straightforward. The environmental justice link has to do with global warming and animal farming, the racial equality link has to do with the fact that most farms are in low-income areas and tend to pollute them, and the immigration and workers'-rights connection has to do with the fact that large numbers of illegal immigrants work in agriculture (and are often afraid to leave the farm for fear of being deported).

However, it is Cappiello's link to feminism that is both creative and revealing. "The meat and dairy industries not only exploit our environmental resources," she writes, "but also continually exploit female bodies in the reproduction of new animals to use and kill for human consumption." In case you missed it, Cappiello is not talking about human females: "Females in the dairy industry are repeatedly and forcibly impregnated to ensure a continuous supply of milk. Their young are ripped from their sides within hours, with the daughters forced into the same generative cycle and the sons killed for someone's dinner."[5]

---

[5] Julie Cappiello, "Here's How Veganism Is Undeniably Linked to Other Social Justice Issues," Mercy for Animals, July 28, 2017, https://mercyforanimals.org/heres-how-veganism-is-undeniably-linked-to.

No, this is not a parody site. This is a real article posted on a real website to be read by real people who nod in real agreement with these unreal claims. *This* is the Critical Social Justice worldview in action.

While few evangelicals promote veganism as social justice, plenty of them promote the worldview behind it. Consequently, several CSJ issues have become part of the evangelical landscape, and more will in the future. In the remainder of this chapter, I will address one of them: Abortion. My goal here is to show the clear link between this issue and the CSJ movement, as well as the evidence of a subtle shift in popular evangelical circles that coincides with the influence of CT/CRT/I in recent years.

Abortion

We touched on abortion previously, focusing on it as a cultural issue in the black community. Here, I want to address the broader question of abortion as it relates to the Critical Social Justice movement and how evangelicals are migrating toward the CSJ pro-abortion position, or at least the rationales that support it.

The abortion debate is strangely absent in the conversation of most Social Justice Christians, and with good reason. While abortion is the number one killer of black people in America (and there is most assuredly a connection to racist, Malthusian eugenics), to the broader Social Justice movement, *access to* abortion is the key issue. In an article titled "Abortion: A Matter of Human Rights and Social Justice," Women on Web notes that the World Health Organization "affirms that medicines used for medical abortion are among essential medicines, which should be available in every country."[6] "Abortion is a social justice issue," says SafeAbortionWomensRight.org, "in that criminalizing, restricting or stigmatising abortion creates barriers that women with unwanted pregnancies face in exercising body autonomy." And in a nod to Intersection-

---

[6] Constitution of the World Health Organization, https://apps.who.int/gb/bd/PDF/bd47/EN/constitution-en.pdf?ua=1.

ality, it adds, "Often these barriers are even greater for women of colour, young women and poor women."[7] The Reproductive Health Access Project leaves no doubt as to its overall political philosophy, noting that the organization "condemns anti-Black, state-sanctioned violence and the brutal murders of Breonna Taylor, George Floyd, Tony McDade, Ahmaud Arbery, David McAtee, and of countless other Black folks lost to the system of white supremacy upon which this country was founded." They finally state, "We stand in solidarity with the Black Lives Matter movement, Black protesters, organizers, and colleagues."[8]

Ironically, the availability of abortion is actually a bit of an embarrassment to the Critical Social Justice movement since, in many ways, it disproves the assertion of disparate impact. For example, if justice equals access to abortion and black women have disproportionate access (that is, they comprise just 12 percent of the population, but have more than 35 percent of the abortions),[9] doesn't that mean America, at least in this area, is … just?

Nevertheless, as the Christian Social Justice movement continues to move along parallel lines with its anti-Christian counterpart, it will have to cross this issue. Unfortunately, the evidence seems to indicate that this is a case of "bad company ruins good morals" (1 Corinthians 15:33).

An example of this is Jesse Jackson. We have already seen his very surprising pro-life quote from 1977 in a previous chapter. However, there is more. He would go on to write, "Human beings cannot give or create life by themselves, it is really a gift from God. Therefore, one does not have the right to take away (through abortion) that which he does not

---

[7] "On World Day of Social Justice, Why Is Access to Safe Abortion a Social Justice Issue?" International Campaign for Women's Right to Safe Abortion, February 19, 2017, https://www.safeabortionwomensright.org/blog/world-social-justice-day.

[8] "From Abortion Rights to Social Justice," Reproductive Health Access Project, May 15, 2018, https://www.reproductiveaccess.org/2018/05/abortion-rights-social-justice.

[9] Susan A. Cohen, "Abortion and Women of Color: The Bigger Picture," *Guttmacher Policy Review* 11, no. 3, August 6, 2008, https://www.guttmacher.org/gpr/2008/08/abortion-and-women-color-bigger-picture.

have the ability to give."[10] However, as his commitment to the social justice movement (and the political left) grew, Jackson eventually would abandon his pro-life stance.

"Fighting social injustice, by caring for migrants and the poor, is just as holy a pursuit for Catholics as opposing abortion," declared Pope Francis in a major one-hundred-page document the Vatican issued in April 2018[11] to discourage so-called "single-issue voting." Likewise, Bishop Mark J. Seitz of El Paso, Texas, argued that "in pursuit of 'single-issue' strategies to end abortion," many Christians "scandalously turned a blind eye to real breakdowns in solidarity and dehumanizing policies, including crackdowns on worker rights and voting rights, the slashing of social support for the poor and sick, racism and the exploitation of immigrants and the environment."[12]

Among Protestants, Jim Wallis, who also decries single-issue voting, is an example of one who holds firmly to liberalism, liberation theology, and the Critical Social Justice movement while attempting to straddle the fence on abortion. Wallis outlines his view in his book *The Great Awakening*, where he writes in favor of "protecting unborn life in every possible way, but without criminalizing abortion." Wallis is a staunch progressive and loyal Democrat, so there is little surprise he holds and promotes such a compromised view. What concerns me is the fact that many in more conservative evangelical circles have begun to promote something similar.

In a series of tweets issued in September 2020 that set off a massive debate about "single-issue voting," Tim Keller appeared to be advancing

---

[10] "From Abortion Rights to Social Justice."

[11] Philip Pullella, "Fighting Social Injustice Is as Important as Fighting Abortion; Pope," Reuters, April 9, 2018, https://www.reuters.com/article/us-pope-document-holiness/fighting-social-injustice-as-important-as-fighting-abortion-idUSKBN1HG1BE.

[12] Bishop Mark J. Seitz, "Bishop Seitz: Single-Issue Voting Has Corrupted Christian Political Witness," *Jesuit Review*, September 30, 2020, https://www.americamagazine.org/politics-society/2020/09/28/bishop-seitz-el-paso-catholics-single-issue-voting-election-2020-biden-trump.

an argument for a more Wallis-like position when he wrote, "The Bible tells me that abortion is a sin and great evil, but it doesn't tell me the best way to decrease or end abortion in this country, nor which policies are most effective."[13] He went on to say:

> The current political parties offer a potpourri of different positions on these and many, many other topics, most of which, as just noted, the Bible does not speak to directly. This means when it comes to taking political positions, voting, determining alliances and political involvement, the Christian has liberty of conscience. Christians cannot say to other Christians "no Christian can vote for …" or "every Christian must vote for …" unless you can find a Biblical command to that effect.[14]

Set aside for a moment the fact that "Thou shalt not kill" is a pretty clear "Biblical command to that effect," and let's put this in a bit of context. First, let's look at the two political parties which, according to Keller, "offer a potpourri of different positions on these … issues." Remember, the primary issue Keller is addressing is abortion. Is it true that the Democrat and Republican platforms offer "a potpourri of different positions" on abortion? The answer is a resounding no! From the Democratic Platform:

> Democrats believe every woman should be able to access high-quality reproductive health care services, including safe and legal abortion. We oppose and will fight to overturn

---

[13] Tim Keller (@timkellernyc), "Some folks are missing the point of this thread. The Bible tells me that abortion is a sin and great evil, but it doesn't tell me the best way to decrease or end abortion in this country, nor which policies are most effective," Twitter, September 16, 2020, 11:24 p.m., https://twitter.com/tim-kellernyc/status/1306433746606977024.

[14] Ibid.

federal and state laws that create barriers to women's reproductive health and rights, including by repealing the Hyde
Amendment and protecting and codifying the right to reproductive freedom.

From the Republican Platform:

We support a human life amendment to the Constitution and
legislation to make clear that the Fourteenth Amendment's
protections apply to children before birth.

We oppose the use of public funds to perform or promote
abortion or to fund organizations, like Planned Parenthood,
so long as they provide or refer for elective abortions or sell fetal
body parts rather than provide healthcare. We urge all states
and Congress to make it a crime to acquire, transfer, or sell
fetal tissues from elective abortions for research, and we call
on Congress to enact a ban on any sale of fetal body parts. In
the meantime, we call on Congress to ban the practice of misleading women on so-called fetal harvesting consent forms, a
fact revealed by a 2015 investigation. We will not fund or
subsidize healthcare that includes abortion coverage.

Far from being a "potpourri of different positions," this is a clear-cut
distinction between two competing worldviews. The two statements
couldn't be more different!

This leads to a second issue: Keller's history and the insight it gives
to his motives in this matter.

Keller has had no problem making clear, unambiguous, authoritative
statements on a host of moral issues from the CRT/I perspective. For
instance, in a recent panel discussion, he declared, "If you have white
skin, it's worth $1 million over a lifetime." This is quite hyperbolic, and
the same has been said about having a college degree, being a man, and
being married (though the last two aren't usually valued at the same

dollar figure), but that is beside the point. What Keller said next is pertinent to the current discussion: "[White people] have to say, 'We don't deserve this!'"

Not "You need to find a biblical command to that effect," but, "you have to say ..." Keller goes on to clarify that white Christians must conclude, "I am the product of and standing on the shoulders of other people *who got that through injustice* ... the Bible says you are involved in injustice ... even if you didn't actually do it."[15] Remember, he is speaking about having "white skin." Your family never owned slaves? Doesn't matter. You have family who fought and died for the Union in the Civil War? Doesn't matter. Your family came here after slavery, segregation, and Jim Crow? Doesn't matter. You are descended from Jews who immigrated to the U.S. to flee oppression after World War II? Doesn't matter! The only thing that matters is "white skin."

To sum up: abortion is a complex web of political potpourri that requires nuance and wisdom, but white privilege, (generational) white guilt, and the need to repent of it is so clear that Keller can use words like "you have to" and "you must."

David Platt, whom we heard from earlier, wrote a book timed for release before the 2020 presidential election titled *Before You Vote*. In it, he recalls a discussion he had with a pastor who said, "In my church, voting for a Democrat could be cause for removal from the church."[16] The pastor asked Platt plainly: "How can a Christian vote for a candidate from a party that holds abortion as a key tenet of their platform?" Platt's response was quite telling: "I considered the implications of the question.... Yes, abortion is abhorrent. That's clear in the Bible.... But is that *the only issue* at stake in an election?"

Then he gets to the heart of the matter. "What about the scores of Christians, including overwhelming percentages of African-American

---

[15] Protestia, "Tim Keller: If You Have White Skin, the Bible Says You're Involved in Injustice," Vimeo, https://vimeo.com/459445613.

[16] David Platt, *Before You Vote: Seven Questions Every Christian Should Ask* (Washington, D.C.: Radical, Inc., Kindle Edition, 2020), 42.

Christians, who consistently vote for Democrats *because of the party's record on other issues that they also deem biblically important?*"[17] Unfortunately, Platt does not enumerate these issues. But others have.

Pro-Life Evangelicals for Biden, led by Fuller Seminary President Emeritus Richard Mouw and touting signatories like Ron Sider, Richard Foster, and John Perkins, echoes the same sentiment. They actually list some of the issues they believe are as important as taking the lives of the unborn, and it looks eerily similar to the CSJ lists I mentioned at the beginning of this chapter:

> Many things that good political decisions could change destroy persons created in the image of God and violate the sanctity of human life. Poverty kills millions every year. So does lack of health care and smoking. Racism kills. Unless we quickly make major changes, devastating climate change will kill tens of millions. Poverty, lack of accessible health care services, smoking, racism and climate change are all pro-life issues.... Therefore we *oppose "one issue" political thinking* because it lacks biblical balance.

The group goes on to add "affordable childcare" and "a minimum wage that lifts workers out of poverty," believing that these policies are more pro-life than—well, being pro-life—because "the most common reason women give for abortion is the financial difficulty of another child."

9Marks founder Mark Dever and editor Jonathan Leeman had an on-stage discussion about single-issue voting in February 2019,[18] during which Dever set off controversy when he opined:

---

[17] Platt, *Before You Vote*, 42.

[18] Although 9Marks went on to address this issue more thoroughly (see "What Makes a Vote Moral or Immoral: The Ethics of Voting," https://www.9marks. org/article/what-makes-a-vote-moral-or-immoral-the-ethics-of-voting), the

African American Christian voters realized a long time ago
that there are going to be a bunch of different issues affecting
us. So I can support a candidate I don't agree with on some
issues, which nothing may get done about anyway, *because I
do agree on other issues where they can help do something.*
Can we, even if we don't accept the position ourselves, can
we make room for that in our church as a morally legitimate
argument and option? (emphasis mine)[19]

Dever would go on to add, "Many white Christians act like [single-
issue voting] is the only morally legitimate way of voting ... I would
certainly like to question that."[20] And therein lies the rub.

First, note how similar these statements are to Platt's. They both
reference "issues" that African American Christians prioritize over
abortion, though neither enumerates those issues. One can only
assume that they would include at least some of those articulated by
Pro-Life Evangelicals for Biden, but we don't know. Dever and Platt
are also concerned with "making room" for Christians who vote
pro-choice.

Second, note that both Dever and Platt ascribe altruistic motives to
black Christians who vote pro-choice and a type of blindness to white
Christians who vote "single-issue." I would take issue with Dever's (and
Platt's) characterization of "African American Christian voters." As
noted earlier, there has been a massive shift in the black community away
from the pro-life position. Personally, I find that I rarely encounter black
Christians who are staunchly pro-life. Among my family, my friends,
and my black ministerial acquaintances, I frequently find that my pro-life
position puts me in the extreme minority (pardon the pun). This became

---

statement is worth analyzing—especially since most people have seen the video,
but haven't read the journal article.

[19] Stop and Think about It, "Mark Dever on One Issue Voting," YouTube, September 13, 2019, https://www.youtube.com/watch?v=cuquvpUEsWE.

[20] Ibid.

painfully clear to me during my time as a professor at the College of Biblical Studies (CBS) in Houston.

At the time, CBS was the largest multi-ethnic Bible college in the United States. Seventy percent of our students were black or Hispanic. One of the classes I taught was Biblical Worldview. Every semester, I addressed the issue of abortion, and every semester, I was disappointed to find the overwhelming majority of the black pastors and church leaders in my class held pro-choice positions. I considered it a win if I had a class with a 50/50 pro-life, pro-choice split among my black students. The idea that most black Christians are voting Democrat in spite of their pro-life convictions is, at best, an overstatement.

I have also witnessed this reality in my work with pro-life ministries. I have preached at many crisis pregnancy center banquets over the years. A common refrain I hear is, "I hope some of our black pastors will come to hear you." As it turns out, most pro-life ministries have a hard time gaining traction with black pastors and churches. These conversations didn't just happen with white Christians. Black board members and volunteers were just as likely to raise this issue.

Finally, I find it rare, in my experience, to run into staunchly pro-life black voters who, for the sake of other issues on which they agree with pro-choice candidates, will do the kind of political calculus Dever and Platt suggest. In 2008 and 2012, black voters voted for Obama 1) because he was a Democrat and 2) because he was black (not necessarily in that order). In 2016, they voted for Hillary supposedly 1) because she was a Democrat and 2) because Trump was "a racist." However, I didn't hear much angst over her position on abortion. Add to this the fact that the largest black denomination, the National Baptist Convention USA, has no official position on abortion and most of the other predominantly black denominations equivocate on it,[21] and the claim of complex political calculus seems dubious at best.

---

[21] See Clare Hepler, "Churches & Abortion," Juicy Ecumenism, January 24, 2020, https://juicyecumenism.com/2020/01/24/churches-abortion. Church of God in Christ: opposes abortion except "in the rare case where mother's life is threatened, abortion is licit as a last resort." National Baptist Convention of

Whether it is Platt, Dever, Wallis, Seitz, Keller, Pro-Life Evangelicals for Biden, or Pope Francis, my big problem with this entire line of argumentation is that "single-issue voting" is a straw man. I am not, nor have I ever met, a single-issue voter. Issues like same-sex marriage, school choice, and religious freedom, to name a few, are all very serious issues to Christian voters. And these voters are more than narrow-minded fundamentalists being led around by the nose for the sake of a single issue. Moreover, this line of argumentation makes light of the vast chasm between the platforms of the two parties on major moral issues while extoling the virtues of sophisticated black voters who carefully weigh important (yet unnamed) issues that white voters apparently do not comprehend.

However, even if abortion were an example of single-issue voting, I reject the idea that murdering the unborn can be subjugated in favor of social issues that are being promoted through the lens of Critical Social Justice. In other words, if I were going to be a single-issue voter, that single issue would be the murder of the unborn.

According to Live Action, an estimated 2,363 pre-born children will die in America today. Every ninety seconds, a child is aborted at a Planned Parenthood facility somewhere in our nation. Under current federal law, pre-born children can be aborted up until the point of birth. A preborn person's life can be ended for any reason.[22] And in the last five years that I have lived in Zambia, I have seen how the UN has worked to advance the same eugenics-based, black- and brown-targeting, abortion-at-any-stage-and-for-any-reason ideology throughout Africa. I think Owen Strachan had it right when, after the first Trump/Biden debate in 2020, he tweeted, "I get the

---

America: is unclear on abortion. AME: "admits exceptions where the mother's life is in danger or a pregnancy from rape or incest." Progressive National Baptist Convention: "opposes abortion outside of reasons of maternal health or fetal disease." AME Zion: opposes with "the exception of the health of the mother or fetal abnormality."

[22] See Live Action, https://www.liveaction.org.

'democracy is being coarsened' point. What an awkward event! But mark this: the moral abomination of abortion has coarsened and soiled America to an untold degree. No other modern evil comes close. Defeat abortion. Vote pro-life."[23]

To those who argue that being pro-life must be about more than abortion, allow me to say a hearty amen! I believe being pro-life should be a comprehensive commitment for the follower of Christ. I also understand that overturning *Roe v. Wade* will not end abortion in America. It simply will return the issue to the individual states, and many will choose to keep abortion legal. While that breaks my heart, I am happy to save every single child I can. I am not a social justice warrior, but I believe God meant it when He said, "Learn to do good; seek justice, correct oppression; bring justice to the fatherless, plead the widow's cause" (Isaiah 1:17). But I don't believe He called me to use the government as a proxy. God calls His people to be His hands and feet in this regard. Believing this transformed my life and that of my family to the tune of adopting seven newborns in nine years as an expression of our pro-life commitment.

We became aware that there was a dearth of black families participating in adoption, so we made ourselves available. After the first adoption, we never had to pursue another. Word got out in the adoption world that a black family was available and "home study ready,"[24] and our phone continued to ring. We received calls from all over the country. We had to turn down several children due to the fact that we were

---

[23] Owen Strachan (@ostrachan), "On the Trump/Biden debate, I get the 'democracy is being coarsened' point. What an awkward event! But mark this: the moral abomination of abortion has coarsened and soiled America to an untold degree. No other modern evil comes close. Defeat abortion. Vote pro-life," Twitter, October 1, 2020, 6:25 p.m., https://twitter.com/ostrachan/status/1311794344429531136.

[24] Adoptive families have to go through an investigative process called a "home study" in order to be approved to adopt. This process can take months, so adoptions that come up suddenly are often very difficult to place. This is especially true if a birth mother specifically requests a black family for her baby. Therefore, "home study–ready" black families are like gold in the adoption world.

engaged in other adoptions at the time. We have also had the privilege of influencing several other families to enter the adoption arena. We couldn't intervene for every child, but we could intervene for some.

So yes, I agree wholeheartedly that being pro-life should go beyond just being anti-abortion. However, it must start there.

I also agree that single-issue voting is irresponsible, but we all know that nobody does that. So why are so many leading evangelicals addressing the issue? I cannot speak for them, but I do have an idea. It is based on several conversations I have had with pastors, ministry leaders, and others dealing with CSJ in their churches, organizations, and families.

Allow me to give you a scenario—one that I have faced numerous times. A pastor is leading a church that he has served for many years. It is a growing multiethnic congregation characterized by broad unity and shared vision. Then the 2008, 2012, and 2016 elections come. In the first two, the overwhelming majority of his black members vote for Obama in spite of his record on abortion, same-sex "marriage," and the broader LGBTQIA+ agenda, to name a few topics. Yet the Church didn't divide, and the leaders of the evangelical movement didn't write articles or participate in panel discussions about black "single-issue" voters (in this instance, the single issue is melanin). Then 2016 happens.

The 2016 elections took place in the wake of several high-profile killings of unarmed black men and the establishment and meteoric rise of Black Lives Matter. Also, race relations had plummeted during Obama's presidency.[25] We know 81 percent of white evangelicals voted for Trump in 2016. Obama received 26 percent and 21 percent of the white evangelical vote in 2008 and 2012, respectively.

---

[25] Overall, 54 percent say relations between blacks and whites have gotten worse since Obama became president, including 57 percent of whites and 40 percent of blacks. See Jennifer Agiesta, "Most Say Race Relations Worsened under Obama, Poll Finds," CNN, October 6, 2016, https://edition.cnn.com/2016/10/05/politics/obama-race-relations-poll/index.html. See also Henry Khachatrian, "A Complete Timeline of Race Relations under Obama," Daily Wire, January 9, 2017, https://www.dailywire.com/news/complete-timeline-race-relations-under-obama-harry-khachatrian.

Unlike the black people in the Church voting for Obama, white evangelicals voting for Trump in 2016 was a fault line. Suddenly, black church members felt afraid. "As an African American who dedicates countless hours and vital energy to racial reconciliation, I feel betrayed," said Jemar Tisby, reacting to the 2016 result. "I mistakenly assumed that American Christians understood each other better across racial lines."[26] Thabiti Anyabwile said, "Mr. Trump's election was ... the worse possible outcome in my mind."[27] A letter signed by seventy-four black church leaders called white evangelicals who voted for Trump a "radical faction."[28] They couldn't possibly have voted for him out of concerns over Hillary's radical policies, Benghazi, email servers, the corrupt Clinton political machinery, the desire to have a businessman and outsider who wouldn't back down against the left or the press, or even sheer pragmatism. It had to be racism! And I say this as someone who supported Ted Cruz in the 2016 primary. I even attended a private Cruz campaign event and lamented the pragmatism of evangelicals who abandoned him in favor of Trump.

In the ensuing four years, the ideologies outlined in this book took root in leading evangelical circles. They also took root in local churches. As that happened, pastors and church leaders who had worked feverishly to establish relationships across ethnic lines, who had promoted, mentored, and discipled black leaders, and who had celebrated diversity in their churches and ministries began to see the fault lines. Suddenly, these pastors and leaders had a choice to make. Addressing these fault lines would result in catastrophic losses and sever cherished relationships—not to mention putting them at risk of being called "racist." Letting them lie

---

[26] Emily Lund, "Trump Won. Here's How 20 Evangelical Leaders Feel," *Christianity Today*, November 11, 2016, https://www.christianitytoday.com/ct/2016/november-web-only/trump-won-how-evangelical-leaders-feel.html.

[27] Ibid.

[28] Jason Lemon, "Black Christian Leaders Rebuke Evangelical Trump Supporters as a 'Radical Faction' in Open Letter," *Newsweek*, January 13, 2020, https://www.newsweek.com/black-christian-leaders-rebuke-evangelical-trump-supporters-radical-faction-open-letter-1481970.

often resulted in disputes in the Church as questions about how black Christians can, in good conscience, associate with neo-Marxist ideologies, policies, and candidates—and, of course, abortion—arose.

So what do you do? One possibility is to get out in front of it by equivocating. Teach your people that "it's not that simple." Argue for a moral equivalency between Joe Biden's pro-abortion position and Trump's abrasive character. "I remain baffled," wrote John Piper in an October 22, 2020, article, "that so many Christians consider the sins of unrepentant sexual immorality (porneia), unrepentant boastfulness (alazoneia), unrepentant vulgarity (aischrologia), unrepentant factiousness (dichostasiai), and the like, to be only toxic for our nation, while policies that endorse baby-killing, sex-switching, freedom-limiting, and socialistic overreach are viewed as deadly."[29] Piper argues that Trump's danger lies in "a pattern of public behaviors that lead to death."

But is this legitimate? Is Trump's character the moral equivalent of the Democrat agenda? Or has Piper joined Dever, Leeman, Keller, and Platt on a fault line?

CRT and the DNC

In order to understand where I am coming from on this, it may help the reader to know a bit more of my history. I made several blog posts in 2008 opposing Obama's presidential candidacy, including one titled "Barack Obama: A Wolf in Sheep's Clothing."[30] The day after the election, I wrote:

---

[29] John Piper, "Policies, Persons, and Paths to Ruin: Pondering the Implications of the 2020 Election," Desiring God, October 22, 2020, https://www.desiringgod.org/articles/policies-persons-and-paths-to-ruin.

[30] Voddie Baucham, "Barack Obama: A Wolf in Sheep's Clothing," Voddie Baucham Ministries blog, May 9, 2015, https://web.archive.org/web/20160222005459/http://voddiebaucham.org/blog/post/barack-obama:-a-wolf-in-sheeps-clothing. The article date is 2015 because the original page is no longer available.

The people have spoken. Barack Hussein Obama has been elected the 44th President of the United States of America. The left-wing press is ecstatic, white guilt has been assuaged, Affirmative Action has been vindicated, and socialist Europe loves us again. Now comes the rub.... It ain't over! If you think this means that the "America is a racist society" crowd will have to shut up, you've got another thing coming. In fact, watch the press closely in the coming days. There will be a concerted effort to press the opposite point. Jesse Jackson (who said he wanted to castrate Obama a couple of months ago because he had the audacity to call black fathers to account), Al Sharpton, and their ilk will argue that this is merely proof that policies like Affirmative Action work, and that such efforts need to be redoubled; not abandoned. They believe we need to continue telling young black boys and girls that they are not smart enough, good enough, industrious enough, capable enough, and America is not "fair" enough for them to succeed without special help that their white (or Asian) counterparts don't need.[31]

Then, as now, I believed neo-Marxist ideology poses a far greater threat to America than race relations. I also see a connection between the infiltration of woke/antiracist ideology and soft-selling the danger of progressive politics.

Remember where we started this chapter? The Critical Social Justice movement goes far beyond just race. As Peggy McIntosh, the mother of the modern white privilege doctrine, wrote, "[S]ince race and sex are not the only advantaging systems at work, we need similarly to examine the daily experience of having age advantage, or ethnic advantage, or physical ability, or advantage related to nationality, religion, or sexual

---

[31] Voddie Baucham, "A Nation of Cowards," Voddie Baucham Ministries blog, May 9, 2015, https://web.archive.org/web/20150918235537/http://www.voddie-baucham.org/blog/post/a-nation-of-cowards. Again, this is an archived article.

orientation." Let's just say the 2020 Democratic National Convention would make McIntosh proud.

Like all political events, this one opened with a nod to God in the form of opening prayers. At the DNC, that task fell upon my fellow Southwestern Seminary alumnus and open-borders advocate Freddie Haynes. "You had the nerve to build a wall while at the same time you have in a harbor there in New York a statue saying, 'Give me your poor, your tired, your huddled masses yearning to breathe free,'" prayed Haynes, a Dallas pastor and long-time civil rights activist, before adding, "Jesus would say, 'America, if you don't get your act together, you may well go to hell.'"

The Pledge of Allegiance at the DNC included the word "someday" at the end but omitted the words "under God." Though many deny the fact, even Snopes acknowledged that "[t]he phrase 'under God' was omitted from at least two recitations of the Pledge of Allegiance at individual caucus meetings during the DNC in 2020."[32] It happened at both the Muslim Delegates & Allies Assembly and the LGBT Caucus meeting. For the National Anthem, participants were told, "You may rise or kneel if you are able, or your preference." I am not nearly as concerned about disrespect for the flag or the national anthem as I am about the deeper issue. All of this was emblematic of the radical, progressive, CRT/I-laden atmosphere that characterized the proceedings.

One speaker was J. Mai, a Duke University student whose preferred pronouns are they/them and who identifies as a "Black-Vietnamese, transgender nonbinary/gender transcendent mermaid Queen-King, currently living out 'their' ever-evolving truths in Winston Salem."[33] Mai recently became a "licensed minister in the Progressive National Baptist

---

[32] Dan Evon, "Did Democrats Omit 'Under God' from the Pledge of Allegiance?" Snopes.com, August 21, 2020, https://www.snopes.com/fact-check/democrats-under-god-pledge.

[33] Debra Heine, "DNC Panel Features 'Mermaid Queen-King' Who Calls for the Abolition of ICE, Police, and Prisons," American Greatness, August 19, 2020, https://amgreatness.com/2020/08/19/dnc-panel-features-mermaid-queen-king-who-calls-for-the-abolition-of-ice-police-and-prisons.

Church." In a caucus meeting, Mai made it clear that those who say the cry to "defund the police" is really just a call for redistributing, retraining, and refocusing police efforts are either misinformed or dishonest. "We're talking about abolishing the police, we're talking about abolishing ICE, we're talking about abolishing prisons...."[34]

During the DNC LGBTQ Caucus Meeting, trans activist Marisa Richmond reiterated the Democrats' position on, among other things, transgender participation in school sports. This is the very ideology that has led to girls being left off the podium at track meets as trans athletes take state championships,[35] girls' high school field hockey and soccer being in danger of being completely transformed, and in one instance, a male-to-female trans MMA fighter breaking his female opponent's skull.[36]

Then there was the Democratic Party Platform. A few planks are worth mentioning here:

> We recognize that quality, affordable comprehensive health care; medically accurate, *LGBTQ+ inclusive, age-appropriate sex education*; and the full range of family planning services are all essential to ensuring that people can decide if, when, and how to start a family.
>
> Democrats will … restore nondiscrimination protections for LGBTQ+ people and people living with HIV/AIDS in health insurance, including coverage of *all medically necessary care for gender transition.*

---

[34] Heine, "DNC Panel Features 'Mermaid Queen-King'."

[35] Pat Eaton-Robb, "Transgender Sprinters Finish 1st, 2nd, at Connecticut Girls Indoor Track Championships," *Washington Times*, February 24, 2019, https://www.washingtontimes.com/news/2019/feb/24/terry-miller-andraya-yearwood-transgender-sprinter.

[36] BJJ World, "Transgender MMA Fighter Breaks Skull of Her Female Opponent. Are We Becoming Too Careful Not to Offend Any Group of People," BJJ World, October 21, 2018, https://bjj-world.com/transgender-mma-fighter-fallon-fox-breaks-skull-of-her-female-opponent.

We will also take action to guarantee that LGBTQ+ people and those living with HIV/AIDS have full access to needed
health care and resources, including by requiring that federal
health plans provide coverage for HIV/AIDS testing and treatment and HIV prevention medications like PrEP and PEP,
gender confirmation surgery, and hormone therapy.
We will work to ensure LGBTQ+ people are not discrimi-
nated against when seeking to adopt or foster children, protect LGBTQ+ children from bullying and assault, and
*guarantee transgender students' access to facilities based on
their gender identity.*
Recognizing that LGBTQ+ youth and adults suffer from
significant health disparities, including mental health and
substance use disorders, Democrats will expand mental health
and suicide prevention services, and ban harmful "conversion
therapy" practices. We will ensure that all transgender and
non-binary people can procure official government identifica-
tion documents that accurately reflect their gender identity
(emphasis mine).

I do not believe the Republicans are beyond reproach. In fact, the
same year I spoke out against Obama, I made waves with another article
in which I chided evangelicals who condemned John McCain's character,
then reversed themselves when he picked Sarah Palin as his running mate.
That piece landed me on Fox News, where the host, expecting me to
whale on the Republicans, almost swallowed her tongue when I pointed
out that Obama was the most radically pro-abortion candidate ever to
run for president.

My point here is this: The Critical Social Justice Movement is vast. Its
influence is broad and deep within evangelical circles. And as that influence
grows, it is causing some among us to make alliances we never would have
forged in the past. A lot of it has to do with the fact that we are afraid to
be called racist or end up "on the wrong side of history" on the race issue.

Unfortunately, some have found themselves on the wrong side of the present. In the next chapter, I will offer a roadmap for moving ahead.

But before I do, allow me to share a part of President Trump's executive order against Critical Race Theory, issued on September 22, 2020. It defines the tenets of CRT/I against which it stands:

> (1) one race or sex is inherently superior to another race or sex; (2) the United States is fundamentally racist or sexist; (3) an individual, by virtue of his or her race or sex, is inherently racist, sexist, or oppressive, whether consciously or unconsciously; (4) an individual should be discriminated against or receive adverse treatment solely or partly because of his or her race or sex; (5) members of one race or sex cannot and should not attempt to treat others without respect to race or sex; (6) an individual's moral character is necessarily determined by his or her race or sex; (7) an individual, by virtue of his or her race or sex, bears responsibility for actions committed in the past by other members of the same race or sex; (8) any individual should feel discomfort, guilt, anguish, or any other form of psychological distress on account of his or her race or sex; or (9) meritocracy or traits such as a hard work ethic are racist or sexist, or were created by a particular race to oppress another race. The term "divisive concepts" also includes any other form of race or sex stereotyping or any other form of race or sex scapegoating.[37]

I continue to be disappointed and at times offended by Trump's behavior. However, as I watch the fault lines of CRT/I shift beneath our feet, I must say I am grateful to God for having put him where he is, for such a time as this. Oh, that more pastors would see the threat

---

[37] "Executive Order on Combating Race and Sex Stereotyping," White House, September 22, 2020, https://www.whitehouse.gov/presidential-actions/executive-order-combating-race-sex-stereotyping.

this clearly and respond to it this boldly! But that is not an issue the president can fix.

CHAPTER TEN

Restoration and Mitigation

By some estimates, the [2010 Haiti] quake left about 33 million cubic yards of debris in Port-au-Prince—more than seven times the amount of concrete used to build the Hoover Dam. [As of September 2010], only about 2 percent has been cleared, which means the city looks pretty much as it did a month after the Jan. 12 quake.[1]

My goal in this chapter is not to offer alternative solutions to America's (or the Church's) "racial injustice problem." I don't believe we have one. I believe there is racism. I believe there are racists. However, I reject the idea that America is "characterized by racism," or that racism is an unavoidable byproduct of our national DNA. In fact, I believe America is one of the least racist countries in the world.

Moreover, the preponderance of evidence shared by those promoting racial justice as the pressing need of the day is rooted either in the

---

[1] Tamara Lush, "Months after Haiti Earthquake, Cleanup Has Barely Scratched Surface of Rubble Piles," Associated Press, September 13, 2010, https://www.cleveland.com/world/2010/09/months_after_haiti_earthquake.html.

assumptions of CRT/I, which views every disparity as *de facto* evidence of racism, or emotional appeals to "facts" that either complicate or completely disprove their claims (i.e., black men are being hunted down and killed). Indulge me while I share a poignant example: the "three-fifths human" myth.

In his book *The Color of Compromise*, Jemar Tisby writes, "Instead of acknowledging the full *humanity* and citizenship of black slaves, political leaders determined that each slave would count as three-fifths of a white citizen."[2] "We were called *three-fifths human* in the Constitution of the United States."[3] writes Latasha Morrison. *White Awake* author Daniel Hill shares, "When they referred to African Americans as *three-fifths human* in this Constitutional provision they literally dehumanized a group of people."[4]

But did they? This common refrain is so ubiquitous few ever question it. Perhaps if they did, people like Tisby, Morrison, and Hill would stop peddling this lie. One need not be an historian to dispel this myth. A simple Google search will suffice. Brittanica.com states:

> Having failed to secure the abolishment of slavery, some delegates from the Northern states sought to make representation dependent on the size of a state's free population. Southern delegates, on the other hand, threatened to abandon the convention if enslaved individuals were not counted. Eventually, the framers agreed on a compromise that called for representation in the House of Representatives to be apportioned on the basis of a state's free population plus three-fifths of its

---

[2] Jemar Tisby, *The Color of Compromise* (Grand Rapids, Michigan: Zondervan, Kindle Edition, 2019), 59. Interestingly, Tisby discusses the relevant issues and includes the relevant evidence, but still draws an inconsistent conclusion.

[3] Latasha Morrison, *Be the Bridge* (New York, New York: Crown Publishing Group, Kindle Edition, 2019), 152.

[4] Daniel Hill, *White Awake* (Westmont, Illinois: InterVarsity Press, Kindle Edition, 2017), 54.

enslaved population. This agreement came to be known as the three-fifths compromise.[5]

If you are not a fan of web searches, no need to worry. Reading the text of the Constitution will dispel this myth. Ironically, Tisby, Morrison, and Hill cite the amendment.[6] Again, one need not be a constitutional scholar in order to see through this myth:

> Representatives and direct Taxes shall be apportioned among the several States which may be included within this Union, according to their respective Numbers, which shall be determined by adding to the whole Number of free Persons, including those bound to Service for a term of years, and excluding Indians not taxed, three-fifths of all other Persons. (U.S. Constitution, Article 1, Section 2, Paragraph 3)

Dear reader, did you catch the last phrase, "three-fifths of all other *persons*"? No mention of the word "slave". No statement that slaves were three-fifths of a person. In fact, the statement affirms the personhood of those to whom it refers while allowing for only three-fifths of those "persons" to be included for the purpose of apportioning taxes and representatives. Anyone who says, as Morrison, Hill, and others do, that the U.S. Constitution calls slaves three-fifths human is ignorant at best. At worst, they are twisting historical facts in order to promote a CSJ view of U.S. history.

Historian David McCullough offers a piece of the puzzle that shines a light on the myth of "three-fifths human." "So another of the ironies of 1800," he writes in his award-winning biography *John Adams*, "was

---

[5] The Editors of Encyclopedia Britannica, "The Three-Fifths Compromise," *Encyclopedia Britannica*, https://www.britannica.com/topic/three-fifths-compromise.

[6] Morrison cites the Article in a footnote and Hill in his main text.

that Jefferson, the apostle of agrarian America who loathed cities, owed his ultimate political triumph [in the presidential election] to New York."

Here's the kicker: "[W]ere it not for the fact that in the South *three-fifths of the slaves were counted in apportioning the electoral votes*, Adams would have been reelected."[7] So the abolitionist Adams was defeated by the slaveholder Jefferson because of the three-fifths compromise that ended up giving Southern states greater representation. Nine of the first twelve presidents would come from Southern states—seven from Virginia and one each from North and South Carolina.

This book is, among many things, a plea to the Church. I believe we are being duped by an ideology bent on our demise. This ideology has used our guilt and shame over America's past, our love for the brethren, and our good and godly desire for reconciliation and justice as a means through which to introduce destructive heresies. We cannot embrace, modify, baptize, or Christianize these ideologies. We must identify, resist, and repudiate them. We cannot be held hostage through emotional blackmail and name-calling. Instead, we must "see to it that no one takes you captive by philosophy and empty deceit, according to human tradition, according to the elemental spirits of the world, and not according to Christ" (Colossians 2:8).

James Lindsay, one of the leading academic critics of the Critical Social Justice movement, offers a warning that the Church should heed:

> For the foreseeable future, online outrage mobs are going to happen, and they will … eventually target your organization. Your only chance of resisting them is to maintain a positive, anti-fragile, team-oriented internal culture that acts as a counterbalance that gets you through the storm (think about it like boarding up your windows against a rhetorical hurricane). That requires making use of organizational leadership to cultivate the right internal values—broadly liberal and

---

[7] David McCullough, *John Adams* (New York, New York: Simon & Schuster, Kindle Edition, 2001), 558.

anti-victimhood—and to treat them like a condition of employment or participation in your organization. Then, you can stand against this obnoxious pressure and keep fulfilling your organization's missions and purposes, as a team.[8]

It may surprise you to learn that Lindsay is an atheist. In fact, by his own admission, he used to be "an angry atheist." He was no fan of the Church. In conversations with him, I have been struck not only by the depth and breadth of his knowledge of the origins, history, and key influences and influencers of Critical Social Justice, but his keen understanding of how dangerous it is to Christianity. He often says jokingly, "If I was still an angry atheist and wanted to destroy the church ... I'd make 'em woke!" It is both ironic and sad that CSJ's attack on the Gospel is so clear that an atheist can see it, yet many churches, denominations, seminaries, leading ministries, and ministers have fallen prey to this movement.

But not all. In this chapter, I will lay out a brief biblical assessment of our current conflict. Then I will apply the principles from that assessment to a key fault line of our day: Black Lives Matter.

Thousands Have Not Bowed the Knee

"Be of good courage, and let us be courageous for our people" (2 Samuel 10:12), for many either have never bowed the knee, or have become "woke" to the dangers of wokeness. Unfortunately, that is usually the beginning of their real problems. I get emails and direct messages from pastors all the time asking, "How do I help my church navigate this mess?"

I wish I had an easy answer. Unfortunately, I believe this fault line is shifting and we have only begun to see the devastation that is coming. Churches are being split, but more will succumb. Ministries are

---

[8] James Lindsay, "How Your Organization Can Resist Woke Social Pressure," New Discourses, August 7, 2020, https://newdiscourses.com/2020/08/how-your-organization-can-resist-woke-social-pressure.

beginning to drift, but they will drift further, and others will join them. Families are being torn apart, and it will get worse. Seminary faculties and denominational factions are being balkanized, and the divide will only get wider. In some ways, American churches are beginning to look like Port-au-Prince after the 2010 quake.

Nevertheless, Critical Social Justice will not have the last word. God's Church will neither fall nor fail. It is "a pillar and buttress of the truth" (1 Timothy 3:15), and God's Word "is firmly fixed in the heavens" (Psalm 119:89). So we can hold on to hope because we know that "[t]he grass withers, the flower fades, but the word of our God will stand forever" (Isaiah 40:8). Therefore, I say with the Apostle Paul, "I am not ashamed, for I know whom I have believed, and I am convinced that he is able to guard until that day what has been entrusted to me" (2 Timothy 1:12).

That is why I wrote this book. I know God will save His people and vindicate His name. I also know that He will do it through Christians who heed the call to "Remember the Lord, who is great and awesome, and fight for your brothers, your sons, your daughters, your wives, and your homes" (Nehemiah 4:14).

We Are at War

Many modern Christians are uncomfortable with "war" language. Perhaps it is because of the aforementioned Eleventh Commandment: "Thou shalt be nice." As a result, anything that looks or sounds remotely aggressive, confrontational, or masculine is deemed "less than Christian." But the Bible is replete with war language (and actual war). And that language is appropriate here because we *are* at war—but we must not rely on ordinary tactics.

> For though we walk in the flesh, we are not waging war according to the flesh. For the weapons of our warfare are not of the flesh but have divine power to destroy strongholds. We destroy arguments and every lofty opinion raised against

the knowledge of God, and take every thought captive to obey Christ, being ready to punish every disobedience, when your obedience is complete. (2 Corinthians 10:3–6)

As we wage this war, the apostle's words will be our guide, and the Kingdom of God, His rule and reign in our lives and our world, will be our goal. But first, we must understand why we are at war. (Spoiler alert! We didn't start it.)

The Critical Social Justice War on Christianity

It is important to note that, in the Critical Social Justice view, the hegemonic power in the United States of America must include, but not be limited to, *all* of the following: white, male, heterosexual,[9] cisgendered,[10] able-bodied,[11] native-born, and Christian.

That's right: Christianity is part of the oppressive hegemony![12] And according to some, it is the *most pernicious* aspect of it; it has and maintains "privilege," and contributes to oppression.

One of the foundational CSJ textbooks, *Teaching for Diversity and Social Justice,* is a mainstay in schools of education. In it, the term "Christian privilege" refers to "the social advantages held by Christians in the U.S. who experience social and cultural advantages relative to non-Christians" derived from hegemony. Hence, it is rooted in "the assumptions underlying institutional rules and the collective consequences of following those rules,"

---

[9] "What Is Heterosexual Privilege?" University of Minnesota, https://www.d.umn.edu/~hrallis/professional/presentations/ally_training/het_privilege.htm.

[10] Sam Killerman, "30 Examples of Cisgender Privileges," It's Pronounced Metrosexual, https://www.itspronouncedmetrosexual.com/2011/11/list-of-cisgender-privileges.

[11] Beth Hendricks, "What Is Able-Bodied Privilege?" Study.com, https://study.com/academy/lesson/what-is-able-bodied-privilege-definition-examples.html.

[12] Maurianne Adams, Lee Anne Bell, and Pat Griffin, eds., *Teaching for Diversity and Social Justice* (London, United Kingdom: Taylor & Francis Group, Kindle Edition, 2007), 256.

and therefore, "is generally unacknowledged by those who hold it, because it is maintained through the pervasive but largely invisible culture of normative religious practices."[13] This is the classic Gramscian-Marxist view of hegemony.

Note how the language here is *exactly the same as the language used to describe white privilege*. That is because the underlying worldview of Critical Theory (and its parent, Conflict Theory) views all norms as not only man-made, but derived from, maintained by, and enforced through hegemonic power.

But these are just the radical, progressive, Neo-Marxist academics outside the Church, right? Wrong!

"Religious freedom … is really code for white Christians being able to do what they want to do," *The Color of Compromise* author Jemar Tisby told *Veggie Tales* creator-turned-antiracist activist Phil Vischer. Tisby added, "It doesn't really include Muslims or Jewish people or other religions."[14] This statement is patently false, considering that the United States has the world's largest Jewish population and has always led the world in religious freedom.

Tisby decries people who "deploy labels such as … Marxism … and critical race theory."[15] Well, now you know why!

In case you still can't see the overt war on Christianity, allow the authors of *Teaching for Diversity and Social Justice* to remove all doubt:

> The significance of Christianity in U.S. life and the challenges it poses for minority religions is a social justice issue that

---

[13] Adams, Bell, and Griffin, *Teaching for Diversity and Social Justice*, 256.

[14] Phil Vischer, "Holy Post Episode 422: The Church's Complicity in Racism with Jemar Tisby," YouTube, September 16, 2020, https://www.youtube.com/watch?v=j84RWjr8lM8.

[15] Jemar Tisby (@JemarTisby), "Opponents of racial justice often deploy labels such as Communism, Marxism, socialism, and critical race theory as attempts to set the limits of discourse and control the conversation. It's not new, but it is a resilient tactic that has deceived too many," Twitter, August 28, 2020, 12:09 p.m., https://twitter.com/JemarTisby/status/1299378580510650370.

requires the kind of historical knowledge and structural/ cultural analysis we use to understand other forms of oppression that stand in the way of social justice.[16]

In other words, substitute "Christian" for "white" and "people of color" for "other religions," then apply the exact same CSJ definitions, principles, standards, and approaches in order to deliver the oppressed from their oppressors. Houston, we have a problem!

How does this branch of the Critical Social Justice tree propose to deal with Christian hegemony and privilege? I think Neil Shenvi has it right when he warns, "If we give carte blanche to anyone waving the banner of antiracism or social justice, we may find ourselves committed to a whole host of ideas and causes whose legitimacy or wisdom we are no longer even permitted to question."[17] If white people need to "check their privilege," then Christians will soon be asked to do the same. Make no mistake about it—we are under attack.

Our War Is Spiritual

For though we walk in the flesh, we are not waging war according to the flesh. (2 Corinthians 10:3)

One reason Christians don't like the Bible's war language is our inability to get past the analogy. We hear words like "war," "fight," "battle," etc., and we immediately envision physical combat. However, the apostle is clearly using an analogy here. The Lord wants us to know that what is happening in the spiritual realm is best understood by its corollary in the physical realm: war. "For we do not wrestle against flesh

---

[16] Adams, Bell, and Griffin, *Teaching for Diversity and Social Justice*, 255.

[17] Neil Shenvi, "Compromised? A Long Review of Tisby's Color of Compromise," Neil Shenvi—Apologetics blog, https://shenviapologetics.com/ compromised-a-long-review-of-tisbys-color-of-compromise.

and blood, but against the rulers, against the authorities, against the cosmic powers over this present darkness, against the spiritual forces of evil in the heavenly places" (Ephesians 6:12).

I am not at war with the men, women, and ministries I have named in this book. I love them. Some of them are actually long-time personal friends. But I am at war with the ideology with which they have identified to one degree or another. I see Critical Race Theory, Intersectionality, Critical Social Justice, and their antecedents—Marxism, Conflict Theory, and Critical Theory—as "cosmic powers over this present darkness."

Our Weapons Are Spiritual

For the weapons of our warfare are not of the flesh.... (2 Corinthians 10:4)

The most important distinction between Christianity and antiracism is the nature of our weapons. And that is rooted in our different understanding of the nature of the war. When the antiracist speaks of "racial injustice," he is 1) assuming definitions inherent to CRT/I, 2) speaking about inequities that he believes can only arise from racism and oppression, and, therefore, 3) proposing solutions that are designed to re-engineer society in order to erase inequities.

We Fight with the Truth of the Gospel

As followers of Christ, we reject the idea that the sin of racism is entirely structural. We believe it is a problem of the human heart—and therefore, its only solution is the Gospel of Jesus Christ. There are most assuredly issues in the culture that are broken, and we should strive to repair them. However, the mission of the Church begins with and works through the hearts of men.

We Fight with the Truth of Biblical Justice

You shall not pervert justice. You shall not show partiality, and you shall not accept a bribe, for a bribe blinds the eyes of the wise and subverts the cause of the righteous. Justice, and only justice, you shall follow, that you may live and inherit the land that the Lord your God is giving you. (Deuteronomy 16:19–20)

We do not pursue equal outcomes, but righteous application of God's Law:

Owe no one anything, except to love each other, for the one who loves another has fulfilled the law. For the commandments, "You shall not commit adultery, You shall not murder, You shall not steal, You shall not covet," and any other commandment, are summed up in this word: "You shall love your neighbor as yourself." Love does no wrong to a neighbor; therefore love is the fulfilling of the law. (Romans 13:8–10)

We have an opportunity to say to a world seeking the false, inadequate, burdensome law of antiracism, "We have something better; something more." God's law in the life of the believer manifests as vertical and horizontal love: We love God, so we keep His commandments, and in doing so, we love our neighbor. This cannot be legislated.

We Fight with the Unity of the Body

One of the sad realities of antiracism is that it is 100 percent correct about race being a construct. But then it goes further by making everything about race. As followers of Christ, we are united to Christ *and* to one another:

But now in Christ Jesus you who once were far off have been brought near by the blood of Christ. For he himself is our peace, who has made us both one and has broken down in his flesh the dividing wall of hostility by abolishing the law of commandments expressed in ordinances, that he might create in himself one new man in place of the two, so making peace, and might reconcile us both to God in one body through the cross, thereby killing the hostility. And he came and preached peace to you who were far off and peace to those who were near. (Ephesians 2:13–17)

Our Weapons Are Powerful

For the weapons of our warfare ... have divine power to destroy strongholds. (2 Corinthians 10:4)

The weapons employed by antiracists in an effort to undo "systemic racism" are woefully inadequate. We know this because much has been done on that front already. "In reality," as Peter Kirsanow points out, "a massive, multi-billion-dollar apparatus [already] exists to identify and eliminate systemic, structural, institutional, and individual discrimination.... That apparatus has existed for more than half a century and continues to expand."[18] Kirsanow goes on to cite a dizzying list of departments, commissions, programs, and laws designed specifically to address so-called racial injustice:

It consists of, *inter alia*, the Civil Rights Division of the Department of Justice, the Civil Rights Division of the Department of Education, the Equal Employment Opportunity Commission,

---

[18] Peter Kirsanow, "The 'Systemic Racism' Canard," *National Review*, July 23, 2020, https://www.nationalreview.com/corner/the-systemic-racism-canard.

the Office of Federal Contract Compliance Programs, the FBI, state civil-rights commissions, local human-rights commissions, state attorneys general, and tens of thousands of investigators, enforcement and compliance officers, local prosecutors, and private attorneys who enforce a sprawling framework of civil-rights and equal-opportunity laws. These laws include, but are not limited to, Title VII of the 1964 Civil Rights Act, Sections 1981, 1982, and 1983 of the Civil Rights Acts of 1866 and 1871, the 14th Amendment, the 15th Amendment, the Fair Housing Act, the Voting Rights Act, and thousands of state and local equal-opportunity and anti-discrimination laws. This mammoth regime doesn't even include the tens of thousands of human-resource officers and diversity and inclusion personnel who guard against systemic/structural racism within their respective institutions.[19]

As we saw previously, Ibram X. Kendi wants to add a constitutional amendment and a new federal department (with state and local authority) to this behemoth.

We, on the other hand, have weapons with unimaginable power. When Paul wrote 2 Corinthians, the world knew only two ways to deal with fortresses: deception (as in the Trojan horse) or siege, which could last weeks, months, or even years as an attacking army built siege works, looked for weak points, and waited for the stronghold's supplies to dry up. None of the apostle's original audience could conceive of a single weapon that would destroy a stronghold.

Of course, you and I have pictures of mushroom clouds burned indelibly into our minds. We can easily conceive of a weapon powerful enough to take out a fortress. However, that is not Paul's point. He is saying that whatever the most powerful defense you can imagine, our weapons are more formidable. And whatever weapon you can conceive

---

[19] Kirsanow, "The 'Systemic Racism' Canard."

of pales in comparison to the weapons of our warfare. Nor does the Bible leave us in the dark as to what those weapons are:

> Stand therefore, having fastened on the belt of truth, and having put on the breastplate of righteousness, and, as shoes for your feet, having put on the readiness given by the gospel of peace. In all circumstances take up the shield of faith, with which you can extinguish all the flaming darts of the evil one; and take the helmet of salvation, and the sword of the Spirit, which is the word of God, praying at all times in the Spirit, with all prayer and supplication. To that end, keep alert with all perseverance, making supplication for all the saints. (Ephesians 6:14–18)

Truth, righteousness, the gospel of peace, the shield of faith, the helmet of salvation, the sword of the Spirit (which is the Word of God), and prayer. If you have been paying attention, you have heard these weapons mocked by big-name evangelicals who call them "simplistic." These things are all fine, they say, but they won't cure racial injustice—as though racial injustice is a new sin that escaped God's attention until now. However, nothing we face today is too powerful for our aforementioned weapons; we just have to know how to deploy them. And that is precisely what comes next.

We Must Destroy Arguments and Speculations

> We destroy arguments and every lofty opinion raised against the knowledge of God. (2 Corinthians 10:5)

The truth is not only to be believed; it is to be deployed. Our atheist friend James Lindsay once again offers sage advice:

The last thing you want to do is bring in a critical diversity, anti-racism, or bias training … because the core purpose of these trainings is to create a subset of your organizational culture that is sympathetic to the (highly seductive) critical view while generating a few genuine agitators and activists— while disarming possible dissenters by, in some cases, creating a paper trail of their "problematic" objections to the training materials.[20]

One of the biggest problems with antiracism is the fact that it is law-based. It condemns based on melanin, and although it constantly uses the words, it holds out no hope of salvation, restoration, or reconciliation. "A few Facebook posts and a sermon or two are not gonna dismantle racism in all its forms," said World Vision Executive Director Michael Chitwood, "but rather it will take a lifelong commitment from each one of us to do everything in our power in all that God is calling us to, day after day, year after year."[21]

Because antiracism is law-based, its ultimate end is changing and establishing laws, then enforcing those laws authoritatively. The leader of the antiracist movement, Ibram X. Kendi, has gone so far as to outline a specific plan of action in keeping with this theological reality, as we saw in Chapter Five.

Nowhere has this been clearer than in evangelicalism's willingness to embrace Black Lives Matter. The number of evangelical leaders jumping on the BLM bandwagon is dizzying. I'm not saying that everyone

---

[20] Lindsay, "How Your Organization Can Resist Woke Social Pressure."

[21] Woke Preacher Clips (@WokePreacherTV), "'A few Facebook posts and a sermon or two are not gonna dismantle racism in all its forms, but rather it will take a lifelong commitment from each one of us to do everything in our power in all that God is calling us to, day after day, year after year.' @TWVCHITWOOD," Twitter, September 21, 2020, 10:10 a.m., https://twitter.com/WokePreacherTV/status/1308045950821298176.

who embraced the phrase embraced the organization; however, the eagerness to incorporate the phrase spoke volumes. Hillsong Church Global Senior Pastor and Founder Brian Houston said in a statement, "Hillsong Church is opposed to racism, and we believe black lives matter."[22] In June 2020, President Trump's personal pastor, Paula White-Cain, made it known that she supported BLM's "Blackout Tuesday" protests on social media. In a speech offered in lieu of his address at the denomination's canceled annual meeting around the same time, Southern Baptist Convention President J.D. Greear called for members of the nation's largest Protestant denomination to declare that "black lives matter."[23]

Nor was this limited to evangelicals. In an odd historical moment, Mormon leaders and the NAACP released a joint statement "expressing solidarity with people outraged by [George] Floyd's death."

But support for BLM is not universal.

In August 2020, the nondenominational Southern Evangelical Seminary (not to be confused with Southern Baptist Theological Seminary) "released a statement simultaneously condemning racism and warning Christians against supporting the Black Lives Matter movement, claiming [it] espouses a 'godless agenda.'"[24]

So what is a Christian to do? Black Lives Matter, and our response to it, has been a source of much division and dispute and offers a perfect opportunity to wrestle with the important question of how we can and must handle such disagreements. To be clear, I oppose BLM and have refused to even say the phrase. Moreover, I think the movement (and by

---

[22] Caleb Parke, "Evangelical Leaders Support Black Lives Matter," Fox News, June 2, 2020, https://www.foxnews.com/us/evangelicals-support-black-lives-matter.

[23] Adelle M. Banks, "Southern Baptist President J.D. Greear Says 'Black Lives Matter'," Religion News Service, June 9, 2020, https://religionnews.com/2020/06/09/southern-baptist-president-j-d-greear-says-black-lives-matter.

[24] Leah MarieAnn Klett, "Evangelical Seminary Condemns Black Lives Matter, 'Wokeness' Ideology," Christian Post, August 20, 2020, https://www.christian-post.com/news/evangelical-seminary-condemns-black-lives-matter-movement-wokeness-ideology.html.

extension, the phrase) is a Trojan horse that poses a clear threat to the witness of the Church. I say this for several reasons, not least of which is the foundation upon which the organization is built.

Black Lives Matter Is Founded on Bearing False Witness

The Black Lives Matter organization was established in 2013 by three "trained radical Black organizers who have long been a part of the larger Black liberation movement"[25]—Patrisse Cullors, Alicia Garza, and Opal Tometi—in response to the acquittal of George Zimmerman, the "white" man (in reality, he is only part white and mostly Afro-Peruvian) who killed black Florida teen Trayvon Martin in 2012. The jury found that Zimmerman acted in self-defense. Those facts did not make a difference to BLM. And the next year, the organization really took off with another protest after the death of Michael Brown.

> It was a guttural response to be with our people, our family—in support of the brave and courageous community of Ferguson and St. Louis as they were being brutalized by law enforcement, criticized by media, tear gassed, and pepper sprayed night after night. Darnell Moore and Patrisse Cullors organized a national ride during Labor Day weekend that year. We called it the Black Life Matters Ride.[26]

The popular narrative surrounding Brown's death at that time was based on now-discredited lies.

BLM contends that these events warrant "an ideological and political intervention in a world where Black lives are systematically and

---

[25] Patrisse Khan-Cullors, "We Didn't Start a Movement, We Started a Network," Medium.com, February 22, 2016, https://medium.com/@patrissemariecullorsbrignac/we-didn-t-start-a-movement-we-started-a-network-90f9b5717668#.kqtcnbi85.

[26] Black Lives Matter, "Herstory," https://blacklivesmatter.com/herstory.

intentionally targeted for demise."[27] This, of course, is patently false, and saying so is bearing false witness. Even when the lie is repeated by Christians like Latasha Morrison.

"Even today," Morrison writes, "governmental powers continue to take the lives of unarmed Black and Brown children, as well as women and men, often without repercussion."[28] She says this in a book where she mentions Michael Brown three times; Ferguson, Missouri, eight times; and references Black Lives Matter directly and favorably.

But bearing false witness may be the least problematic thing about BLM.

Black Lives Matter Is an Openly Pagan, Marxist-Leninist Organization

In a now-viral video, Cullors identifies herself and her cofounders as "trained Marxists."[29] Nor is this hyperbole. Cullors is the protégé of Eric Mann, "former agitator of the Weather Underground domestic terror organization." From him, she spent several years absorbing the Marxist-Leninist ideology that contributes significantly to her worldview.[30] The organization's revolutionary Marxist origins and ethos are antithetical to the message of Christianity.

The founders also have been quite open about the fact that they practice witchcraft. In a June 2020 video call, both Cullors and Los Angeles BLM chapter founder Dr. Melina Abdullah discussed how they

---

[27] Black Lives Matter, "Herstory."

[28] Morrison, *Be the Bridge*, 139.

[29] The Real News Network, "A Short History of Black Lives Matter," YouTube, July 22, 2015, https://www.youtube.com/watch?v=kCghDx5qN4s&feature=youtu.be.

[30] Yaron Steinbuch, "Black Lives Matter Co-Founder Describes Herself as 'Trained Marxist'," *New York Post*, June 25, 2020, https://nypost.com/2020/06/25/blm-co-founder-describes-herself-as-trained-marxist.

channel spirits to accomplish their objectives, using the Yoruba religion of Ifá, which involves ancestor worship.

"In my tradition, you offer things that your loved one who passed away would want, whether it's like honey or tobacco, things like that," Cullors said. "It's so important, not just for us, to be in direct relationship with our people who have passed, but also for them to know we've remembered them. I believe so many of them work through us."[31]

Abdullah detailed how she "laughs a lot" with "Wakiesha"—the spirit of a black woman found dead in a Los Angeles jail cell in 2016.[32]

Black Lives Matter Is an Openly Feminist, Pro-LGBTQIA+ Organization

All three of BLM's founders are lesbians who were bothered by the fact that "Black liberation movements in this country have created room and space and leadership mostly for Black heterosexual, cisgender men, leaving women, who are often queer or transgender, either out of the movement or in the background to move the work forward with little or no recognition." They "recognized a need to center the leadership of women," particularly queer and transgender women. "Among our movement mentors," says Cullors, "were queer and trans people whose labor had been erased and replaced with an uncontested narrative of male leadership."[33]

This commitment to LGBTQIA+ as the core impetus behind BLM was evident on its website's "What We Believe" page. I say "was" because the page has since been deleted—a move I anticipated, so I copied it

---

[31] This is also why they emphasize saying the names of the deceased. It is an integral part of their ancestral worship.

[32] The Apostolic Mind, "BLM Founder Witchcraft Confession," YouTube, September 8, 2020, https://www.youtube.com/watch?v=gV5ZG4E4YGI.

[33] Patrisse Marie Cullors-Brignac, "We Didn't Start a Movement. We Started a Network," Neighborhood Funders Group, February 21, 2016, https://www.nfg.org/resources/we-didn-t-start-movement-we-started-network.

before it disappeared. (It also has been archived, so the evidence is still there.)[34] I did so because I knew it would be problematic for BLM—and for the Church. (Or at least it should be.) From the website:

> We are self-reflexive and do the work required to *dismantle cisgender privilege and uplift Black trans folk*, especially Black trans women who continue to be disproportionately impacted by trans-antagonistic violence.
>
> *We foster a queer-affirming network*. When we gather, we do so with the intention of freeing ourselves from the tight grip of heteronormative thinking, or rather, the belief that all in the world are heterosexual (unless s/he or they disclose otherwise) (emphasis mine).

In case you are wondering, biblical Christianity would not only be an example of "heteronormative thinking," but the very source of it.

Black Lives Matter Is Openly Anti-Male and Anti-Family

In true Critical Social Justice fashion, BLM is at war with every aspect of "the hegemony." However, its animus is particularly strong when it comes to the biblical family and men:

> We build a space that affirms Black women and is free from sexism, misogyny, and *environments in which men are centered*.
>
> We make our spaces family-friendly and enable parents to fully participate with *their children*. We *dismantle the patriarchal practice* that requires *mothers* to work "double shifts" so that they can *mother* in private even as they participate in public justice work.

---

[34] Black Lives Matter, "What We Believe," http://archive.is/oARH0.

> We disrupt the Western-prescribed nuclear family struc-
> ture requirement by supporting each other as extended fami-
> lies and "villages" that collectively care for one another,
> especially our children, to the degree that mothers, parents,
> and children are comfortable.[35]

While the obvious problem with this part of the BLM statement is that its members are committed to "disrupting the Western-prescribed nuclear family structure," a few other things are worth noting. First, note that the word "father" appears nowhere in the BLM statements on family. "Women," "children," and "parents," but not one mention of fathers.

Also, the statement decries "the centering of men." In case you are unfamiliar with the term "centering," it refers to the practice of making something the standard and is common in woke, antiracist, CSJ parlance. Robin DiAngelo, for example, refers to an "inauthentic, white-norm-centered, and thus hostile environment."[36] Elsewhere, she condemns "centering white people and the white voice."[37] Ibram X. Kendi also refers frequently to "not centering White."[38] Latasha Morrison refers to being "centered in whiteness."[39] I am not suggesting that everyone who uses "centering" is an SJW. The term has become common parlance. However, it has clear meaning in the CRT/I world.

Finally, note the reference to "villages." This is an allusion to a communal, matriarchal view of family reminiscent of early Marxist teaching.

---

[35] Black Lives Matter, "What We Believe," http://archive.is/oARH0.

[36] Robin J. DiAngelo, *White Fragility* (Boston, Massachusetts: Beacon Press, Kindle Edition, 2018), 127.

[37] Ibid., xiv.

[38] Ibram X. Kendi, *How to Be an Antiracist* (New York, New York: Random House Publishing Group, Kindle Edition, 2019), 130.

[39] Morrison, *Be the Bridge*, 66.

We Must Take Every Thought Captive

We ... take every thought captive to obey Christ, being ready to punish every disobedience, when your obedience is complete. (2 Corinthians 10:5–6)

Racism is real. Injustice is real. No matter how many times I say those things, I still will be accused of turning a blind eye to them—not because I deny them, but because I deny the CRT/I view that they are "normal" and at the basis of everything.

But there is another way of seeing. "The history of the USA is neither purely wicked and racist, nor perfect," writes Thomas Sowell. "Correlation is not causation, disparity is not necessarily discrimination. Complex problems require complex solutions.... To make racism the driving force behind slavery is to make a historically recent factor the cause of an institution which originated thousands of years earlier."

The CSJ worldview flows from presuppositions about hegemony, then interprets everything in that light. Therefore, dealing with CSJ requires taking thoughts captive.

Again, the Black Lives Matter movement serves as a useful example of what this looks like.

We Must Confront the Lie and Hold to the Truth

Black Lives Matter is a Trojan horse. The movement has a name that Christians find attractive because we love God and our neighbor and have a desire to see justice done. And for some, that has come to mean embracing the false narrative of "state-sponsored terror against black and brown bodies." We must love our God, His Gospel, and our brothers enough to challenge this false narrative. However, in doing so, we need to go deeper.

We Must Listen with Discernment

There is a reason people gravitate toward the false narrative of "state-sponsored terror." For some, it is their own negative personal experiences. For others, it is the constant barrage of the media's repetitions of the false narrative. For a few, the attraction lies in the inordinate power they suddenly have as the world seeks to "listen to and 'center' their voice." For many white Christians, it is the opportunity to assuage their guilt. In all these instances, we must listen to our sisters and brothers and show compassion. However, we must also remember our first commitment and tell them the truth. We must take these thoughts captive.

We Must Correct Them

The facts about Black Lives Matter are not in dispute. The organization is Marxist, revolutionary, feminist, misandrist, pro-LGBTQIA+, pro-abortion, and anti-family, with roots in the occult. It is unacceptable for Christians to partner with, celebrate, identify with, or promote this organization. And that includes being bullied or pressured into using the phrase "black lives matter."

When I say this, people always ask, "Are you saying black lives don't matter?" Allow me to respond.

First, I reject the premise of the question; it presumes that black lives did not matter until 2013 when Cullors, Garza, and Tometi created the hashtag. Until then, black people could be killed like dogs in the street and nobody cared. This is preposterous! We don't live in the Jim Crow South. The era of public lynchings is long past. We don't need a hashtag for black lives to have meaning and significance.

Second, I am a Christian. I believe all men are made in the image of God. Therefore, I most certainly believe that the lives of people matter regardless of how much or how little melanin is in their skin. The idea that saying the phrase or using the hashtag "Black Lives Matter" is now a litmus test for whether somebody is an antiracist ally is absurd. Nor do I need to see a hashtag on any of my white sisters' or brothers' social media accounts to know they were appalled by the death of George Floyd. I don't sit around wondering if white Christians care when black people are gunned down in the streets. I believe they belong to Christ and love humanity until they demonstrate otherwise.

This will not repair the fault lines. Nothing will. These divisions are both real and necessary. As I said at the outset, the goal here is to be on the right side of the fault line when the catastrophe comes. In the meantime, we must love. I do not mean that we must accept the world's faulty, emasculated, unbiblical version of love—the version that sees any disagreement or confrontation as inherently unloving. No, we must love each other with a tenacious, biblical, Christlike love.

Dear reader, I know it is hard. I don't like losing friends, being called names, or being ousted from platforms any more than you do. However, you and I must love the truth more than we love our friends, our reputations, or our platforms. I am not suggesting that we go out and be rude, obnoxious, or disrespectful. I hope I have not done so in these pages. Instead, I hope I have heeded the apostle's words and encouraged you to do the same:

> Now who is there to harm you if you are zealous for what is good? But even if you should suffer for righteousness' sake, you will be blessed. Have no fear of them, nor be troubled, but in your hearts honor Christ the Lord as holy, always being prepared to make a defense to anyone who asks you for a reason for the hope that is in you; yet do it with gentleness and respect, having a good conscience, so that, when you are slandered, those who revile your good behavior in Christ may be put to shame. For it is better to suffer for doing good, if that should be God's will, than for doing evil. (1 Peter 3:13–17)

Of course, this only applies if the righteousness for which we suffer is the "righteousness of our God and Savior Jesus Christ" (2 Peter 1:1), the righteousness "which comes through faith in Christ" (Philippians 3:9). Antiracism's false religion, false priesthood, and false canon cannot grant this righteousness.

Ironically, antiracism is also powerless against racism. It is Christ, and Christ alone, "who has made us both one and has broken down in his flesh the dividing wall of hostility" (Ephesians 2:14). This doesn't mean that black and white Christians won't offend or sin against each other. It also doesn't mean that the sin of racism will not raise its ugly head in the broader culture, or even in the Church. What it does mean is that we have an answer.

CHAPTER ELEVEN

Solid Ground

I n August 2006, I stood on African soil for the first time. It was an amazing two weeks.

One Sunday, I was scheduled to preach at Evangel Baptist Church, pastored by Dr. Grave Singogo. When I arrived at the church, a spry eighty-seven-year-old man approached me. He was Pastor Singogo's father. He introduced himself, shook my hand, gave me a giant African smile, then a hug. Then he asked me, "Is this your first time in Africa?" I said yes.

Somehow, his smile got even bigger. He raised his left hand (his right never stopped shaking mine), grabbed my face, kissed me, and exclaimed, "Son, welcome home!"

I completely lost it. There I stood in the dirt parking lot of a church I had never been to before, and I just started sobbing.

When I finally got myself together, I greeted more of the brethren, then found my way to my seat. As the service began, I was overcome with emotion once again. I thought about Papa Singogo's greeting and how much it had meant to me. I thought about how much my father, who had died four months before my trip, would have loved to be there with me.

But there was more. I thought about the fact that my ancestors once inhabited the continent of Africa. That was, until for one reason or another, other Africans sold them into slavery—probably after taking them as slaves themselves. I thought about the horrors of the Middle Passage and the indignities of bondage in America. I thought about the fact that slavery had robbed me of so much that I didn't even know which African country my ancestors had come from, let alone which tribe.

Then I thought about the moment at hand, and something switched.

Suddenly, I realized that I had traveled thousands of miles from the place of my ancestors' oppression to the place of their betrayal. And for the first time in my life, I forgave. I didn't forgive because I was big enough, or a godly enough man. Nor did I forgive because anybody asked me to. I forgave because I was overcome by the weight and majesty of God's providence.

By God's providence, my ancestors survived their ordeal. By God's providence, one of their descendants (me) had returned—not as a slave of men, but as a slave of Christ. By God's providence, I was born a free man and a citizen of the greatest Republic in the history of mankind. By God's providence, I was numbered among the healthiest, freest, most prosperous people (of any race, not just black people) on the planet. By God's providence, I had received the best theological education available in the world. And by God's providence, He had brought me back to Africa to bless the descendants of the people who sold my ancestors into slavery. So I forgave.

I forgave the Africans who took my ancestors' freedom. I forgave the Americans who bought and exploited them. I forgave the family that replaced my identity with their German name. I just forgave! I did not harbor any ill will. I did not feel entitled to any apologies or reparations. By God's grace, I recognized that Providence had blessed me beyond my ancestors' wildest dreams—or my own. I couldn't help but remember Joseph's words: "As for you, you meant evil against me, but God meant it for good, to bring it about that many people should be kept alive, as they are today" (Genesis 50:20).

The Way Forward

In the end, it is forgiveness that will heal our wounds. My hope is not that white Christians can feel sorry enough for their past or that ministries and organizations can dig up and grovel over enough historical dirt. That is not the powerful, life-changing, world-confounding message of the Gospel. That is the message of the world.

I have heard a mantra lately that rings hollow in my ears: "There can be no reconciliation without justice." When I hear that, I want to scream, "YES! AND THE DEATH OF CHRIST IS THAT JUSTICE!" All other justice is proximate and insufficient. It is because of Christ's work on the cross that that we can heed the apostle's admonition: "Let all bitterness and wrath and anger and clamor and slander be put away from you, along with all malice. Be kind to one another, tenderhearted, forgiving one another, as God in Christ forgave you" (Ephesians 4:31–32). Who am I to tell a white brother that he cannot be reconciled to me until he has drudged up all of the racial sins of his and his ancestors' past and made proper restitution? Christ has atoned for sin!

Consequently, the most powerful weapon in our arsenal is not calling for reparations: it is forgiveness. Antiracism knows nothing of forgiveness because it knows nothing of the Gospel. Instead, antiracism offers endless penance, judgment, and fear. What an opportunity we have to shine the light of Christ in the midst of darkness!

I realized in 2006 that I had been blessed in order to be a blessing. I had been given much so that I could give much. A decade earlier, the Lord had called me to lead my family away from churches where everybody looked like us, and we became strangers in a strange land. Now, He was calling me to go to a place where most everybody looked like us, and we would remain strangers in a strange land (Jeremiah 14:8).

I am not an African. I am not an African American. I am an American, and I wouldn't want to be anything else. America doesn't owe me anything. America has blessed me beyond measure. If anything, I owe America. More importantly, I owe my Savior, and by extension, I owe my brothers and sisters in Christ.

This book was hard to write. I knew that no matter how careful I was, how irenic, deferential, or gracious, the very content of this book would be deemed offensive, unkind, and insensitive. Some will go as far as calling it "violence." So why write it?

I wrote this book because I love God more than life, the truth more than others' opinion of me, and the Bride of Christ more than my platform. My heart is broken as I watch movements and ideologies against which I have fought and warned for decades become entrenched at the highest and most respected levels of evangelicalism. I want this book to be a clarion call. I want to unmask the ideology of Critical Theory, Critical Race Theory, and Intersectionality in hopes that those who have imbibed it can have the blinders removed from their eyes, and those who have bowed in the face of it can stand up, take courage, and "contend for the faith that was once for all delivered to the saints" (Jude 3).

I harbor no animosity against anyone named in these pages, and if you happen to agree with my perspective on these issues, I hope you don't either. My goal is not to destroy, but to expose (Ephesians 5:11), warn (2 Timothy 3:15), and correct (2 Timothy 2:25) in hopes that "they may come to their senses and escape from the snare of the devil, after being captured by him to do his will" (2 Timothy 2:26). And yes, I do mean to call these ideologies demonic.

Rise to the Challenge

The history of the Church is replete with moments like these; moments where dear brothers disagreed passionately and publicly over issues they saw as threats to the Gospel. This is such a moment. A moment like the one faced by Charles Spurgeon in the Downgrade, and

J. Gresham Machen facing modernism. In his moment, Machen made a statement that could absolutely be made in ours:

> Men tell us that our preaching should be positive and not negative, that we can preach the truth without attacking error. But if we follow that advice we shall have to close our Bible and desert its teachings. The New Testament is a polemic book almost from beginning to end.[1]

I hope this book helps better equip you to be "a worker who has no need to be ashamed, rightly handling the word of truth" (2 Timothy 2:15). I also hope to embolden you to pull back the curtain and expose the wizard, call out the boy who cried wolf, proclaim that the emperor has no clothes, and any other metaphor you can think of for shedding light on these fault lines. Not so you can defeat your brethren in an argument, but so that you can engage them with the hopes of winning them.

Love your brothers and sisters enough to contend with them and for them.

Pastors, I beg you to consider what I have written here. I believe the Church—your church—is under attack. As shepherds, we must defend the sheep. We must repel the wolves. And yes, the wolves are many. However, this one is within the gates and has the worst of intentions. He desires to use your genuine love for the brethren as leverage. Don't let him! Recognize the difference between the voice of the Good Shepherd who calls you to love all the sheep and the voice of the enemy that tells you some of them are guilty, blind, ignorant oppressors and that others are oppressed—all based on their melanin. Reject cries that take principles and stories of individual restitution (Numbers 5:7; Luke 19) and eisegetically twist them into calls for multi-generational reparations. Reject the cries of those who twist the repentance of Daniel and Ezra 1) on behalf of theocratic Israel and 2) for sin that took place during their

---

[1] John Gresham Machen, AZ Quotes, https://www.azquotes.com/quote/679085.

lifetime, in an effort to promote multi-generational, ethnic guilt that rests upon all white people by virtue of their whiteness.

"From now on, therefore, we regard no one according to the flesh" (2 Corinthians 5:16). And why is this? Because "There is neither Jew nor Greek, there is neither slave nor free, there is no male and female, for you are all one in Christ Jesus. And if you are Christ's, then you are Abraham's offspring, heirs according to promise" (Galatians 3:28–29). Beyond that, remember Ezekiel's words:

> The word of the LORD came to me: "What do you mean by repeating this proverb concerning the land of Israel, 'The fathers have eaten sour grapes, and the children's teeth are set on edge'? As I live, declares the Lord GOD, this proverb shall no more be used by you in Israel. Behold, all souls are mine; the soul of the father as well as the soul of the son is mine: the soul who sins shall die." (Ezekiel 18:1–4)

If you are a person who has imbibed this ideology, let it go! Find freedom in Christ. "For Christ also suffered once for sins, the righteous for the unrighteous, that he might bring us to God" (1 Peter 3:18). Why, then, would you hold on to guilt for sins committed by or against your distant grandparents? And if you do, why only stop at slavery and Jim Crow? What about the other commandments broken by our distant kin? No, beloved, "If we confess our sins, he is faithful and just to forgive us our sins and to cleanse us from all unrighteousness" (1 John 1:9). That is who we are, since "as far as the east is from the west, so far does he remove our transgressions from us" (Psalm 103:12). And because of this, we can rest in the reconciliation that Christ has secured for us:

> For he himself is our peace, who has made us both one and has broken down in his flesh the dividing wall of hostility by abolishing the law of commandments expressed in ordinances, that he might create in himself one new man in place

of the two, so making peace, and might reconcile us both to God in one body through the cross, thereby killing the hostility. And he came and preached peace to you who were far off and peace to those who were near. For through him we both have access in one Spirit to the Father. (Ephesians 2:14–18)

The Jew-Gentile divide was far more significant than the black-white one. If Christ took care of *that* on the cross, how much more did He take care of any man-made divisions we face today? Does that mean there is no more racism? Of course not! Does that mean it is not important for us to get to know each other, to hear one another's stories? If I believed that, I wouldn't have written the first two chapters of this book. What this does mean is that we do not occupy the space of oppressors and oppressed based solely on our melanin. Does that mean our ethnicity is irrelevant? I leave you with God's answer to that:

After this I looked, and behold, a great multitude that no one could number, from every nation, from all tribes and peoples and languages, standing before the throne and before the Lamb, clothed in white robes, with palm branches in their hands, and crying out with a loud voice, "Salvation belongs to our God who sits on the throne, and to the Lamb!" And all the angels were standing around the throne and around the elders and the four living creatures, and they fell on their faces before the throne and worshiped God, saying, "Amen! Blessing and glory and wisdom and thanksgiving and honor and power and might be to our God forever and ever! Amen." (Revelation 7:9–12)

APPENDIX A

The Dallas Statement on Social Justice and the Gospel

I n view of questionable sociological, psychological, and political theories presently permeating our culture and making inroads into Christ's
church, we wish to clarify certain key Christian doctrines and ethical
principles prescribed in God's Word. Clarity on these issues will fortify
believers and churches to withstand an onslaught of dangerous and false
teachings that threaten the gospel, misrepresent Scripture, and lead
people away from the grace of God in Jesus Christ.

Specifically, we are deeply concerned that values borrowed from
secular culture are currently undermining Scripture in the areas of race
and ethnicity, manhood and womanhood, and human sexuality. The
Bible's teaching on each of these subjects is being challenged under the
broad and somewhat nebulous rubric of concern for "social justice." If
the doctrines of God's Word are not uncompromisingly reasserted and
defended at these points, there is every reason to anticipate that these
dangerous ideas and corrupted moral values will spread their influence
into other realms of biblical doctrines and principles.

We submit these affirmations and denials for public consideration,
not with any pretense of ecclesiastical authority, but with an urgency that

is mixed with deep joy and sincere sorrow. The rapidity with which these deadly ideas have spread from the culture at large into churches and Christian organizations—including some that are evangelical and Reformed—necessitates the issuing of this statement now.

In the process of considering these matters we have been reminded of the essentials of the faith once for all handed down to the saints, and we are recommitted to contend for it. We have a great Lord and Savior, and it is a privilege to defend his gospel, regardless of cost or consequences. Nevertheless, while we rejoice in that privilege, we grieve that in doing so we know we are taking a stand against the positions of some teachers whom we have long regarded as faithful and trustworthy spiritual guides. It is our earnest prayer that our brothers and sisters will stand firm on the gospel and avoid being blown to and fro by every cultural trend that seeks to move the Church of Christ off course. We must remain steadfast, immovable, always abounding in the work of the Lord.

The Apostle Paul's warning to the Colossians is greatly needed today: "See to it that no one takes you captive by philosophy and empty deceit, according to human tradition, according to the elemental spirits of the world, and not according to Christ" (Colossians 2:8). The document that follows is an attempt to heed that apostolic command. We invite others who share our concerns and convictions to unite with us in reasserting our unwavering commitment to the teachings of God's Word articulated in this statement. Therefore, for the glory of God among his Church and throughout society, we offer the following affirmations and denials.

Scripture

WE AFFIRM that the Bible is God's Word, breathed out by him. It is inerrant, infallible, and the final authority for determining what is true (what we must believe) and what is right (how we must live). All truth claims and ethical standards must be tested by God's final Word, which is Scripture alone.

WE DENY that Christian belief, character, or conduct can be dictated by any other authority, and we deny that the postmodern ideologies derived from intersectionality, radical feminism, and critical race theory are consistent with biblical teaching. We further deny that competency to teach on any biblical issue comes from any qualification for spiritual people other than clear understanding and simple communication of what is revealed in Scripture.

Imago Dei

WE AFFIRM that God created every person equally in his own image. As divine image-bearers, all people have inestimable value and dignity before God and deserve honor, respect and protection. Everyone has been created by God and for God.

WE DENY that God-given roles, socioeconomic status, ethnicity, religion, sex or physical condition or any other property of a person either negates or contributes to that individual's worth as an image-bearer of God.

Justice

WE AFFIRM that since he is holy, righteous, and just, God requires those who bear his image to live justly in the world. This includes showing appropriate respect to every person and giving to each one what he or she is due. We affirm that societies must establish laws to correct injustices that have been imposed through cultural prejudice.

WE DENY that true justice can be culturally defined or that standards of justice that are merely socially constructed can be imposed with the same authority as those that are derived from Scripture. We further deny that Christians can live justly in the world under any principles other than the biblical standard of righteousness. Relativism, socially constructed standards of truth or morality, and notions of virtue and vice that are constantly in flux cannot result in authentic justice.

God's Law

WE AFFIRM that God's law, as summarized in the ten commandments, more succinctly summarized in the two great commandments, and manifested in Jesus Christ, is the only standard of unchanging righteousness. Violation of that law is what constitutes sin.

WE DENY that any obligation that does not arise from God's commandments can be legitimately imposed on Christians as a prescription for righteous living. We further deny the legitimacy of any charge of sin or call to repentance that does not arise from a violation of God's commandments.

Sin

WE AFFIRM that all people are connected to Adam both naturally and federally. Therefore, because of original sin everyone is born under the curse of God's law and all break his commandments through sin. There is no difference in the condition of sinners due to age, ethnicity, or sex. All are depraved in all their faculties and all stand condemned before God's law. All human relationships, systems, and institutions have been affected by sin.

WE DENY that, other than the previously stated connection to Adam, any person is morally culpable for another person's sin. Although families, groups, and nations can sin collectively, and cultures can be predisposed to particular sins, subsequent generations share the collective guilt of their ancestors only if they approve and embrace (or attempt to justify) those sins. Before God each person must repent and confess his or her own sins in order to receive forgiveness. We further deny that one's ethnicity establishes any necessary connection to any particular sin.

Gospel

WE AFFIRM that the gospel is the divinely revealed message concerning the person and work of Jesus Christ—especially his virgin birth, righteous life, substitutionary sacrifice, atoning death, and bodily resurrection—revealing who he is and what he has done with the promise that he will save anyone and everyone who turns from sin by trusting him as Lord.

WE DENY that anything else, whether works to be performed or opinions to be held, can be added to the gospel without perverting it into another gospel. This also means that implications and applications of the gospel, such as the obligation to live justly in the world, though legitimate and important in their own right, are not definitional components of the gospel.

Salvation

WE AFFIRM that salvation is granted by God's grace alone received through faith alone in Jesus Christ alone. Every believer is united to Christ, justified before God, and adopted into his family. Thus, in God's eyes there is no difference in spiritual value or worth among those who are in Christ. Further, all who are united to Christ are also united to one another regardless of age, ethnicity, or sex. All believers are being conformed to the image of Christ. By God's regenerating and sanctifying grace all believers will be brought to a final glorified, sinless state of perfection in the day of Jesus Christ.

WE DENY that salvation can be received in any other way. We also deny that salvation renders any Christian free from all remaining sin or immune from even grievous sin in this life. We further deny that ethnicity excludes anyone from understanding the gospel, nor does anyone's ethnic or cultural heritage mitigate or remove the duty to repent and believe.

The Church

WE AFFIRM that the primary role of the church is to worship God through the preaching of his word, teaching sound doctrine, observing baptism and the Lord's Supper, refuting those who contradict, equipping the saints, and evangelizing the lost. We affirm that when the primacy of the gospel is maintained that this often has a positive effect on the culture in which various societal ills are mollified. We affirm that, under the lordship of Christ, we are to obey the governing authorities established by God and pray for civil leaders.

WE DENY that political or social activism should be viewed as integral components of the gospel or primary to the mission of the church. Though believers can and should utilize all lawful means that God has providentially established to have some effect on the laws of a society, we deny that these activities are either evidence of saving faith or constitute a central part of the church's mission given to her by Jesus Christ, her head. We deny that laws or regulations possess any inherent power to change sinful hearts.

Heresy

WE AFFIRM that heresy is a denial of or departure from a doctrine that is essential to the Christian faith. We further affirm that heresy often involves the replacement of key, essential truths with variant concepts, or the elevation of non-essentials to the status of essentials. To embrace heresy is to depart from the faith once delivered to the saints and thus to be on a path toward spiritual destruction. We affirm that the accusation of heresy should be reserved for those departures from Christian truth that destroy the weight-bearing doctrines of the redemptive core of Scripture. We affirm that accusations of heresy should be accompanied with clear evidence of such destructive beliefs.

WE DENY that the charge of heresy can be legitimately brought against every failure to achieve perfect conformity to all that is implied in sincere faith in the gospel.

Sexuality and Marriage

WE AFFIRM that God created mankind male and female and that this divinely determined distinction is good, proper, and to be celebrated. Maleness and femaleness are biologically determined at conception and are not subject to change. The curse of sin results in sinful, disordered affections that manifest in some people as same-sex attraction. Salvation grants sanctifying power to renounce such dishonorable affections as sinful and to mortify them by the Spirit. We further affirm that God's design for marriage is that one woman and one man live in a one-flesh, covenantal, sexual relationship until separated by death. Those who lack the desire or opportunity for marriage are called to serve God in singleness and chastity. This is as noble a calling as marriage.

WE DENY that human sexuality is a socially constructed concept. We also deny that one's sex can be fluid. We reject "gay Christian" as a legitimate biblical category. We further deny that any kind of partnership or union can properly be called marriage other than one man and one woman in lifelong covenant together. We further deny that people should be identified as "sexual minorities"—which serves as a cultural classification rather than one that honors the image-bearing character of human sexuality as created by God.

Complementarianism

WE AFFIRM that God created mankind both male and female with inherent biological and personal distinctions between them and that these created differences are good, proper, and beautiful. Though there is no difference between men and women before God's law or as recipients of his saving grace, we affirm that God has designed men and women with distinct traits and to fulfill distinct roles. These differences are most clearly defined in marriage and the church, but are not irrelevant in other spheres of life. In marriage the husband is to lead, love, and safeguard his wife and the wife is to respect and be submissive to her husband in all things lawful. In the church, qualified men alone are to lead as pastors/elders/bishops and preach to and teach the whole congregation. We further affirm that the image of God is expressed most fully and beautifully in human society when men and women walk in obedience to their God-ordained roles and serve according to their God-given gifts.

WE DENY that the God-ordained differences in men's and women's roles disparage the inherent spiritual worth or value of one over the other, nor do those differences in any way inhibit either men or women from flourishing for the glory of God.

Race/Ethnicity

WE AFFIRM God made all people from one man. Though people often can be distinguished by different ethnicities and nationalities, they are ontological equals before God in both creation and redemption. "Race" is not a biblical category, but rather a social construct that often has been used to classify groups of people in terms of inferiority and superiority. All that is good, honest, just, and beautiful in various ethnic backgrounds and experiences can be celebrated as the fruit of God's grace. All sinful actions and their results (including evils perpetrated between and upon ethnic groups by others) are to be confessed as sinful, repented of, and repudiated.

WE DENY that Christians should segregate themselves into racial groups or regard racial identity above, or even equal to, their identity in Christ. We deny that any divisions between people groups (from an unstated attitude of superiority to an overt spirit of resentment) have any legitimate place in the fellowship of the redeemed. We reject any teaching that encourages racial groups to view themselves as privileged oppressors or entitled victims of oppression. While we are to weep with those who weep, we deny that a person's feelings of offense or oppression necessarily prove that someone else is guilty of sinful behaviors, oppression, or prejudice.

Culture

WE AFFIRM that some cultures operate on assumptions that are inherently better than those of other cultures because of the biblical truths that inform those worldviews that have produced these distinct assumptions. Those elements of a given culture that reflect divine revelation should be celebrated and promoted. But the various cultures out of which we have been called all have features that are worldly and sinful—and therefore those sinful features should be repudiated for the honor of Christ. We affirm that whatever evil influences to which we have been subjected via our culture can be—and must be—overcome through conversion and the training of both mind and heart through biblical truth.

WE DENY that individuals and sub-groups in any culture are unable, by God's grace, to rise above whatever moral defects or spiritual deficiencies have been engendered or encouraged by their respective cultures.

Racism

WE AFFIRM that racism is a sin rooted in pride and malice which must be condemned and renounced by all who would honor the image of God in all people. Such racial sin can subtly or overtly manifest itself as racial animosity or racial vainglory. Such sinful prejudice or partiality falls short of God's revealed will and violates the royal law of love. We affirm that virtually all cultures, including our own, at times contain laws and systems that foster racist attitudes and policies.

WE DENY that treating people with sinful partiality or prejudice is consistent with biblical Christianity. We deny that only those in positions of power are capable of racism, or that individuals of any particular ethnic groups are incapable of racism. We deny that systemic racism is in any way compatible with the core principles of historic evangelical convictions. We deny that the Bible can be legitimately used to foster or justify partiality, prejudice, or contempt toward other ethnicities. We deny that the contemporary evangelical movement has any deliberate agenda to elevate one ethnic group and subjugate another. And we emphatically deny that lectures on social issues (or activism aimed at reshaping the wider culture) are as vital to the life and health of the church as the preaching of the gospel and the exposition of Scripture. Historically, such things tend to become distractions that inevitably lead to departures from the gospel.

Original Resolution on Critical Race Theory and Intersectionality

Author's note: This is the first draft of the resolution that was submitted to the Southern Baptist Convention's Resolutions Committee for consideration at its annual meeting in 2019.

WHEREAS, all Scripture is totally true and trustworthy and reveals the principles by which God judges us, and therefore is, and will remain to the end of the world, the true center of Christian union, and the supreme standard by which all human conduct, creeds, and religious opinions should be tried; and

WHEREAS, critical race theory and intersectionality are founded upon unbiblical presuppositions descended from Marxist theories and categories, and therefore are inherently opposed to the Scriptures as the true center of Christian union; and

WHEREAS, both critical race theory and intersectionality as ideologies have infiltrated some Southern Baptist churches and institutions—institutions funded by the Cooperative Program; and

WHEREAS, critical race theory upholds postmodern relativistic understandings of truth; and

WHEREAS, critical race theory divides humanity into groups of oppressors and oppressed, and is used to encourage biblical, transcendental truth claims to be considered suspect when communicated from groups labeled as oppressors; and

WHEREAS, intersectionality defines human identity by race, social background, gender, sexual orientation, religion, and a host of other distinctions, and it does so at the expense of other identities; and

WHEREAS, intersectionality reduces human beings to distinguishable identities of unequal value and thus reduces human identity down to differences rather than commonality; and

WHEREAS, intersectionality encourages rage as its driving energy and conclusion; and

WHEREAS, intersectionality magnifies differences while deeming as more favorable the individuals who combine the highest number of oppressed identities; and

WHEREAS, both critical race theory and intersectionality breed division and deny humanity's essential commonality; and

WHEREAS, the Scripture provides God's narrative on such matters; and

WHEREAS, the book of Genesis grounds humanity in that which unites us, namely our common identity as the Imago Dei, which itself is the foundation of every biblical, ethical command to love one's neighbor and to seek justice for all; and

WHEREAS, the Bible acknowledges differences—male and female, slave and free, Jew and Gentile—it does not begin with human differences, but instead begins with what unites humanity, namely the Imago Dei; and

WHEREAS, the sameness of humanity built upon the Imago Dei, justifies the value of all individuals in something that transcends race, gender, and other identity intersections; and

WHEREAS, the New Covenant further unites by creating a new humanity that will one day inhabit the new heavens and the new earth, and that the people of this new humanity, though descended from every nation, tribe, tongue, and people, are all one in Christ; and

WHEREAS, this new humanity is comprised of people from every ethnicity and race, of every socio-economic background and culture, and yet these people enter this new humanity through belief in the Gospel of Jesus Christ; and

WHEREAS, Christian citizenship is not based on our differences but instead on our common salvation in Christ; and

WHEREAS, we find our true identity in Christ; and

WHEREAS, the Scriptures have categories and principles by which to deal with racism, sexism, injustice, abuse—principles found in prior Southern Baptist resolutions such as On The Anti-Gospel of Alt-Right White Supremacy, for example, that are not rooted in Marxist anti-gospel presuppositions; and

WHEREAS, the rhetoric of critical race theory and intersectionality found in some Southern Baptist institutions and leaders is causing unnecessary and unbiblical division among the body of Christ and is tarnishing the reputation of the Southern Baptist Convention as a whole, inviting charges of theological liberalism, egalitarianism, and Marxism; and

WHEREAS, the Southern Baptist Convention is committed to racial reconciliation built upon biblical presuppositions, and is committed to seeking biblical justice through biblical means; now, therefore, be it

RESOLVED, That the messengers to the Southern Baptist Convention, meeting in Birmingham, Alabama, June 11-12, 2019, decry every philosophy or theology, including critical race theory and intersectionality, as antithetical to the Gospel of Jesus Christ, since they divide the people of Christ by defining fundamental identity as something other than our identity in Jesus Christ; and be it further

RESOLVED, That we deny any philosophy or theology that defines individuals primarily by non-transcendental social constructs rather than by the transcendental reality of all humans existing as the Imago Dei; and be it further

RESOLVED, That while we denounce critical race theory and intersectionality, we do not deny that ethnic, gender, cultural, and racial distinctions do in fact exist and are a gift from God that will give Him absolute glory when the entire gamut of human diversity worships Him in perfect unity founded upon our unity in Jesus Christ; and be it further

RESOLVED, That Southern Baptist Churches will seek to paint this eschatological picture in a proleptic manner in our churches in the present by focusing on our unity in Christ and our common humanity as the Imago Dei rather than dividing over the secondary matters than make us different; and be it further

RESOLVED, That Southern Baptists Churches and institutions will take a prophetic stand against all forms of biblically defined injustice, but we will do so in a manner consistent with the biblical worldview rather than unbiblical worldviews; and be it further

RESOLVED, That Southern Baptist institutions need to make progress in rooting out the intentional promulgation of critical race theory and intersectionality in both our churches and institutions; and be it further

RESOLVED, That we earnestly pray, both for those who advocate ideologies meant to divide believers along intersectional lines and those who are thereby deceived, that they may see their error through the light of the Gospel, repent of these anti-Gospel beliefs, and come to know the peace and love of Christ through redeemed fellowship in the Kingdom of God, which is established from every nation, tribe, people, and language.

SBC Resolution 9 on Critical Race Theory and Intersectionality

Author's note: This is the version of the resolution that the Southern Baptist Convention's Resolutions Committee wrote and subsequently adopted without removing the original author's name.

WHEREAS, Concerns have been raised by some evangelicals over the use of frameworks such as critical race theory and intersectionality; and

WHEREAS, Critical race theory is a set of analytical tools that explain how race has and continues to function in society, and intersectionality is the study of how different personal characteristics overlap and inform one's experience; and

WHEREAS, Critical race theory and intersectionality have been appropriated by individuals with worldviews that are contrary to the Christian faith, resulting in ideologies and methods that contradict Scripture; and

WHEREAS, Evangelical scholars who affirm the authority and sufficiency of Scripture have employed selective insights from critical race theory and intersectionality to understand multifaceted social dynamics; and

WHEREAS, The Baptist Faith and Message states, "[A]ll Scripture is totally true and trustworthy. It reveals the principles by which God judges us, and therefore is, and will remain to the end of the world, the true center of Christian union, and the supreme standard by which all human conduct, creeds, and religious opinions should be tried" (Article I); and

WHEREAS, General revelation accounts for truthful insights found in human ideas that do not explicitly emerge from Scripture and reflects what some may term "common grace"; and

WHEREAS, Critical race theory and intersectionality alone are insufficient to diagnose and redress the root causes of the social ills that they identify, which result from sin, yet these analytical tools can aid in evaluating a variety of human experiences; and

WHEREAS, Scripture contains categories and principles by which to deal with racism, poverty, sexism, injustice, and abuse that are not rooted in secular ideologies; and

WHEREAS, Humanity is primarily identified in Scripture as image bearers of God, even as biblical authors address various audiences according to characteristics such as male and female, Jew and Gentile, slave and free; and

WHEREAS, The New Covenant further unites image bearers by creating a new humanity that will one day inhabit the new creation, and that the people of this new humanity, though descended from every nation, tribe, tongue, and people, are all one through the gospel of Jesus Christ (Ephesians 2:16; Revelation 21:1–4, 9–14); and

WHEREAS, Christian citizenship is not based on our differences but instead on our common salvation in Christ—the source of our truest and ultimate identity; and

WHEREAS, The Southern Baptist Convention is committed to racial reconciliation built upon biblical presuppositions and is committed to seeking biblical justice through biblical means; now, therefore, be it

RESOLVED, That the messengers to the Southern Baptist Convention meeting in Birmingham, Alabama, June 11–12, 2019, affirm Scripture as the first, last, and sufficient authority with regard to how the Church seeks to redress social ills, and we reject any conduct, creeds, and religious opinions which contradict Scripture; and be it further

RESOLVED, That critical race theory and intersectionality should only be employed as analytical tools subordinate to Scripture—not as transcendent ideological frameworks; and be it further

RESOLVED, That the gospel of Jesus Christ alone grants the power to change people and society because "he who started a good work in you will carry it on to completion until the day of Christ Jesus" (Philippians 1:6); and be it further

RESOLVED, That Southern Baptists will carefully analyze how the information gleaned from these tools are employed to address social dynamics; and be it further

RESOLVED, That Southern Baptist churches and institutions repudiate the misuse of insights gained from critical race theory, intersectionality, and any unbiblical ideologies that can emerge from their use when absolutized as a worldview; and be it further

RESOLVED, That we deny any philosophy or theology that fundamentally defines individuals using categories identified as sinful in Scripture rather than the transcendent reality shared by every image bearer and divinely affirmed distinctions; and be it further

RESOLVED, That while we denounce the misuse of critical race theory and intersectionality, we do not deny that ethnic, gender, and cultural distinctions exist and are a gift from God that will give Him absolute glory when all humanity gathers around His throne in worship because of the redemption accomplished by our resurrected Lord; and be it finally

RESOLVED, That Southern Baptist churches seek to exhibit this eschatological promise in our churches in the present by focusing on unity in Christ amid image bearers and rightly celebrate our differences as determined by God in the new creation.